Gaffers,
Grips,
and
Best Boys

Gaffers, Grips, and Best Boys

ERIC TAUB

St. Martin's Press
New York

To Carol

Acknowledgments

I wish to thank all those people who agreed to be interviewed for this work. Without their talents, insights, and intelligence this book would not exist. In addition, I thank Richard Anobile, who initially convinced me that I was the right man for this job; Margie Bresnahan, for her excellent transcription of the interviews, which were always accompanied by precise, appropriate evaluations of the work, as well as of the interviewees; Barbara Anderson, my editor; Jane Flatt, who helped me see the light in the first place; Doug Dutton, Los Angeles bookstore owner, for his unflagging interest in my progress and enthusiasm for my work; and Carol Zulman, my wife and my most demanding, insightful, and supportive critic and friend.

GAFFERS, GRIPS, AND BEST BOYS (revised edition). Copyright © 1994, 1987 by Eric Taub. All rights reserved. Printed in the United States of America. No part of this book may be used or reproduced in any manner whatsoever without written permission except in the case of brief quotations embodied in critical articles or reviews. For information, address St. Martin's Press, 175 Fifth Avenue, New York, N.Y. 10010.

Design by Barbara Bert

Library of Congress Cataloging-in-Publication Data

Taub, Eric.
    Gaffers, grips, and best boys / Eric Taub. — Rev. and updated ed.
        p.   cm.
    Includes index.
    ISBN 0-312-11276-9 (pbk.)
    1. Cinematography—Biography.   2. Motion pictures—Production and direction—Biography.   I. Title.
    TR849.A1T38   1994
    791.43'092'2—dc20   94-28113
                                                  CIP

10 9 8 7 6 5 4 3

Contents

Postproduction

Preface to the
Second Edition

My interest in creating this new, second edition of *Gaffers, Grips, and Best Boys* was piqued in large part by my continuing involvement in the digital world. The first edition of this book, now over seven years old, was written on a Macintosh computer with 128 kilobytes of RAM; storage space consisted of one 400-kilobyte floppy drive. The five new chapters in this edition were created using a machine four times as fast as its predecessor, with sixty times as much RAM and three hundred times as much storage capacity. In addition to creating text, I now use my computer to manipulate color photographs that are stored on CD-ROM disks, to dabble in off-line film editing, and to wander through and around three-dimensional rooms and shapes that I have created in virtual worlds that exist solely on-screen.

The rapid advancement in computer capabilities has radically altered the way motion pictures are created, and this new edition explores those changes. Unwanted scenes from a movie are no longer left on the cutting room floor; increasingly, they're being dragged to a computer's trash can, as film editors abandon their Movieola and Steenbeck editing machines for Macintoshes with twenty-one-inch monitors and enormous storage capacities. Today, writers are using computers to assist in plot development and to ease the task of formatting their work into the proper screenplay style, while line producers create budgets and schedules on their notebook models. Motion picture special effects wizards are creating digitized animals, reptiles, and even humanlike creatures that stretch our ability to define what is real and what is only illusory in this most deceptive of businesses.

This new edition also explores the shift in the filmmaking culture from the 1970s—a time when film's creators enjoyed unprecedented artistic freedom—to today, when more motion picture executives are interested solely in profiting from films rather than in making them. The rapid technological expansion in the industry is coming at the same time as a financial contraction; over the past several years, motion picture studio executives have given ever greater lip service to the need to contain costs. The reasons are not hard to find: the enormous and spiraling salaries of the few "bankable" stars, the ever more colossal budgets needed to make even "small" films, the daunting losses that result from the failure of such extravaganzas as the Arnold Schwarzenegger epic, *Last Action Hero*.

The growing need to turn huge profits has pressured filmmakers to create projects that can attract wide audiences. Artistic freedom increasingly takes a back seat to finance; the wrong rating from the Motion Picture Association of America's ratings board—what many regard as a de facto system of censorship—can mean a difference of millions of dollars at the box office. The mechanics behind the ratings system, the goals and motivations of the board and its members, are elucidated in the following pages.

Even if a film is favorably rated, no amount of promotion will make a poorly received film a hit. Still, skyrocketing feature film costs have created a parallel increase in the amount of money spent to market a production. As a result, no account of the filmmaking process—a process unique in that it produces both an artistic statement and a highly valuable mass-market commodity—can be complete without an understanding of what it takes to sell a film throughout the world, to exploit the channels of profit that have grown to encompass, in less than ten years, home video, laser disc, pay-per-view, pay and free cable TV, direct-to-home satellite, standard broadcast television, and interactive video games. It's all done with the goal of maximizing revenues, of building careers as well as the riches that are the dream of everyone who has ever wanted to get involved in that most unique of fantasy worlds, the one known in every country as simply, "Hollywood."

Introduction

The motion picture business is one of the most talked about, debated, and critiqued industries in the world. It is also an industry about which people know almost nothing.

What people do know is gleaned from the popular media: scandalous rumors about actors, tidbits about studio executives' enormous power and astronomical salaries, notes on where the Hollywood elite are eating this week. But the fact is that filmmaking, the prolonged and extraordinarily intricate process of preparing, producing, and promoting a motion picture, remains a murky business at best.

Everyone knows that motion pictures involve people known as writers, directors, and film editors; and some obsessed movie-goers, unwilling to relinquish their seats until the last credits roll up and off the screen, have even heard of gaffers, grips, and best boys. But few have any idea what these jobs are, what acting, directing, photographing, or pushing a dolly around a motion picture set actually entail.

This book attempts to answer those questions, to get beyond the glamour of motion pictures, to demystify the inner workings of what may be the most mystifying industry in the world.

The reader will notice that there are certain credits that appear in films that are not discussed in these pages. That's because the purpose of this book is not to serve as an encyclopaedia of job descriptions for people looking for movie careers. Its purpose is to give students of motion pictures, through interviews with some of Hollywood's most successful artists and craftspeople, an overall understanding of the entire filmmaking procedure, from the germination of an idea to its development, scripting, and sale to a studio; from the selection of a director to the director's edited version of the film; from the finished product to its first release to the theaters.

Through an understanding of the steps in this process will come an appreciation that motion picture production is, by necessity, not a solitary but an inherently collaborative act. Not one individual, from successful producer to first-time set carpenter, works alone; rather, the skills, experiences, and ideas that each brings to his or her task are always applied, modified, or even rejected in consultation with others.

One last note: several of the participants in this book have the same last names. That's no coincidence; it's because they're fathers and sons. The motion picture business is to a large extent a nepotistic business, and for obvious reasons: children of film workers grow up surrounded by "the industry"; they understand it and know others in it. Consequently, they need no leap of the imagination to picture themselves involved in Hollywood, as might be necessary for someone growing up in Buffalo or Baton Rouge.

Still, while it might be easier for the son or daughter of a film worker to get a start in the motion picture business, he or she will have no better luck in it than anyone else if they can't succeed on their own. The individuals profiled in the following pages have been chosen not because they are someone's relative, but because they are universally regarded as the best in the business.

—Los Angeles, 1987

Preproduction

Executive Producer, Producer

▬ Charles Joffe
Midge Sanford
Sarah Pillsbury

In the beginning, there is the idea. And in the business of film-making, that idea often stems from the work of the producer, the individual—or individuals—charged with perhaps the most complex and far-reaching job in the filmmaking process. For while many other people perform necessary and indeed integral roles in making a motion picture, only the producer has so much involvement in the overall product.

It is often the producer who develops the idea for the film in the first place, who comes up with the idea of obtaining the rights to a story that may already exist in book, play, or even magazine form. It is usually the producer who tries to get a major or minor studio interested in making a film and financing it, who tries to get a distributor to guarantee that it will place the film in movie theaters and supply enough money to advertise it properly.

It is the producer who must hire the director, the actors, the major technical people, and the person who will oversee the film on a day-to-day basis. Indeed, it is only the producer who will so thoroughly live with the film, twenty-four hours a day, for years at a time, as he or she goes through the extremely complicated and time-consuming job of placating egos, putting out fires, and encouraging members of an industry to say yes when they're often more inclined to say no.

On the other hand, the "producer" may do none of these things. With the extremely fluid job definitions in the filmmaking business, some people may be producers in name only, granted what amounts to an honorary Hollywood peerage, a title of "executive producer" for having helped raise necessary funds, for having written a script that was eventually bought—or even just as a favor to a friend.

But assuming that the title is indeed accurate and deserved, then it is the producer—not the actor or even the director—who has the most to gain or lose with the success of a motion picture.

. If the picture is a critical or financial disaster, then it is the producer who takes the blame for having suggested the project in the first place. The actor may get rave reviews for his work even if the film is a mess; the director may come out smelling like a rose, being praised for managing to salvage something out of what is now called a terrible hodgepodge of scenes. But it is the producer whom the studio will see as carrying the burden of disaster.

Producing is never easy, even for those who, from the outside, now look to be the most successful in their field. "Show business is the most unrealistic business," says industry veteran Charles Joffe. Joffe, along with his partner Jack Rollins, has served as producer or executive producer of every Woody Allen picture, including *Annie Hall, Interiors, Hannah and Her Sisters,* and *Radio Days,* as well as other films such as the comedy *Arthur,* starring Dudley Moore.

"More people who hate insecurity go into this business, yet it's the most insecure business—for stars, for anyone. What is commonly true in any business is certainly true in ours: nothing is easy. Everybody would think with our clients everything is easy. But that's not true."

By his clients, Joffe means the likes of Woody Allen, Billy Crystal, Robin Williams, David Letterman, and Martin Short. And even with them, pictures are never automatic "go's."

"Even as successful a producer as Bob Chartoff was saying to me a few weeks ago that he's got a small picture that he's in love with and the studios aren't letting him do it. He's fighting with the studios to do it. You would think with his successful background he could walk right in with a not-very-high-budget film.

"I don't know of any producer that really has 'go' pictures," Joffe adds. "I'm going to get a damn good hearing when I bring a project to a studio. And usually they think it's going to be for one of my clients.

"Only Woody Allen has total, total, total control. The studios don't even have to read a script. We have a three-pic deal with the studio. If one picture costs $12 million to make, then the other will cost $8 million. The studio executives don't even see it, don't read it. Woody's the only one in the business who has that kind of deal."

But even Woody Allen is faced with commercial constraints. "Woody wrote *Interiors* before *Annie Hall*, because he always wanted to do a serious picture, but Jack and I wouldn't let him do it [first]," recalls Joffe.

"I mean, we discuss it, and discuss it, and discuss it, and whoever's logic wins out, wins out. We don't dictate. We're the only voices Woody has to deal with, as we've been with him for twenty-eight years, and he knows we're all on the same side."

But Allen also understood he had to have a commercial picture before he could try *Interiors.* "After *Annie Hall* won an Oscar, United Artists said 'We don't expect to make ten cents on [*Interiors*] but you deserve it, go make it,'" Joffe said. "It was that easy. 'You deserve it, the script is wonderful, just no one will go and see it.' I think now it's pretty close to having earned its money back."

First and foremost, Joffe is a talent manager, not a producer.

He, along with his two partners, spends the majority of his time managing the careers of some of America's top comics, not producing films.

He felt that Woody Allen's early pictures were fraught with problems, due partially to the fact that studio executives often did not know what to make of them. "When we did *Take the Money and Run,* we brought it to the distributor and they walked out of the room without saying a word. I got a call later in the day from them, and they didn't know if they'd distribute it at all. I said 'Put it in one theater and try it there.'

"They agreed. They found a theater in New York that had never played a first-run picture before—the 68th Street Playhouse. The reviews were incredible—they put on extra ushers, brought in cops; there were lines around the block—then of course the distributor called and asked if we'd make another picture.

"But I never stopped knocking on doors. If I sat home, who was going to call me and say 'Hey, kid, do you want to be a producer?' But that's the fantasy of a lot of people."

That fantasy was not shared by Midge Sanford and Sarah Pillsbury, the producing team whose first picture, *Desperately Seeking Susan,* took three years to see the light of the screen. They had met each other through mutual friends and decided to go into the producing business together. "I knew Midge wasn't a crazed, ambitious, glitzy Hollywood-type person who would, as soon as things looked bad, take a $50,000-or $75,000-a-year development job somewhere else," Pillsbury says.

They wanted to raise over $400,000 to get their business started. But before that had happened, they read the screenplay of *Desperately Seeking Susan,* and decided to try and **option** it with their own money. That was in early 1981.

"We won the option in a bidding war in the winter of 1981," Pillsbury recalls. "And we paid a lot of money—$15,000—for those rights."

An option would give them permission, for a period of six months, to try and get the project made. If they were unsuccessful during that time, they could extend the option for another six months, as long as they paid the rights holder an additional fee.

Even before they formally optioned it, they got the right from the writer to show it around without paying any money—a "free option." Their first contact was director Martin Brest (*Scent of a Woman*), to whom they sent a draft of the script.

Brest was only the first of many people who would ultimately see the script—and reject it. "We were working as hard on the project as anyone could," Pillsbury said. "After our initial option was up, we reoptioned it two more times, and in that subsequent negotiation we got the rights from the agent to act as the film's producers.

"After a year of optioning and reoptioning, we were able to get it for a reduced amount of money. By that time, we had shown the script to a zillion people. It was no longer a fresh project, so it was unlikely that they'd be able to option it to anyone else."

Sanford and Pillsbury continued to exist on their own monies. But by August 1982, eighteen months after they had optioned *Desperately Seeking Susan*, they did go into business, raising $450,000 through a limited partnership and taking office space near MGM studios in Culver City, California.

"When we first met and decided to work together, we didn't know each other that well," Sanford recalls. Up to that time, Sanford had been working for a film editor-turned-producer who "didn't like all this raving and ranting and didn't like having luncheon meetings and meetings with writers and agents. I started out reading scripts for him [*see pages 36–44 for more information on the role of a reader*], and then because he really didn't like doing what producing entails, I got to do the next step when I felt ready.

"I would say, 'Well, I got through [reading] all this [script] material and I found some writers that I really like, so I think maybe I should meet with them.' He'd say 'Fine.' Then I'd say 'I think I should go to Universal with this writer and discuss some of his ideas.' He'd say 'Fine.' So whenever I felt like I knew what the next step was, he encouraged me to do that for the company."

In the winter of 1981, when Sanford and Pillsbury decided to work together, they began to look for projects. Pillsbury had just won an Academy Award as the producer of the short film *Board and Care*. The first project that they optioned was not *Susan*, but *Eight Men Out*, a book about the Black Sox scandal. Writer-director John Sayles had written a number of drafts of a screenplay and by 1988, seven years after they had first purchased the option, Sanford and Pillsbury were able to make the film.

At the beginning of the option of *Desperately Seeking Susan*, Sanford and Pillsbury had no "elements" attached to the project, that is, no director or well-known actor had committed him- or herself to working on it, a factor that often influences a studio's interest. But the two women were still relatively inexperienced with the Hollywood system.

"We were positive that a studio would option the script by itself," Pillsbury says. "We thought this was the cat's meow. We knew women executives at high levels within the studios who really liked the script, but none of them could convince the men there who had to say yes that this was a viable, exciting, fresh idea."

At about the same time, the team started to approach directors with the project. More than thirty were sent the script, including Jonathan Demme, George Roy Hill, Hal Ashby, Louis Malle, Claude Lelouch, Stanley Donen, and even Clint Eastwood.

All sorts of scenarios began to develop. Somebody at Universal loved the project and wanted Lily Tomlin to star in it, because Tomlin had a deal there. It never happened.

Jonathan Demme loved it, and wanted to do it if Diane Keaton wanted to do it. Diane Keaton didn't want to do it.

Jonathan Sanger, it was said, would become executive producer while Jack Fisk would direct the picture and Sissy Spacek would star in it. "There were months when nothing happened with the project, and then every once in a while one of these scenarios would appear," Sanford says.

Meanwhile, Midge Sanford had seen the independent feature film *Smithereens*, and decided that its director, Susan Seidelman, would have the perfect sensibility for their project. Since Sanford's husband, a literary agent, was a partner of Seidelman's agent, Sanford was able to find a direct route to get Seidelman the script.

Seidelman read it and decided she wanted to direct the picture. The only problem was that, given the fact that many people in the Hollywood community didn't know who Seidelman was or what her first picture was about, she did not add much additional credibility to the film. "When Seidelman committed herself to this project, we went back to the people we had seen before with this new element," Sanford recalls. "We had to educate people about Seidelman. We set up a special screening of *Smithereens* for about fifty industry people because the picture hadn't opened in Los Angeles.

"We tried to develop a Susan Seidelman fan club of sorts, and then went back to various places and really pitched the project. We had to talk about what the movie would be, as opposed to what the screenplay was that they were looking at, which was much more cerebral. At the same time, we commissioned the writer to do a rewrite."

Then came a stroke of good fortune. A new Orion executive, Barbara Boyle, "adored" Susan Seidelman. "She just loved the idea of pushing a woman director and getting her going, and she loved the idea that we were women producers. She thought that this was a great woman's project, and she was very supportive." Unfortunately, Boyle could not convince the other people at Orion to back the project.

Then, virtually out of the blue, Warner Bros. decided to option *Susan* in the early spring of 1983. They had the writer come in and do a rewrite. They had seen the project before but no one at the studio in Los Angeles had been very enthusiastic about it; it found a great audience with a Warners' executive in New York, however, who decided to pick it up.

But fortunes were soon to change once again. Just two weeks after handing in a revised draft, the script went into turnaround, a polite way of saying that Warner Bros. suddenly lost interest in the project. They offered the producers the right to buy back the rights as long as the studio would recoup its financial investment.

Sanford and Pillsbury did so, and remained active in promoting the script. "Not a week went by that we didn't do something to try to advance the project," says Pillsbury. "But there were times when we were just waiting. The first time we went to Orion and Barbara Boyle was so excited about the project, even then we waited from August 1982 to February of 1983 to hear something, and they finally said maybe. And then in March, this deal from Warners came out of nowhere."

The producers always had other projects they were working on—about eight other projects in addition to *Susan*. They had optioned *River's Edge* (released in 1987 by Hemdale); *A Chinaman's Chance*, an action adventure picture set in the 1870s; and a picture called *The Investigator*, among others. They were working on other things, but were always working the hardest on *Susan*.

The draft written for Warners was virtually unrecognizable from the one done previously. After it went into turnaround, Sanford and Pillsbury decided to send it out once more. At the beginning of January, they delivered the new draft to twelve different studios and production companies, noting that the project had gone into turnaround and that they wanted to discuss their new ideas for making the film, which included the fact that it would star Rosanna Arquette or Meg Tilly or Madonna. They also decided to take it back to Orion once more, as Barbara Boyle, the executive who had been enthusiastic about it previously, now had been promoted. And with the promotion, the producers surmised, came more power for getting things done.

"This time we were going back to Orion with this fixed idea in our heads that we would cast Rosanna Arquette or Meg Tilly, that we were going to make the picture for under $5 million, and that we'd have all this fresh young talent involved, such as Susan Seidelman."

The first new meeting with Orion took place in January 1984. Within three weeks, a relatively short time in Hollywood but a period that can seem like an eternity, they received their answer.

"I was very nervous about this meeting," recalls Pillsbury. "And Midge said, 'Why are you so nervous? Nothing is going to happen. Nothing ever happens at meetings.'

"So we went in and Barbara Boyle just said, 'Well, we're going to make this movie.' We were flabbergasted." It was now three years after the fledgling young producers had first optioned the screenplay.

Orion said that they would make it, but with several caveats: they didn't like the rewrite done for Warners—they wanted to use the original one previously shown to Orion. They approved Sanford and Pillsbury as producers, Seidelman as director, and they needed the right to approve the budget, cast, and final script, to all of which the producers agreed.

Contracts began to be drawn up, but no money was forthcoming to the producers. Orion officials had told the producers that the film would be made; so why would they need money at this point, Orion asked?

That's the kind of position that raises a red flag in front of lawyers' eyes. Talk is always cheap; in Hollywood, it often seems it's even on sale.

"Lawyers always tell you that you should get paid, but we believed that they were going to make the movie. We were not going to stop this process by demanding cash up front," says Sanford.

"It was as if there was a train that was starting [with Orion] and we had to keep the train moving. And if we had said, 'Hey, wait a minute, we're not doing anything, you can't get involved in this project unless we get paid,' that would have stopped the train. Our goal was to keep the train moving."

Orion got involved in numerous story conferences to iron out differences in the script. Four or five were held between February and June of that year, some of them fairly extensive. It wasn't until March 15 that they all came up with a new version of the story that Orion agreed to have written into a new draft of the screenplay.

As new producers, Sanford and Pillsbury had to go through that process of heavy involvement with studio executives, each one of whom believes he or she has important contributions to make to the development of the film. It's a process that, fortunately, Woody Allen and Charles Joffe can now avoid.

"If Woody's scripts went through [the] studio [process] forget it," says Joffe. "One person would like this joke, one would like that joke. There'd be no consensus of what's funny.

"When we released *Arthur* I had no idea if we had an audience for it, if anyone would sit still for a forty-year-old Englishman being drunk for an entire picture, if kids or older folks would relate to it, even though I knew it was funny. Funny, I had.

"The film was special, but the studios don't know how to operate that way, they want everybody in the whole room to feel the same about a picture, so that nobody's on the line. So they have these huge staffs of development people, creative people, and vice presidents and presidents of production. And everybody's got a voice."

After the latest draft of *Susan* was finished, there ensued another week of "intense" meetings with Orion and all-day meetings between Sanford and Pillsbury, the writer, and the director, Seidelman. Seidelman decided to try to prepare something herself. She came up with what was basically the story that already existed, but in her own voice; she wanted to tell the story to Orion in her own way, to convince the studio that the project was truly cinematic.

"We were very adamant with Orion that this was a woman's picture," Pillsbury says, "and we were not going to have some male character in the film solve the problem. The studio had difficulties with the fact that the character Susan was such a larcenous person, the kind of person who would lie and steal and that she was like a little brat, which she was.

"But we thought that she should be that way. That she should absolutely be as antibourgeois a character as she could be and that was her appeal, in contrast to Rosanna Arquette who played an entirely bourgeois character."

The studio meetings proved useful to the producers, in that they helped to bring up ideas that could be incorporated into the work. "What we had to do in those meetings," Sanford says, "was to listen to what they said, not to the specific ideas, but to the direction that they wanted to go in and then try to come up with original ideas that would satisfy them.

"We had to reject their ideas without alienating them, without blowing the deal, the deal that didn't exist as of yet on paper. We had to make sure that we didn't blow the possibility of them making the movie, and at the same time come up with something that they would accept.

"It was scary, because they're telling you they want to make the movie, and then they're telling you how they want to make the movie, and then you're telling them that you don't like the way they want to make the movie. It was pretty risky."

But the producers were able to walk the very narrow line. They came up with a script that Orion approved. By May, they were ready to begin **preproduction,** the phase of filmmaking at which a number of key production personnel are brought in to the project.

The first thing that Sanford and Pillsbury did was to hire a **line producer,** one who knew New York City, the location of *Susan,* very well. The line producer served as a production manager, but also had greater responsibility than the manager, in the sense that he or she was also responsible for hiring, in conjunction with the producers and director, the heads of the various production departments.

The producers needed a high-powered, knowledgeable

line producer who would know the ropes of shooting in New York. Given the relatively low budget of the picture, $5 million, the producers couldn't afford to shoot a union film. They needed someone who could go in and talk to the president of the union that governed the workers in New York to allow the shoot to take place.

The man they chose for the position was Michael Peyser, an individual who has played a similar role on a number of Woody Allen's films. Peyser, in turn, brought in a number of key crew people who also worked regularly with Allen, including the gaffer (*see pages 151–162*).

Susan Seidelman, having shot only one independent feature before with a small crew, felt a bit intimidated by working with an experienced New York crew. To ease the situation, Peyser tried to hire not the old timers but the sons of the veteran New York technical people, "younger guys who were more open to working out" an equitable financial agreement. In fact, the grip, gaffer, and set dresser all came from a long line of people who held the same professions.

While Peyser was hired as a line producer, he received the title of **executive producer,** with Sanford and Pillsbury taking the **producer** credit.

"We wanted the producer credit, because we wanted people to know that we had done the work in terms of making the movie," Sanford says. (If a picture wins an Academy Award for best picture, it is the producer who will be named.) The executive producer is often the person who is perceived as having come up with the financing for a picture, someone who has worked in a hands-off way on the production. In addition, sometimes directors who are working closely with a studio will actually hire a producer to work on the film, rather than the other way around.

"What's happened," says Charles Joffe, "is that **production managers** have grown up and are now called **associate producers.**" Production managers run the day-to-day aspects of film management, and are also involved creatively. They're on the set every single day. They make all the deals for locations, for transportation, arranging airplane tickets for the stars. They set up locations and ensure that extras needed for scenes are available and ready.

"They're physically running the picture. The problem is they grew up and they wanted a bigger title than associate producer. So some people started making them executive producers, so that they could keep the producer title for themselves in case the film was nominated for an Oscar. If they knew it was a commercial picture that wouldn't win any awards, then they'd say, 'I'll take the title of executive producer, and you'll be the producer.'

"I think [the title situation] is always arbitrary. When I produced *Popeye* with Robin Williams, during the first meeting I had with the studio president and the producer—the man who had worked a year and a half on the script—I was told that I could be called the executive producer and get an executive producer's fee. I said no, I don't want it. I'm here not as Robin Williams's producer, but as his manager. But there are those managers to superstars who will do that."

Occasionally, powerful directors will also want a producer's title. So the *actual* producer, the person who brought the director in on the project, takes the executive producer credit. Or the director may take both the executive producer and director titles.

On Sanford and Pillsbury's film, *River's Edge*, the picture's financiers, John Daly and Derek Gibson of Hemdale, were named as executive producers. They had little actual involvement with the shaping of the screenplay, according to the producers, as the film was basically shot from a script that Sanford and Pillsbury optioned and that went through just slight changes, never having been redeveloped in the way that *Susan* was.

The script of *Desperately Seeking Susan* went through nine separate drafts before it was ready to be shot. But *River's Edge* remained intact. Daly and Gibson had minor impact, according to Sanford. They commented on some characters, the producers said they didn't agree with the comments, and the changes were not made. "They left us entirely alone when we were making the movie; then they wanted to see the movie when it was done, and they had a couple of comments when it was finished. A couple of changes were made, and now they're very involved in getting the print and ad money together."

After the line producer, the next person to be hired on *Susan* was the **casting director**. While producers have certain definite ideas about who they want to hire to play various roles in the film, the casting director enhances the selection process, suggesting actors that may not have occurred to the producer and/or director. In addition, the casting director facilitates the selection process by acquiring résumés, photographs, and examples of an actor's work, and is often involved in helping negotiate the terms of a proposed contract between the actor's agent or attorney and the producer.

Sanford and Pillsbury hired two young women who came out of the New York theater and had no experience in casting for a film before. (Since *Susan* they have gone on to cast *At Close Range* and *Something Wild.*) The film was cast with a mix of individuals who had been in low-budget films and off-Broadway New York stage productions.

Both Seidelman and the producers agreed on the director of photography, Ed Lochman. Michael Peyser suggested that Santo Loquasto, one of Woody Allen's production designers, be brought in to serve the same function on *Susan.*

"All of these people who were hired were either partly our decision, or totally our choice," Pillsbury says. "It worked out that the director and the two of us completely agreed.

"We wanted to hire Woody Allen's editor, Susan Morris, but she was starting to work on *Hannah and Her Sisters* that fall. We met with another editor and talked to him about the script. His take on it was pretty good, where he thought the film should go and where it might be slow and that sort of thing. Susan actually hired the editor—but a lot of hiring *should* be done by the director, with the producers having the veto power."

By June of 1984 the producers had picked office space, formed a new company, and Orion opened a bank account on their behalf. At that point, they became pretty confident that this movie was actually going to get made.

"Midge was getting very excited," Pillsbury says. "Checks would come by her desk and she would see that Orion had spent some amount of money. She would call me and tell me how much they had spent that day. We were so thrilled . . . like how could they close down a movie when they had just made out a check for $50,000?

"But of course they could—they could close it down and save $4 million—but who's thinking that way?"

At this point, casting was well under way. Madonna had been interviewed for the role; she had actually been spoken to early on, but only took a screen test in July. The executives at Orion saw it and thought that she looked very good. After briefly considering other people, the producers made an offer to Madonna, who had already expressed her strong interest in playing the part.

Throughout the filming of *Desperately Seeking Susan*, the producers showed up on the set each day. "Our main concern was what was happening with the script, not the cost overruns or changes of locations, which were Michael Peyser's responsibility.

"Susan Seidelman was doing a lot of rewriting. She had changed some lines that, in her mind, made it easier to shoot. And we got very upset, definitely more upset than we needed to be, although there were some things that were changed and got lost."

The producers had to mediate between the actors and Susan at times, because the actors were upset about script changes that didn't work for them. They would come to Sanford and Pillsbury for help. That wound up putting the producers in a very difficult situation, when they realized the inappropriateness of placing themselves between an actor and the director.

"Nobody should be between the actor and the director," says Sanford. "The producer should be facilitating everything to make sure it goes well. The producer should talk to the actors, should be supportive, should discuss the scenes—but the actors have to trust the director.

"If an actor is running to a producer and saying 'The director's changing this' and 'Will you go and talk to the director?' that's just a nightmare. So we had to try to push them back into the right course of action, to deal directly with the director. We had to talk to Susan a lot about the script, what was happening, and the effect it was having on the actors. We really tried to make sure that every scene, even if it was changed, was at least working."

Another problem that the producers had to face was the turmoil caused on the set by a series of script rewrites. The original screenplay had been rewritten a number of times. In July, during preproduction, a second writer was brought in after the first got tired of the entire process. "She was burned out on the whole thing, and didn't want to be someone else's scribe," Pillsbury recalls.

A second writer did play that role, adding some jokes and structural changes requested by the director. At the same time, some of the dialogue began to ring less true, according to the producers, who brought in yet a third writer to perform a "dialogue polish."

"The crew was really upset that we were going to make changes that were going to affect the things like locations and props. They were doing all the planning for locations, production design, art, props, etc., based on one script draft, and then they found out that certain scenes were no longer in the film. One person said that, by our actions, we had forfeited every opportunity to create any kind of look for this picture.

"So we were looked at as the bad producers from Hollywood. We were seen as somewhat interfering, and why didn't we just shut up. In the end, the person who probably resented our presence the most was Susan, who thought we were just sort of a pain in the neck. But on the other hand she would listen to us and say during the screening of **dailies** [the prints of the scenes shot the day before] that she was glad she had done something we had asked her to do.

"So the big lesson of the movie for us was that you don't have to get along with everybody all the time. It was all right to have real disagreements. And the film is certainly one that had a lot of contributors."

Sanford and Pillsbury were not involved in the editing of the film; contractually, the studio was not obligated to include them. They did see the picture about ten times during the editing period, a process that took about ten weeks before they had a first version of the film from Seidelman and the editor.

They then took the picture on the road, "previewing" it, showing it to audiences around the country who were told little about the picture before it was screened for them. After the picture was shown, each member of the audience was asked to fill out a card and that posed several questions about the production (see also page 90).

"The previews told us that the ending didn't work," Pillsbury says. Part of it was that Aidan Quinn was just so strong in the movie. What turned out to be emotionally satisfying to the audience was the thought that Quinn would end up with the female lead. "Initially we thought that it was so much more the story of the two women and that we could have the two of them off on camels in the middle of the desert together. We jokingly said that would have worked in the seventies, but now in the eighties audiences were turning their interests back to romance." The necessary scenes had already been shot, so altering the ending was mostly a matter of editing out two segments.

The producer's role continues through the marketing phase to the eventual release of the picture. It became clear to Sanford and Pillsbury that the marketing approach favored by

Orion did not match their own. The decision was made to hire their own marketing consultant to help steer the studio's campaign in a direction they would approve.

"Our representative was much more aggressive than we were and not afraid to step on anybody's toes [at the studio]. He was really adamant about things, which was just not our style. But it helped us in terms of creating the movie poster, and I think we were able to improve the trailer somewhat," says Sanford.

"We also had our own publicist, someone who worked as a publicist on the film, and we wanted to keep him on to help open the picture. We fought incredibly hard for that. Orion had to pay for him. We pointed out how much publicity he had gotten for the movie while it was being made, but they wanted to know why they needed an outside person, when they had their own. We went back three times and just kept fighting and saying 'The independent publicist is really going to help.' And finally they agreed. Studios just don't like to say no to you. They hem and they haw and think about it. We were always able to go and re-open the discussion and talk about things some more."

"On some level a producer cares more about a picture than anybody," says Charles Joffe. "Nobody stands to gain more by a movie being successful than a producer does. If it's not a critical success, if it's not a financial success, then it means absolutely nothing to a producer's career."

Why did *Desperately Seeking Susan* get made? "So much of it was luck and timing," Sanford says. "And the configuration of who had the power, and where, and was it the right moment.

"We just never took no for an answer. We kept going back to places. Every time we had a new element on the project we tried to reopen discussions even if they had already said no.

"It's perseverance. It wasn't so much what we did specifically, as that we kept doing it. It makes us feel that, in a certain way, there's a Zen to producing."

The Changing Face of the Motion Picture Business
Marshall Herskovitz

In the eight years since the first edition of *Gaffers, Grips, and Best Boys* was written, the motion picture industry has undergone a dramatic transformation. Production costs have soared far faster than the rate of inflation. Several of the major film studios, including Columbia and Universal, are now owned by Japanese conglomerates such as Sony and Matsushita; both have poured billions into their acquisitions. And high technology has captured large parts of the production process, transforming the look and even the content of motion pictures.

Many of these changes have been fueled by the enormous sums required to make a film. The Arnold Schwarzenegger action epic and financial failure *Last Action Hero* cost more than $130 million to create and market. Major film stars regularly receive multimillion-dollar salaries for several weeks' work. Added to that are the enormous amounts of money needed to market a picture. As a result, the cost of making a film today has risen eight to ten times over typical costs of the early 1980s.

To make its money back, Hollywood now searches as never

before for the major hit. The film industry is not interested in low-budget pictures that return minimal but nevertheless respectable profits; more than ever, it's the potential blockbuster that gets all the attention.

Terrified by rising costs, studios have cut spending in many areas, forcing directors to keep within their budgets and shooting schedules. The studios have refused to put money into projects that may never get made, and they attempt to anticipate the size of the audience for a film before it is given the go-ahead.

While some see these steps as prudent business measures, an insidious shift has widened the gulf between art, as represented by a movie's creator, and commerce, the corporation's need to make money. As a result, the worlds of *show* and *business* are closer than ever before.

Technology is often worshipped for its own sake, rather than as a new way to enhance a good story. High-budget, "high-concept" films have become laboratories for special effects creativity. Once rarely seen outside of a classroom, computers are now used for everything from creating the dinosaurs that roamed *Jurassic Park* to such everyday tasks as typing screenwriters' rejection letters.

Low-budget films are still being made, but they are increasingly relegated to the video market, that is, they are distributed by Hollywood's major studios directly into the video stores, without a major theatrical release. This has become a lucrative part of the movie business, particularly for action-adventure, horror, fantasy, and erotic films. Writers and directors with something to say, artists who are intent on making "smaller," personal stories, are learning that Hollywood is not the place to bother to try and say it.

The process has come as a rude and disturbing awakening to Marshall Herskovitz, who in the eighties rose to fame as one of the television's industry's most creative and substantive thinkers. In conjunction with his partner, Ed Zwick, Herskovitz created *Thirtysomething*, a television series that, with its ensemble cast of memorable characters, reflected upon and touched the souls of the baby-boom yuppie generation as it approached middle age. Despite overwhelming television success, Herskovitz has been stymied in his attempts to make a name for himself in the feature film business.

"The film business is changing enormously," says Herskovitz. "The boom is dropping. Ten years ago, there was an uneasy alliance between the great filmmakers and the studios, a sense that you needed each other, and a sense of pride in film as an art form, even among executives who knew they had a bottom line to worry about. We are now watching the business divest itself of the last trappings of 1960s and 1970s auteur filmmaking. The kind of films we all grew up with in the early 1970s—*McCabe and Mrs. Miller, Bonnie and Clyde,* and *Taxi Driver*—films that had a dark, difficult vision of life and that demanded a lot of the audience, are terribly difficult to sell to an audience today, and therefore terribly difficult to sell to a studio.

"Once the most famous film executives were those who had the closest relationship to filmmakers. In the last five years we've seen the final overturning of that, not just by the executives, but by audiences as well. Like so many things in life, there's just a sense that there's no room anymore for anything soft, anything that doesn't pay off. We've seen an incredible tightening of budgets, scheduling, and salaries. There's this no-nonsense attitude. It's a real change in philosophy."

A slender, bearded, soft-spoken and thoughtful man in his early forties, Herskovitz received his training at the American Film Institute. He first received industry attention in 1982, when he and Zwick won Emmy Awards for producing and writing *Special Bulletin,* a television movie-of-the-week that recreated a fictitious nuclear disaster in Charleston, South Carolina, as told through the lens of an equally fictitious local television news show. The similarity to Orson Welles's adaptation of *The War of the Worlds* was so strong that an extremely cautious NBC in-

sisted on running a continuous this-is-a-work-of-fiction dis-
claimer across the bottom of the screen.

Like so many others, Herskovitz did not want to remain in
the television business but hoped to move on to the more prestigious realm of filmmaking. Yet television was where Herskovitz
made his start and as with most people, he needed to earn a
living.

"*Thirtysomething* was a concept that we came up with in
one day," Herskovitz recalls. "It was a pure concept, and it
worked because it was pure. We really didn't want the network
to pick up the show idea because we didn't want to do television.
So when the network said that they hated the name we had come
up with—which we actually thought of in one instant while typing the cover page—we decided to play hardball, hoping that
they would agree *not* to create the show.

"The network complained about the name *Thirtysomething*. They said it didn't mean anything. I told them it was just
the name of the show, but they wanted to call it *Grownups*. That
was a stupid name, but luckily Jules Feiffer owned it and he
wasn't about to let us use it. So, in the end, they let us go with
our own name."

It's a measure of Herskovitz's humility that he refuses to
bask in the fact that the moniker of the show he never wanted to
do has become part of American and English lexicon. "The whole
experience of *Thirtysomething* taking off was so bizarre to me
that I've never gotten used to it. I tend to ignore all those refer-
ences to the 'Thirtysomething generation' because I can't quite
relate to it. We went into this show ass-backwards, and it totally
changed our lives and careers, because when we started the series, no studio head would consider me to be a director. I used
to joke that the only way I could get hired as a director would be
to create a series and hire myself. And that's what I did. Nobody
wanted me to direct the pilot of *Thirtysomething*, but I did, and
I got some recognition for that. I was a very hot item for a while."

It was this flush of success that convinced Herskovitz it was time to try and develop a feature film project based on a subject that had been his passion for close to five years. Both he and his wife, writer Susan Shilladay, saw themselves as "unhappy denizens of the twentieth century." They loved reading about the Middle Ages and were fascinated with the idea of creating a film on the life of Robin Hood; not one more film that mythologized the character, but a project that would ask "how could a legend like this happen? We wanted to make a stab at the real event and understand how it could have led to this famous legend. We started writing, and we came up with a romantic story that had a different take on almost every part of the legend, yet it still resonated with the story as we all know it."

At the same time, Herskovitz knew that two other production companies were exploring the Robin Hood myth. (That's not an unusual occurrence: with a finite number of dramatic tales in the public domain, producers are constantly looking to mine new or lately unexplored concepts. At times, two versions of one story may even make it to the screen simultaneously, as with the 1992 release of *Christopher Columbus: The Discovery* starring Tom Selleck and *1492*, starring Gerard Depardieu. John McTiernan, the director of *Die Hard* and *The Hunt for Red October*, had started development of his own Robin Hood project at 20th Century-Fox, as had a group based at the independent film production company Morgan Creek.

"In the spring of 1990, I heard that both the McTiernan and the Morgan Creek projects were going nowhere. I called my agent and said, 'I'll never live with myself if I don't try to get this made.' She told me to go for it." In the end, it would be Herskovitz's passion for his idea that would allow him to move forward. But it would also be his passions that would result in his greatest disappointments.

The fledgling feature film director took the script he and his wife had been working on to Tri-Star. The next day, the head of the production company telephoned Herskovitz.

"How soon can you come in for a meeting?" Mike Medavoy

wanted to know. Medavoy told Herskovitz that they loved the concept and were ready to commit a large sum of money to the film. They wanted Herskovitz in England within the week to scout locations and prepare the picture for production. Medavoy immediately hired production designer Norman Garwood, (see pages 93–104), who had recently served the same role on Ed Zwick's Civil War epic, *Glory*.

In Hollywood there are few secrets. Once a third entry in the Robin Hood sweepstakes was announced, all three companies raced to secure the biggest, most recognizable name to star in their films.

"We were trying to get Alec Baldwin, but of course everyone wanted Mel Gibson," Herskovitz recalls. "Gibson *is* Robin Hood. Then we heard that Morgan Creek had hired Kevin Reynolds (*The Beast*) to direct, and that he'd approached Kevin Costner to star, and that Costner was considering it."

Still devoid of a star, Herskovitz was in England researching locations and assembling a stellar crew to create the look of the film. His team included Steve Rosenblum, the Academy Award–nominated editor of *Glory*; Vic Armstrong, Harrison Ford's stunt double in the Indiana Jones films; and John Malo, the costume designer for *Star Wars*. In the midst of this preproduction work, Alec Baldwin made it known he wasn't available because he had decided to play the lead in *The Fugitive* (ultimately Baldwin would be replaced by Harrison Ford). Tri-Star's Mike Medavoy called Herskovitz and told him that, lacking a star, the studio was reluctant to pump hundreds of thousands of dollars into a project that might be beaten to market. The studio had decided to delay the start of set construction by one week, by which time the progress of the competition would be clearer. That decision shocked Herskovitz, who had already spent weeks lining up key locations. Time was clearly of the essence. The competing films were on such similar trajectories that Herskovitz, while investigating a location in Shropshire, missed bumping into the director of one of the other two Robin Hood projects by just minutes.

"You don't understand," Herskovitz told Medavoy from England. "This is a game of chicken we're in now. If you delay the start of construction one week, that will be the signal Kevin Costner is looking for. He'll sign within that week, because he'll know there's no competition. Right now, we're seven weeks ahead of them. They can't catch up." Herskovitz begged Medavoy not to stop, to spend the necessary money and forge ahead.

"I'm sorry, Marshall," Medavoy told Herskovitz. "I can't countenance spending one hundred thousand dollars to build sets when you don't have a star."

"It's seven weeks before shooting," Herskovitz argued. "We can get a star in seven weeks." Medavoy refused to budge.

The next week, as Herskovitz had predicted, Kevin Costner signed with Morgan Creek to play Robin Hood.

Herskovitz was too involved to give up. He wanted to keep construction going, even offering to pay the $50,000 needed for the next week out of his own pocket. Tri-Star eventually anted up the money, and Herskovitz flew back to Los Angeles to plead his case.

Once back in town, he was never given a straight answer. He was never directly told that the project was going to be stopped. Returning to London, he received an urgent phone call in the airline lounge. It was Steve Randall, from Tri-Star.

"Don't get on the plane, Marshall," Randall said. "Mike and I want to meet with you tomorrow."

"Why? What's there to talk about?"

"I don't know, but Mike wants to meet."

"Has anything new come up?"

"No."

"Steve, I think this is bullshit," Herskovitz said.

"They could never tell me the truth," he maintains. "Even down to the last week, they were giving me mixed signals. So I got on the plane and went back to England. When I told the crew that we were shutting *Robin Hood* down, one man who had seen his own film industry in Britain devastated came over to me and said, 'We know no one could have tried harder than you.' He made it sound so heroic, as if we had lost a battle during wartime."

What Herskovitz had lost was a bit of his innocence. He began to realize that his enthusiasm, his passion for filmmaking was not shared by his employers. For the studio, this project interested them because it looked to be profitable. What might have been a partnership in creativity a decade earlier had turned into a cold business venture.

"I learned an important lesson developing *Robin Hood*," Herskovitz says. "I was so full of passion for this project. And the studios are so afraid of passion. The film business has always been a collision between art and commerce, but now commerce is more powerful than it was in the 1970s."

The change is felt at all stages of production. For example, studios have recently decided that they shouldn't be spending so much money optioning the rights to as many projects as they have in the past. Most have severely reduced the number of scripts they'll develop.

That's no problem for them because, with so many people in Hollywood hungry to break into the film business, the studios have never had a paucity of scripts to read. While many complain that "there are so few good scripts available," the studios are now showing more willingness to get writers to create for free, "on spec." This way, the studios avoid investing any of their own money until they're quite convinced that the project is something they want to create.

"Three years ago a studio would commission you to write a script, but now that's much less likely to happen. Their opinion of the idea is the same, but they've cut the number of scripts actually produced by thirty to sixty percent each year."

With a reduction in the number of ideas that a studio is now willing to develop comes a desire, especially in these times of rapidly rising costs, to play it safe, to concentrate on ideas that appear to have a guaranteed audience. Of course, there is no evidence that any studio is consistently good at picking the right ideas—if they were, they'd have hits most of the time.

This new emphasis on bigger films geared to larger audiences comes as a sad fact to filmmakers like Herskovitz, who always assumed that, no matter what, there would still be room in the American film business for pictures that expressed an individual vision, films for which an audience might not be readily apparent.

"Given that so many of us in the business are baby-boomers, and we all came of age with the same movies, it's only come to us recently that we can't make those movies anymore. The studios won't make or even develop those movies; it specifically has to do with dark themes. Hollywood has no interest in things that are dark. Audiences don't want to see films that are dark."

Herskovitz discovered this while developing and directing *Jack the Bear*, his first feature film, a drama about the small-time host of a local late-night horror-movie TV show, who impulsively moves from Syracuse to Oakland with his two young children after his wife is killed in a car crash. The father, played by Danny DeVito, must come to terms with his irresponsible and aggressive behavior after his youngest child is kidnapped by an evil neighbor.

The episodic film, a series of vignettes depicting an inner journey of the soul, was panned by most critics and seen by few others. Taking over two years to create, twice the time it takes to make the average picture, Herskovitz experienced the changing nature of the relationship between the filmmaker and the executive suite. Expecting to be "the primary creative voice in the making of this film," Herskovitz saw his powers as director systematically removed as 20th Century-Fox, fearful of a large financial loss, decided to take control.

Herskovitz's involvement with *Jack the Bear* was serendipitous. His partner on *Thirtysomething*, Ed Zwick, had been sent the script to see if he wanted to direct. The project had been in the hands of Bruce Gilbert, a former associate of Jane Fonda's who had produced her films *Coming Home, Nine to Five,* and *On Golden Pond.*

Gilbert had been involved in the story for twelve years, having optioned *(see page 6)* the book on which it was based. Steven Zaillian, the writer of *Awakenings* and later, *Schindler's List,* was hired to write a draft, which drew the attention of Danny DeVito, who expressed strong interest in starring in the film.

Zwick had already committed himself to directing *Leaving Normal,* with Christine Lahti. He gave the script to Herskovitz, who loved the story and, after meeting with Bruce Gilbert, Joe Roth, and DeVito, was approved as director.

Herskovitz first sensed that something might be wrong when he went to the studio to scout for temporary office space. One of the executives told him that they had found wonderful, large space for them to work in. "You're going to love it," she told Herskovitz.

"It was terrible. They wanted us to be in the former film vaults. There were no windows, it was tiny, and all our people would be separated. I told her it was unacceptable."

"Well, you have to take it," the executive said. "We already promised the other space you were looking at to Larry Kasdan."

"So there it was," muses Herskovitz. "This wasn't about office space, it was about the way things were already being handled, the way the studio was treating people.

"It immediately went from there into the toilet," Herskovitz recalls. As a director, Herskovitz expected to have the final say on the film; he thought the screen draft as it existed was "unwieldy and too atmospheric. I didn't have a sense of where we were going with the film. If we shot that version, we'd lose the audience." But he found that Zaillian, a screenwriter with a vision of his own, was little interested in Herskovitz's approach. The two could not work together, and Zaillian left the project. At that point, the real difficulties began.

By the fall of 1990, Herskovitz had taken over the writing, changing the script to remove the structural problems he saw and making the DeVito character more important. He turned in a draft to Gilbert in November, and both Gilbert and the studio said they loved it. But that wasn't true. In fact, Gilbert didn't even like it, and DeVito absolutely hated it.

"DeVito demanded that my version be thrown out and that we go back to the Zaillian script," Herskovitz says. "DeVito saw the film as a collection of very powerful images and vignettes—a cult film. He didn't care if it was a popular film; he wanted to keep the integrity of the project. I thought I was keeping the integrity of it and making it work better. I was strengthening De-Vito's character, but he didn't care about that."

It looked as though DeVito would leave the film, unless Herskovitz did first. They eventually ironed out their difficulties and compromised, using a hybrid script that was mostly Zaillian's. But Herskovitz wasn't satisfied. "As brilliant a script as I thought it was, it had enormous structural liabilities." He decided that during shooting he'd film some additional bridge materials that he could add in the editing room later to make the story more comprehensible.

As is typical for many films, *Jack the Bear* went over schedule and over budget. Not by much: it took eleven days longer than planned to complete the shooting, but it was over budget by only $100,000, rather than the $600,000 Herskovitz had expected with so many extra days of photography. Nevertheless, the studio came down hard on Herskovitz, berating him for being over schedule, threatening to fire his staff and to remove scenes from the script. At one meeting, things deteriorated so far that Fox's Joe Roth became verbally abusive, calling Herskovitz a "motherfucker."

"This is part of what's happening at the studios today. It's too adversarial. It's not just 20th Century-Fox, it's the business in general. You're over schedule, they beat the shit out of you. There's no point in being understanding–being understanding is just being weak. I fought them all the way, so the shooting was a miserable experience."

The picture was scheduled for a Christmas 1991 release. By September, six weeks after shooting stopped, the studio was worried. They didn't see how the picture could be finished in time for a Christmas release, and they didn't see how this film was going to make them any money. *Jack the Bear* was not cheap: costing $26 million to make, this picture needed to bring in forty or fifty million just to break even. That couldn't be accomplished unless there was a large repeat audience of young people, with theater seats occupied not just on Friday and Saturday evenings but also during the week. The problem was that studio heads knew that "dark" films like this were no longer drawing large audiences.

Unable to wait any longer, the studio executives demanded to see the work in progress. "They were very disappointed in what they saw," Herskovitz recalls. "The problem was they didn't tell me that at the time."

Instead, the studio heads said that they liked the film. They understood, they said, that there were some problems but, after all, this was only the first cut. "You're on your way," they disingenuously told Herskovitz.

"The truth is Elizabeth Gabler (a Fox vice president) and Roger Birnbaum (Fox's head of production) were very concerned about the film. They were concerned about my ability to finish it well, and about Steve Rosenblum's ability to edit it. It was unwieldy, it had 300 scenes, twice the number of a typical film, and it had little vignettes of life on the street; it didn't really go in any direction. The film had all these problems we had to solve. I couldn't edit at the same time, so I told Steve to go on hiatus. We stopped editing for the next four to six weeks, and all we did was argue about the structure of the film, and how to reshoot scenes."

The film took its toll on the relationship between Herskovitz and his producer, Bruce Gilbert. Both men agreed that the film had problems, but their approaches to fixing it were antithetical. "Bruce wanted to radically remake the film, to do a tremendous amount of reshooting, to make Danny more the center of the film, as I had wanted. But I knew you couldn't do that any longer. You can't remake a film in the editing room. It's too late. Having done eighty-five episodes of a television series, I had a good sense of how structure works."

By now, the relationship between the two had reached a new low. Gilbert was speaking to the studio independently, offering his suggestions on how to fix the film. This only alienated Herskovitz, who assumed Gilbert was trying to wrest control from him. Fox decided to fire Steve Rosenblum, the editor, but Herskovitz balked. The studio backed down but, in a slap in the face to Rosenblum, hired another editor to work alongside him.

After toiling for several more weeks, even with the new associate editor in place, the picture still was not working. In a move unusual for a producer, Gilbert told the studio that he wanted a chance at a cut, that he had an idea he thought would make the film work. By asking for this, he was stepping directly into the territory of the director and usurping his power.

"Are you saying you want Marshall to stop working on the picture?" Joe Roth asked Gilbert. "Because if we want to, we can hire another editor for you, you can create a new version, and if some of the cuts you make work out, that will be better for the film." Herskovitz wasn't sure what position to take on Roth's suggestion. He thought it might even be a trap to remove him from the film entirely.

The following weekend, Herskovitz and Gilbert got together, spending much of their time arguing and shouting over who had the proper approach to solving this picture's problems. Herskovitz had already decided he would not allow the producer to try his hand at a cut. A director relinquishing control of his film is tantamount to a general ceding control of the battlefield to the secretary of defense. "I can't give you a cut," Herskovitz told Gilbert. "It goes against everything I've ever been taught."

But Herskovitz's agent had been prodding him into easing his position. Any ideas that Gilbert could generate, the agent suggested, would only help. Herskovitz agreed on a compromise: he'd let Gilbert into the editing room, but only to work side-by-side, not to take over.

"It was the worst six weeks of my life," Herskovitz reflected several years later. "I kicked myself for letting it happen, because I basically did give him a cut. I decided I was a wuss and a wimp. The truth is, I was so sick of fighting and tired of the battle and feeling like I was going to be fired all the time, that I felt this was the only way to resolve it." Six weeks later, Bruce Gilbert came up with a new version of the film that required a great deal of new footage. As a result, the thrust of the film would have shifted from DeVito's son to the DeVito character himself. Artists' renderings of the new sequences had been sketched, but according to Herskovitz, by following Gilbert's prescription the emotional heart of the film, which had been the young son, was being removed. "Everyone agreed that Gilbert's cut wouldn't work."

Herskovitz was now back in control. He was given a third cut by the studio and, after three days of shooting several new scenes, felt that he had a real breakthrough, that he had succeeded in making the picture comprehensible. The studio had been showing the film all along to selected audiences, and with each successive cut, approval ratings kept rising. Finally, two years after the start of production, *Jack the Bear* premiered nationwide.

Opening on a Friday night, the film was immediately burdened by poor reviews. Exit polls were devastating. By Saturday morning, it was clear that *Jack the Bear* would be a box-office disaster.

The critics were no kinder to the film than were its few patrons. From Richard Schickel in *Time* to Janet Maslin in *The New York Times*, reviewers failed to appreciate the film that Herskovitz had tried to create.

"People wanted to know what a neo-Nazi was doing chasing a boy in a tree. This movie doesn't take place in the real world, it takes place in an inner world. I thought that would be clear to everyone. Some people saw this film as a factual depiction of events on a particular street in Oakland. It wasn't that; it was an inner journey."

Herskovitz is convinced that if only he had been given the support he needed and expected from the studio, he could have created a depiction of the dark side of life, an example of how "the darkness in one's heart will awaken a much greater darkness in others."

"I was trained to believe that the director was the primary creative voice in a film, and I walked into this project believing this. If I had been [the primary creative voice], I could have solved the problems. Instead, I became a victim of the new studio system, of the lack of honesty, directness, and forthrightness. I was pushed into a shooting schedule that couldn't be met. Ten years ago, this wouldn't have happened. There would have been more of a sense of partnership between the filmmaker and the studio. The executives would have paid more attention to the production people; they would not have tried to take as much power away from me as they did.

"When you're on the set and there is this feeling that the studio is against you . . . when you know you're doing the best you can, you're not being lavish, you're not being self-indulgent, and yet you still expect the rug to be pulled out from under you, it's horrendous. First they try to maneuver you. When that doesn't work, they tell you what to do. That's how the film business has changed."

Story Analyst
■ Joe Davis

One of the most oft-repeated mistaken beliefs of fledgling screenwriters is that having been signed by an agent, they have passed the major stumbling block to success, and are now on their way to taking their rightful role in the film business. Final-year film students often go about campus bragging to their colleagues that they've become associated with a top literary representative; if the William Morris Agency is brilliant enough to recognize the true genius of this budding writer, can 20th Century-Fox be far behind?

The answer, unfortunately, is yes. A contract with a literary agency often means little. While an agent may see talent, there is no guarantee that anyone else along the lengthy chain of movie decision-makers will as well.

It is easy to forget that hundreds if not thousands of people are simultaneously going through the same process: writing a script of sufficient quality to attract the attention of an agent, and then trying to sell that screenplay to a production company. But with the exception of a few very well-known or newly successful screenwriters, virtually everyone's screenplay—no matter how well written or how well received by an agent, no matter how well connected the writer or producer is to a highly placed studio executive—will have to go through the same production-company screening process. And that screening process begins, in virtually every instance, with a **reader.**

The reader, more formally known as a **story analyst,** is the first way station along the road of a studio's acceptance or rejection of a literary property. His or her role is to act as a filter for **production executives** *(see pages 49–50)* whose schedules prohibit them from reading every script sent by anonymous agents or even personally given to them by close industry friends.

"Most writers generally deplore the idea of what we do," notes Joe Davis, a veteran Hollywood story analyst for Lorimar-Telepictures. "When you've spent four to six months laboring over a 120-page manuscript, it's quite normal for you to fear 'What if the reader got up on the wrong side of the bed; what if he or she had a fight with their spouse? What if the reader read half of the script on a Friday and the other half on a Monday? How do I know that I'm getting a fair shake from this reader on the evaluation of my script?'"

The answer is that one doesn't ever know. When a dispassionate individual is swamped on a daily basis with more scripts than he or she can possibly read with the attention to detail that is expected and necessary, mistakes are bound to occur. And there is no question that those mistakes, when made, can be costly, dooming a project to oblivion, or a writer to less recognition than he or she may deserve.

"But this is the only way yet devised to cope with the huge mass of written material that we must get through," Davis believes. "Our work is used as an aid for the studio decision-makers. It's a shortcut for them."

The reader is the low man on the totem pole, the individual who sees virtually all submissions sent to a studio, but who ironically has virtually no power to get any of them made into a film. "If we are negative about something," says story analyst Davis, "it's quite likely that nobody else in the company is going to take time to read it. They will trust [our opinion]. If we are strongly positive about something, [the executives] will look at it, but it does not mean that our company is going to buy it."

Fortunately for the studio executives, there are few scripts that readers get very excited about. The number of outstanding properties is minuscule. "To think that because almost all submissions come through a literary agency, they are therefore of a highly professional nature, would be incorrect," Davis says. "The vast majority of submissions are average to mediocre."

For legal reasons, studios tend not to accept submissions without the backing of a literary agency. Past experience has indicated that writers who submit work without agency representation may later try to sue a studio, claiming that their work became the basis for a project for which they did not receive credit or compensation.

Davis reads and evaluates an average of seven to ten scripts per week. "Perhaps one out of ten is worth calling to the attention of the executives. And maybe two or three times a year, one script out of a hundred, do I find myself really excited about something." That excitement can come from the story itself, the way it is written, or the "elements" attached to the project, i.e., the pledged involvement of a major star, director, or producer.

Virtually all studios follow the same procedure in their story "coverage" requirements. A reader prepares a report that, on its front page, lists basic facts of the **literary property**, that piece of material—be it screenplay, novel, magazine article, or book galleys—that an agent has submitted to a studio in the belief that it will make a good, financially successful film.

Manuscripts of novels come either from agents or, in the case of Lorimar-Telepictures, from the company's New York office, which, being physically and intellectually closer to the publishing industry, keeps a special eye out for appropriate books. Those New York submissions are then reviewed by the Los Angeles office for their suitability for the screen. The review is necessary because New York story analysts are not always as attuned as their Hollywood-based colleagues to the requirements for adaptation to film or television.

The front page of the reader's report lists the name of the property, its author, the type of material, length, and its elements: committed star, director, or financing, if any. In addition, a two-sentence "log line" gives a summary of the story. The final statement on the front page indicates whether or not the reader recommends the work.

Attached to the first page is a separate two-page story synopsis. "If we find something that we're really wild about—which is very rare—then we'll write something longer to capture more of the flavor, the nuances of the story," says Davis. Regardless of the length of the synopsis or the reader's feelings about the literary property, the story analyst will make every attempt to be as objective as possible in his summary section of the report. For instance, the reader will write "a wild chase ensues through Los Angeles," rather than "an amateurishly conceived wild chase ensues through Los Angeles."

The analyst's comments are reserved for the third section. It is here that the reader gets the chance to talk about the problems and strengths of the material, and whether or not it can work as a film. Even if the screenplay will not be recommended, the reader may find that the writer has particular talents of which the production executives should be made aware.

Elements that do not impress analysts are fancy, multicolored script covers; carefully rendered full-color drawings meant to illustrate various scenes as they could be photographed; or the professed, though unsubstantiated, involvement of a particular actor or high-powered director in the making of the film.

That's because Hollywood is a community that thrives on exaggeration; story analysts know that a claim of interest on the part of an Arnold Schwarzenegger or a Chevy Chase may mean, at best, that the writer ran into the star outside a supermarket and told him about the script; perhaps the star, to get the writer off his back, asked the writer to send a copy to his agent. At worst, the claim may be an outright fabrication.

"It's not infrequent that I get a script that says that Robert Redford or Chuck Bronson is committed to playing in it," says Davis. "And you read it and say, 'This is crazy, this is the worst stuff ever.' While we have to write these claims, on the front page we may put them in quotes. It almost seems that the more the exaggeration about supposed interest in the script, the worse the submission."

Despite the fact that many fledgling writers fear that their material will get lost as it winds its way through the maze of agents, readers, and production executives, the fact is that story analysts are, rather than a bored bunch of cynical slackers, a conscientious group of individuals, many aspiring writers themselves, who are devoted to searching out good work. And many of them have a much better grasp of the elements necessary to make a good screenplay than their bosses, the production executives.

"To be a good story analyst," Davis believes, "you have to have a recognition and appreciation of good dramatic writing, a thorough familiarity with writers working in the movies, and a knowledge of movies that have been made, as well as a historical perspective on film in general. It doesn't mean that you can read a script and say 'This is just like the 1990 film, such-and-such.' But it does mean that you can examine the basic structural elements of a screenplay, as a craftsperson, and recognize where the acts end and begin, where the climax of the acts and of the whole story happen, the denouement, if and where it must happen, if and where the characters grow and change.

"We must be able to recognize what makes for good dialogue. We need to understand such intangibles as pacing, mood, tone, and rhythm. We also need to understand what distinguishes our art form from other art forms, what makes a film different from a play or a novel. We can't let the writing fool us. It's relatively common to be able to use the language well. But the talent to tell a story in a pure form is very rare."

That knowledge is gained in part by being a well-read individual, by enjoying reading, and by knowing about the world's important literary works.

"If I were a music critic, I would probably not do as good a job analyzing the opera *Salomé* without knowing the biblical version, or Oscar Wilde's version. If I read a screenplay that is an adaptation of a Hemingway short story, I should understand Hemingway, what his contribution was to American letters. It's important for story analysts to read book reviews, to keep up on book publishing and know what books are selling well, know what books are being adapted into films.

"I'm not saying that every story analyst at Lorimar-Telepictures read Norman Mailer's *Ancient Evenings* when it was published, but everyone knew that he had a new book out, knew roughly what it was about, knew that it was circulating amongst the film companies for possible purchase.

"The more information like that that you have to call upon, the more professional a job you're going to do, and the better service you can render the studio executives."

Finally, the analyst needs to keep abreast of the film industry, and the world in general; he must know what films are about to be produced, what films have just been released, and which of those have been successful. He must know what themes the United States seems to be generally concerned with, which have been overplayed, and which, if possible, look like they may be coming to the fore in the next year or so.

"I am of no use to a production company if tomorrow I read a script about young guys in the air force who are the greatest fighter pilots, and there's a romance involved and friendship, and somebody dies, and I say: 'This is a great script and it should be made,' because the executives will think I'm an idiot if *Top Gun* is playing at the same time, and I don't know anything about it."

Similarly, when the Reagan Administration declared its public antipathy toward drugs, and Nancy Reagan made "Just Say No" the famous battle cry of the last decade, it would have been foolish to have recommended a script that showed its he-

roic characters disseminating the message that marijuana, co-
caine, and heroin are harmless, positive parts of life.

These dictums may sound elementary, but any number of
hopeful and even professional screenwriters violate them on a
daily basis, and are shocked to find out later that nobody is interested in their screenplay. While a novel depicting activities that
are currently out of favor in the culture can be financially
successful, film studios, faced with the enormously high costs of
producing a picture, are not prepared to take that large financial
risk with a project that may receive a lot of adverse publicity due
to its themes. Story analysts are consequently charged with the
dual role of finding projects that are both artistically successful
and commercially promising.

"Badly written things come to us that we recognize right
away have no commercial appeal, and we'll tell the production
executive that. Other things that are well written may still have
no commercial appeal. For instance if I read something that is
very much of a downer, I'll have to think twice about it because
in this day and age it seems that executives think people want
happy endings."

On the other hand, the story analyst may find that a work
that neither appeals to his tastes nor impresses him as well written may nevertheless contain something in the treatment of its
subject, a certain raw sense of storytelling, that makes it clear
that the writer has a special understanding of contemporary
youth culture. "We have to keep in mind that what may be abom-
inable to us may be the greatest thing in the world to a fifteen-
year-old," Davis notes. In such a case the analyst may "flag" the
script so that the executive takes another look at it. While the
studio may not want to make the film, it's a good opportunity to
meet a writer that might be useful for another project that the
studio happens to own.

Sometimes disagreeable subjects do get in the way of the
analyst's attempt to make an objective opinion. For instance, less
professional writers may realize that a particular genre of film
has proven successful at the box office. Assuming that they've hit

upon a formula for success, they will then try to write a film that carries that same style to the *n*th degree, but without the inherent understanding or sense of style that made the original film successful. That trend seems to be particularly evident in the action genre. Readers often find that certain films generate imitators whose main goal seems to be to write the most action-filled, sexually violent scripts possible, in the belief that the visual excitement will make up for the lack of a coherent story line, or believable characters.

"There are times when any story analyst is pushed to the wall by a simple matter of taste," says Davis. "If I read a lot of gratuitous violence or sexually abusive material, it's very difficult for me not to be angry."

After scripts receive their coverage from the story analysts, they are passed up the chain to one of a number of production executives. Each weekend, the executives take home a number of scripts that have been recommended during the week by the reader. If they have received poor evaluation, the executive may read only the coverage and a few pages of the material. Generally speaking, the better the evaluation from the reader, the more intensive the reading from the executive.

Writers who believe that their scripts have been passed over because they do not have well-placed studio contacts are making a mistake, according to Davis. All scripts are read by analysts, whether they are written by the best friend of a studio executive or an unknown writer.

In the end, it will be the story analyst upon whom studio executives rely for their basic summary of and approach to the material. They will be confident in doing so because, in many instances, they have been reading the same analyst's work for years, and have come to trust his or her opinions.

Writers who understand studio executives know this, even though the executive may tell a writer the little lie that he will "personally" read the writer's script, without waiting for a story analyst's report.

"It's just not reasonable for an executive to read a script without first having an analyst look at it," says Davis. "This is a business *made* of contacts and connections. *Everyone* has them. If they read the script of one friend without getting our comments first, where would executives finally draw the line?"

Production Executive
▬ Miguel Tejada-Flores

Walk into a production office in most major film studios, and you'll be confronted with a wall full of scripts. These are not all the films that the studio will make; they are all the scripts that the studio has "under development."

Out of that mass of material will come the handful of films produced that year. To hedge its bets, the studio "options" many more, paying writers and producers sometimes a very large sum of money either to obtain the rights to a screenplay on a short-term basis or to buy them outright.

Those scripts arrived on the production office bookshelf through a time-consuming and sometimes convoluted process beginning, as we have seen, with an evaluation of the material by a reader or story analyst.

Once a reader has reviewed a script or book, the "coverage" of the material is passed on to a **production executive.** When this individual has time, usually on weekends or at night, he or she will read the story analyst's evaluation. If the material or its analysis intrigues him, he'll read the script, or at least part of it, to formulate his own opinion. If he likes it, he'll recommend its purchase.

Hollywood is unlike other industries, in that one cannot always discern an individual's job responsibilities, or even skills, from a title. Assistant editors may not edit; executive producers do not always produce; and production executives are not necessarily involved in production. Often titles are given out as sops, favors that are easier to grant than an increase in salary. At other times, titles may indicate the desire of a company to puff itself up, to indicate to the world that they are bigger and more successful than they really are. "Senior vice president of business affairs," for instance, sounds considerably more important than "house attorney."

"You can call my title 'misnomer production,' " says Miguel Tejada-Flores, an executive at Vista Productions, an independent (independent of major studios) film production and financing company based in Los Angeles and founded in 1986. While his title is indeed "production executive," Tejada-Flores is actually the senior production executive amongst his group of three at the company. And none of them is actually involved in production.

What they all should really be called is "creative affairs executives," a nebulous term indicating that these people choose which projects to make, negotiate the initial financial terms with the owner of the property, then guide the development of the script through to the point where it's ready to begin actual production.

It is not always this way throughout the film industry. "Different places use different titles to mean different things," Tejada-Flores points out. "In most studios, there will be a production executive, or vice president in charge of production. Those people have as their job to find new ideas, find new writers, develop the scripts, develop the writers, get the scripts or properties together with agents, find the stars, the directors, get the picture ready to be shot.

"Yet the **production divisions** at studios contain the people who are really producing the film. A typical vice president of production may or may not have any experience in the actual physical nuts-and-bolts production process, that is, the work of hiring people, finding locations, etcetera.

"On the other hand, in some studios a production executive, regardless of his or her title, can actually be in charge of the production of a given film. That all depends on the operating philosophy and the management of the studio. Sometimes the two separate entities of 'creative affairs' and actual production can merge. There are just lots of different kinds of combinations." Those combinations can even vary within the same studio. One film may require a production executive who can also be a hands-on executive during the production, while another may not.

Tejada-Flores came to Vista after spending two years as vice president of film production at Lorimar, which, before its merger with Telepictures, was best known to the public for its production of television series such as *Dallas*. His present company previously operated like virtually every other production competitor: after it selected a project that it wanted to try and make, executives would meet with a major studio or other company that was actually in the position of financing such ventures, and try to convince them to get involved.

Vista's goal was to become the overall producer of the project, thereby receiving a production fee for bringing the movie to the attention of a studio, but not have to put up any money of its own. Today, Vista can eliminate that final step, thanks to a public offering that raised for the company, founded by producers Herb Jaffe and Gabriel Katza, around $70 million with which to do its own financing of features. As a result, Tejada-Flores and his colleagues now act just like their counterparts at the major studios; they no longer have to try and convince an external financial and production entity to get involved in the project.

Nor do they need a commitment from an outside entity to put up the funds for the picture's distribution, money normally needed to buy prints of the film and pay for advertising. This is the result of a joint venture between Vista and New Century/SLM, whereby the two groups have formed a third division for the distribution of their own work.

"Our basic theory is that if we're spending a lot of money on making films, then we should spend a certain amount of money to ensure that those films are distributed as well as they can be, rather than handing our films over to a third party that doesn't care as much about them as we do."

Tejada-Flores does not just sit and wait for projects to come to him. He actively scours the sources of information on material, *The New York Times Book Review*, magazines, and newspapers, for interesting books or ideas that could be turned into screenplays.

"It's like a disease. You wind up looking at everything for a potential story idea, and I know some people like myself who are avid readers but who tend to have gotten slight brain rot from reading years of only film material. Once you go on vacation you make a point of taking with you pleasurable reading which has nothing to do with anything that could possibly be a film.

"Even so this disease still rears its ugly head. You find yourself reading things and starting to say, 'Well, we could compress the first half of this into a short first act.' Once you've trained your brain to think in a certain way, you can't help it."

Material additionally arrives on Tejada-Flores's desk via agents, producers, and writers or directors who are known to various members of the company. After "coverage" by the company readers, the executives take home the material to review for themselves.

As previously mentioned, the readers are always the first rung in a studio's evaluation process. Even well-placed film industry workers, be they stars, producers, or directors, have their material read first by readers, except in the most unusual circumstances. Here's one instance where connections don't work. Since everyone in Hollywood has connections, how can exceptions to the evaluation process be made?

"Often a fiction is maintained," Tejada-Flores confirmed.

"In many companies the person to whom the submission is made, the studio executive such as myself, tells the submitter that yes, they will read the script [first]. Everyone knows they won't. They send it first to the story department.

"No matter what is said to you when you're submitting a script, whether you're a powerful producer or director, the person you're submitting the script to is equally powerful. Odds are they're not going to read the script first."

Submitters of material must also be aware that executives are notorious for being overworked; consequently, they have little time to actually read, even though they try to get through ten or more scripts per week. It is not unusual for someone to scour no more than the first twenty or thirty pages of the normal 120-page script. Writers know this when their copies of the work are returned, with only the first few pages bent back to a reading position.

In addition, it's always possible that a story analyst, a studio executive, or both, will not be the type of person who likes the kind of material that the writer writes. They'll come up with a negative opinion of the material for the wrong reasons.

Or they'll come up with a positive opinion for equally wrong reasons. "If Harrison Ford wants to star in a film and Steven Spielberg wants to direct it, those factors will make people who read the script read it in a different fashion psychologically," Tejada-Flores says.

"The readers give us a synopsis, which is a fancy term for a book report. Attached to their synopsis is their opinion of the material. That's important. Just as important is the book report, because that gives us a quick shorthand of the story. Often the synopsis will be better written than the script itself, the script being a piece of shit."

Even if the script is poorly written, the production executive must be careful not to alienate the agent who submitted it. That's true even if most of the material sent by that agent turns out to be of poor quality. "You can't totally dismiss that agent, take him off your list of good agents. Every once in a while he'll submit something really good. We just can't tell. But it's my job as a production executive," Tejada-Flores says, "to maintain that relationship with that agent. It's also the job of the story department, the home of the readers, to ensure that *that* one good script from that generally poor agent doesn't fall through the cracks."

Those who have established themselves as capable writers or producers have another opening through which to try and sell their ideas: they can have a **pitch meeting** with the production executive, at which they are able to suggest ideas that they think would make a good screenplay. The executive, knowing their work, trusts their judgment and is consequently prepared to recommend that the studio go ahead and develop an idea based on little more than a few minutes' conversation.

But for the fledgling writer, completed works are the only entrée. "Samples from new writers get put at the bottom of my pile due to time constraints," says Tejada-Flores. On the other hand, if an agent has a new writer that he wants the executive to consider, then a quick meeting with that writer will often encourage the executive to go back and read his script.

Major Hollywood studios are prepared to produce only about five or ten percent of the films they have in development. Vista, on the other hand, wants to produce about fifty percent of the work that it options. "What that means is that we as production executives, or creative affairs executives, or development executives, or whatever we call ourselves, have to do an immense amount of work during the writing process to help the writer. That work entails helping the writer with everything from characterization to structure to dialogue. Everything.

"Initially, the writer and I will come up with a basic concept or outline for the story—the essence of the story in a couple of sentences. And then we'll construct a short idea of what happens during the three acts, the beginning, the middle, the end. We'll construct the main characters.

"And then we'll do more work on it, we'll broaden it. The next step is to construct scenes, perhaps not a scene-by-scene construction, but most of what's going to happen in the first act, the second act, etcetera. Here are most of the major kinds of motion, what is going to happen with the characters, what the dramatic moments are, where the humor is, the good guys and bad guys, etcetera.

"The specific scene-by-scene construction, the actual development of what happens at every moment, is difficult. And that you can't do with the writer. The writer has to do that alone. I'm not writing the script, the writer is.

"My goal is simply to help guide and direct the writer as much as possible. Some writers don't like to do this. Some writers like to just sit down and write from scratch. But most writers of screenplays tend to write better if they know where they're going from the beginning, which is our job to help them learn. Or at least to be there for them if they get into trouble with the story."

In general, Tejada-Flores will periodically read chunks of the script, rather than waiting for the writer to finish the entire project. The purpose of all of this hand-holding is to avoid a situation in which a writer turns in his finished product, a very serious work of drama, and the production executive then says, "I like it very much. But can you make it into a comedy and change the male black lead into a Chinese woman, and set it in Canada instead of Singapore?"

While this sounds like an absurd scenario, such situations too often occur when production executives, up to their eyeballs in work, fail to take the time to sit down with their writers in the early stages of the work to ensure that they share a complete and accurate understanding of what the writer is trying to accomplish, and that the writer's goals have something in common with those of the studio's.

"My personal theory is that the reason why so many scripts are rewritten by writers and writers and writers at studios, which is a common phenomenon, is because of lack of time," Tejada-Flores says. "When you bring in another writer you're basically saying that this writer failed. My theory is that not only is the writer responsible, we're responsible. We, the production executives, are equally responsible for the success or failure of the writer's draft."

When the writer feels that the script is finished, it is read by every production executive at Vista. Everyone who has any power or ultimate authority to accept or reject a script discusses whether the script works or not; whether the written product has stayed at least as exciting as the original concept; whether it appears that the company's multimillion-dollar investment will certainly not lose it any money and more than likely return it a healthy profit. At that point, a decision is made as to whether to go forward with the film, continue to rework and revise the script, or pass on the project, allowing it to go into turnaround.

If the decision is positive, the production executive next sets out to find an appropriate and interested director for the film, one who would be available to shoot the picture within the time frame set out by the studio to allow for the film's release on an appropriate date.

Directors at times may be brought in on the project even before the completion of the screenplay. In the case of a new Vista picture, *Maid to Order,* starring Ally Sheedy, Tejada-Flores contracted with director Amy Jones to work on the project early in its development. The script had been written by two first-time writers who had never worked before on assignment. To maximize the project's chances of success, Jones worked alongside them for several years as they constructed the script, and then ultimately rewrote the finished screenplay. "Ultimately I think that that strategy paid off very well for us."

Contracting a director onto a project also means that the script will usually go through another rewrite, as directors bring their own opinions, orientation, and worldview to a story. The rewrite may barely change the script or, on the other hand, radically alter it.

The next step is to set a formal budget for the picture. While the studio has had a rough idea of what the film would cost, it will now call in a professional movie **budgeter,** who will be able to break down the expenses for every item on the shoot. Those costs are divided into two large categories: **above the line** and **below the line** costs. "Above the line" refers to items associated with **talent,** i.e., the producer, director, and actors. "Below the line" includes all production and postproduction expenses, such as crew, food costs during the shoot, transportation, film stock and processing, editing, special effects, costumes, and lighting.

Budget costs are more accurately determined once a team of people travel to various proposed locations to see what kinds of logistical problems may be associated with shooting there. Such a trip may be made by a newly hired **production manager,** a **location manager,** and the director, in order to determine such things as how difficult it will be to bring a crew into a mountainous region for three weeks or, if the film calls for shooting in a coal mine, what apparatus would need to be built to allow the camera to move freely inside that mine. If a chase scene is to be shot in Manhattan, then the costs associated with the provision of police services, crowd control, and automobiles must be factored into the budget.

"If the budget is on target with what we thought it would be and what we were committed to spend, we can proceed," says Tejada-Flores. If not, it may be necessary for the production executive, in conjunction with the producer and/or the writer, to tinker with the script, reducing costs by eliminating certain characters from the story, cutting out a chase scene, relocating an event from the West Indies to Florida, or changing a locale from a large discotheque to a small, intimate club.

Vista expects to spend between $5 million and $6 million for one of its average features. That's a relatively small amount of money for American-made films these days, when picture budgets can easily reach double-digit figures. But the low expenditure is no guarantee that the company will make its money back on the project. The reality is that, in addition to that $5 million, the cost of making prints of the film to distribute to the hundreds of movie theaters across the country, and the cost of purchasing advertising in newspapers, magazines, radio, and television to promote the picture adds, as a rule of thumb, fifty percent to the budget.

In this case, that would be an additional $2.5 million. Suddenly, the studio needs to earn not $5 million, but $7.5 million just to break even. Given the fact that roughly fifty percent of the price of a ticket is returned to a studio by the theater owner, this typical "low-budget" $5 million film now needs to reach $15 million in ticket sales just for the studio to make its money back.

Consequently, the studio will want to hedge its financial bets. To increase the likelihood that enough people will go to see the film, the company will try to get a commitment from one or two major stars to play roles in the film. The inclusion of well-known actors, while not a guarantee of success, will encourage many people to take a second look at a picture that they might otherwise have decided to skip.

"We do this," Tejada-Flores notes, "because of a very conservative theory which says, 'Even though we know the script is great and even though we're totally confident in the director, what if everything goes wrong, everything totally screws up? What if we wind up with an unreleasable piece of shit?' At least if we had a couple of stars or names of one sort or another in the roles, we could use that to advertise the film as a way to get some of our money back, in addition to our attempts to get our money back from the expected sales of the picture to television, pay television, home video, and airlines. You always want to get the best actor for the role, but if you have a choice between two actors and one of them is a name and the other one isn't, the one with the name can ultimately protect you financially."

As a small company, Vista also saves money by producing its films in-house. Outside producers usually command a high production fee: $100,000 to $200,000, plus a percentage of the profits. By assigning the producer's responsibilities to one of the company's own executives, the budget can be lowered by as much as five percent.

At this point, the beginning of so-called **preproduction**, the production executive's job often ends. But there are also times when his or her work will continue into the production phase of filmmaking.

"On a given picture, I may be responsible for giving the director a lot of advice in the story and scripting phases. The director may want my opinion on whether or not this or that star will be good, for example, so I may become a resource for the director to rely upon.

"During production we may also run into difficulties that require script or story changes. My goal is to ensure that the script we all loved before somebody found out it was too expensive to make doesn't get lost in a mad orgy of budget hacking, and that we don't wind up throwing the baby out with the bathwater."

With film budgets regularly reaching levels that were almost unimaginable ten years ago, there is a natural and understandable tendency for production executives to tread carefully and slowly before making a final decision to shoot a picture. As we've seen in the case of *Desperately Seeking Susan* (*see pages 6–12*), a decision by a studio to get involved in producing a project can often take years. "It's psychologically difficult for us to take the step of saying 'Yes, I'll spend $5 million to $8 million on a film,'" Tejada-Flores agrees. "There is no getting around the fact that even $5 million is a lot of money to spend for a movie."

Unfortunately, all of the thought, work, and testing of a concept never guarantees that a film will be a success. "*Back to the Future* floated around for years and no one wanted to do it because it was too 'soft,'" says Tejada-Flores. "'Nobody likes time-travel movies,' production executives said. Now those people feel that they made a mistake.

"On the other hand, other film projects have been rejected for years for equally mindless reasons, and then when they are finally produced they do indeed belly-flop. And the production executives say 'See, we were right to pass on that film all this time.'"

In order to maximize a film's chances for success, a production executive should not be looking for a particular type of script, Tejada-Flores believes. Attempting to replicate the popularity of a recent film by producing scores of identical knock-offs, as many production executives have done with horror and teenage sex films, is the wrong approach. Rather, the search for screenplays should concentrate on those that, in one way or another, transcend the boundaries of a limited genre, thereby becoming timeless.

In order to accomplish this, they must follow the classic rules of literature, utilizing structures and themes that are the basis of all great Western writing. It's a fact that young screenwriters often find hard to swallow, impressed as they are with their own abilities, and confident that they have invented a story or a form that has never been seen before.

"You can make an argument that the same rules about great story construction apply both to Academy Award-winning films and to films like *Porky's* or *Animal House*," says Tejada-Flores. "You can analyze films and the way mass audiences react to them and come up with certain story points which are valid for all. And the more I know about great literature and story construction, the more I can apply whatever I know to the script I'm currently working with.

"It doesn't matter whether you're a production executive, the head of a studio, or a reader at the bottom of the totem pole. If you read scripts, you find the same thing: one or two will be exceptional, a lot will be bad, and a lot will be terrible. It doesn't matter if you're in my position or in the lowly position of the lowest reader on the bottom rung. We're still doing basically the same job—looking for good scripts."

Entertainment Attorney
■ Frank Gruber

In Hollywood, it is often said that people do not make motion pictures, they make deals. And for many film executives, the "deal"—the legal document setting forth the agreement between a producer and a major studio or independent production company—is of consuming importance.

Executives discuss not the attractiveness of the projects in which they are involved, but the people with whom they have struck a contract. Peers are classified as to their ability to be tough negotiators. And negotiations drag on—sometimes for years—as studio bosses are fired and a new management team comes into place. The result is that often the actual concept, the screenplay or stage adaptation or novel that is to be bought by a studio for production, seems to take second place to the mélange of meetings, telephone calls, and legal documents that set forth the parameters of every contract.

Arrangements to make a film regularly take years to complete, as overworked studio executives try to eke out a moment on an airplane to read a script; as business and legal affairs persons at the major film studios try to ensure, through their contracts, that their companies are protected against every single unexpected turn of events; as new studio heads typically throw out all existing projects from the previous regime and start anew, forcing producers, those people who own the rights to a project, to make the rounds once again looking for interest in their film.

Behind all of this wheeling, dealing, and maneuvering between producers, actors, directors, and the studios is the **entertainment attorney**, a lawyer who specializes in the drafting and evaluation of contracts (and litigation) that allow film projects to come to fruition.

Entertainment attorneys also act as agents from time to time, procuring scripts, approaching studios with projects that their clients are interested in becoming involved in, helping to package material with stars, or financing, or both. But this dual role is reserved for the best-known directors and actors, those who do not need an agent to promote them, because the studios are constantly knocking at their doors. All these people require is a lawyer to write the contract after they choose the deal they want.

Making motion pictures is far from easy; getting motion pictures made may be even more difficult. That's because putting together the cast and crew for a film is not that much different from starting a new business from the ground up every twelve months. New employees must be hired, financing must be arranged, facilities must be contracted for, and lawyers must be present to make sure it all happens in a way that protects their clients, be they a studio, a director, a producer, or an actor.

During the contract system in the 1930s, studios were able to keep a stable of talent under their wing. By negotiating one single contract, the studio could have a producer, director, or actor on call for several years at a time, and could require him or her to work on a project whenever the executives decided he or she was needed. But without the studio system, each film worker is a free agent, a free-lance talent who wants to ensure that each project he or she is involved in offers better financial remuneration than the previous one. The best way to guarantee this is to employ one's own personal negotiator, the entertainment lawyer, an individual who makes his or her living by attempting to extract the most from an employer while giving up the least.

Once abhorred as little more than industry hangers-on, attorneys today play a key role in the filmmaking process; and as their responsibilities have increased, so too has their status. It is an attorney like Thomas Pollock, not a talented director or producer, who is looked to to head Universal Studios. Thanks to the growing complexity of getting a picture made, it is the attorney who is presumed to have a familiarity with all aspects of the filmmaking *business*. It is the profession of attorney that has become the newest way station to the film-studio hierarchy.

"Scratch the surface," says entertainment attorney Frank Gruber, "and you'll find many if not most entertainment lawyers considering going into production themselves, or interested in getting a studio job."

Gruber entered the legal profession because he was looking for an area that "was a little bit more intellectual" than the film business, a profession that would give him credibility, but still allow him to preserve his options if he later decided to get into production per se. Gruber typically represents independent producers and writers who have a film project that they want to complete, who have lined up the financing through a studio, or nonstudio "independent" production company, and now need an attorney to iron out the fine points.

Much of Gruber's negotiations are carried on between his producer clients and so-called "independent" production companies; that is, companies "independent" of the major studios: 20th Century-Fox, Paramount, Warner Bros., Universal, Disney, and Columbia. With the growth of ancillary financial markets, such as home video, and syndicated and pay television, smaller companies are now able to amass enough money to allow them not only to distribute films that have been financed elsewhere, but also to finance these films themselves. Companies such as Atlantic Releasing, Samuel Goldwyn, and Island Pictures all began as firms looking to fill a particular motion picture niche by acquiring specialized feature films, and have now moved more and more into making them.

This was not always possible. Before the development of other nontheatrical outlets as viable sources of revenue, independent producers looking to make their picture outside of the studio system were usually forced to deal with nonentertainment industry individuals for their money. The cliché that groups of rich Pennsylvania dentists, acting through limited partnerships, were one of the prime sources for independent feature film financing was not that far from the truth.

The fact that an independent studio is smaller than a major studio allows it to make deals more quickly and with fewer artistic and bureaucratic obstacles. It does not mean that the deal will be any more favorable to the producer, or that the producer will be able to retain more power than if he went to a major studio.

There is no typical scenario that would describe the process in which a lawyer is involved in the negotiations leading up to the production of a film. Every deal is different and, as studio head producer Peter Guber (*Midnight Express*) is fond of saying, "Anything can be negotiated. Anything."

In one deal that began over four years ago, a group of independent producers that Frank Gruber represented became interested in a classic film to which the director owned the rights. They met the director, who still worked in the industry, they all got along famously, and they all agreed to attempt to do a remake of the picture. The deal between the director and the producers was quick, informal, and never formally solidified. "It was just a handshake agreement," Gruber points out.

After some period of shopping the concept around, presenting the project to studio executives in "pitch meetings," they eventually were offered a development deal. That is, in exchange for a certain fee, they would hire a writer to put together a new screenplay version of the idea. A studio executive, the **vice president of production**, would supervise the project through its various stages. Enter the entertainment attorney.

Frank Gruber proceeded to negotiate the contracts between the studio and the producers. The **business affairs department**, after coming to an agreement with Gruber, the attorney representing the producers, then consulted with the legal department, asking them to draw up a proper contract that reflected the arrangements agreed to with the producers' representative. In this case, the discussions involved "a lot of complicated negotiations about vesting schedules," a legal term that defines, again according to negotiation, what percentage of a previously agreed-to share in a movie's profits one is entitled to if, through no fault of one's own, work is not finished on a picture.

They wrote several drafts, and held the usual story conferences with studio executives. But when there was a change in management at the top of the studio, the new executives lost interest in the project and it went into **turnaround**. Turnaround defines, according to an agreement negotiated between attorneys, the period of time that must pass before the rights to a project will revert from the studio back to the producer, if the studio decides not to go ahead and make the film.

But the studio does not want to lose the money that it put into the project. So, as part of the original agreement, the studio and the producer will agree on how much money will be paid by the producer in order to obtain his rights back, an amount that ensures the studio will not have lost money on the development.

In addition, even though the studio will no longer be involved, it often demands a small percentage of ownership in the project; if the film gets made somewhere else, the original studio doesn't want to lose out on participating in its success. It feels justified in asking for a percentage because it nurtured the project in the first place.

This holds true if the project is eventually placed at an independent studio. If one of the major studios makes the film then, as a gentleman's agreement between companies, the studio will not demand its percentage of ownership. "The studios have a sort of comity or courtesy relationship," Gruber says. "They don't want to be charged for all this stuff when they pick up a picture that was at another studio, so they'll do nice things to each other. If you take a project to something other than a [major] studio that they don't perceive to be as valuable to them, they will generally be harder and stick you with everything."

During the negotiations, it was Gruber's intent to provide the first draft of the agreement between his producer clients and the studio, rather than waiting for the studio's legal department to send the initial paperwork.

"It's better for the first writing to come from our side than from their side. There are certain ways you can shade things; you can bring up issues. In general, it's easier to get a point from a studio the earlier it's raised as part of the deal, because the studio is most vulnerable to giving you something before you are committed to them. Once you're committed to them, they know you can't really go anywhere else, and that's when they start putting on all the pressure."

One of the studio's common tactics, according to Gruber, is to state that by agreeing to a client's demands, they would be setting an unacceptable precedent in their relationship with producers. That's not an unexpected approach; in fact, it's one which Gruber, and most negotiators, use whenever *they* don't want to budge from a position. It's just not very palatable when one is on the receiving end of the argument.

The studios have developed a scenario, whether through intent or not, that starts with a production executive who becomes very enthusiastic about a particular concept; he wants to make the project and to guide it along. Next, the business affairs person, while wanting to support the creative affairs person, is more down to earth, explaining that while the creative executive did indeed promise certain things during the early stages of negotiations, he didn't really mean exactly what he said. The legal affairs department executive finally states that what the business affairs person promised can't be honored, because that would set a precedent and there are certain procedures involved in writing contracts that must be followed.

"It goes beyond a good cop, bad cop routine," says Gruber. "It's good cop, bad cop, *miserable* cop."

The aim of negotiating is to get as much for one's own side as possible, while giving up as little as one can to the other side. Possessing most of the clout, the studio is usually on the winning side. But there are times when Gruber feels that he has gotten the better of the deal.

One of his writers was asked to stay on and do an exhausting number of rewrites on a script for which he had written the original draft. Gruber knew that the studio would rather have the same writer than try to find a new one, so his client was psychologically in the driver's seat. "We were reasonable in our negotiations for his services, I like to think," says Gruber. "The studio said that we handled ourselves very reasonably.

"But we held them up. We were able to do to them what they are usually doing to artists. Believe me, the people representing Sylvester Stallone have a very positive dynamic when they go and deal with United Artists."

After the remake project went into turnaround, Gruber was faced with another problem. The producer's **option** to develop the property had expired, and had to be renegotiated. An option is a legal agreement whereby the owners of that work allow another individual, for a reduced fee, to attempt to exploit that property for a fixed period of time. At the end of that option period, the option holders can either renegotiate another option, buy all the rights to the project in perpetuity for a substantially larger fee, or drop the idea altogether.

The producers still wanted to develop the project, so Gruber had to negotiate a new option agreement. But the rights owners weren't happy with the way the first rights period turned out. They didn't like the fact that the property essentially languished for over a year at a studio without the picture being made. Rightly or wrongly, they felt they had lost valuable time during that period. "We did a lot of negotiating to retain those rights," Gruber says.

Simultaneously, the producers were attempting to bring elements into the picture, such as particular actors, that would make the project more attractive to an independent studio. They began looking for stars, but that brought one more contractual point into play: the **changed elements clause**. Under the contract signed with the studio that had originally tried to develop the project, the studio still reserved the right to reevaluate the project if there was some important change in its composition, such as the addition of a particular actor or director. This was true despite the fact that the script had gone into turnaround, and the studio had thereby essentially said that they were no longer interested in working on the film.

The producers had assembled a list of four actresses whom they were considering for the lead; they asked the studio if the employment of any of them would cause it to want to exercise its changed elements clause. The studio said no, so the producers went after and obtained the services of one of the actresses.

An independent studio now liked the package enough, with the inclusion of that actress, to make a deal to produce the picture. The film was on its way.

The new distributor picked up the project on a thirty-day-option basis. That is, despite the fact that they had a script that had already gone through three rewrites when it was being developed at the major studio and now had a star attached to it, there were still other concerns. The parties agreed that a refined, detailed budget would be prepared and that the writer would discuss the script and do one more rewrite before a final commitment would be made to produce the film.

These terms were spelled out in a **deal memo** sent by Gruber to the distributor. A shortened version·of a contract, the deal memo sets forth the essential points of an agreement, without including much of the boilerplate surrounding it. Typically, the deal memo also states that a longer, more formal agreement will be negotiated and signed at an unspecified later date.

The project has been approved and the picture's planning begins—once, the deal memo could have been left unsigned without a problem. But with increased competitiveness and sky-high budgets, the more elements that are resolved, the better. Still, some continue to operate on trust.

"Whatever people hear about the entertainment industry being full of cutthroat people," Gruber says, "I don't know of other industries that work this way. There's no business that I know of that runs so reliably on not even a handshake deal. I'll make deals on the telephone with people that I've never even met face-to-face. And ninety-nine percent of them are completely reliable."

While documents setting forth ownership rights must be executed, the fact is that many deal memos *never* get signed. As long as a letter is written indicating the facts as understood behind the deal, and the other party acts on that arrangement in some way, then it's usually accepted that that deal is in force.

On the other hand, negotiations can get bogged down for any number of reasons. There may be disagreement over the terms of the contract or, in the worst case, the attorneys may virtually forget why they're negotiating, entering the legal discussions as if they're a personal quest for self-aggrandizement.

Gruber recalls one instance where he was negotiating a director's contract on behalf of a client who was the producer of a motion picture. "I knew that the producer and director get along fabulously well," Gruber said. "In fact, the two of them worked out a deal memo between themselves, without any attorneys." But that's when the complications began. The director's attorney, part of a large entertainment law firm, "is known as a screamer, as one of the most rabid, difficult people to deal with. I'm not negotiating with him, because the contract is fairly routine stuff. But his junior must be under certain pressure, because I'm getting condescending things from him, ridiculous things, needlessly inflammatory things, when I know for a fact that he hasn't talked to his client for weeks, and the client feels completely different. He's asking for things that were never negotiated, never part of the deal. For instance, he wants a 'film by' credit. We won't give him this credit; the picture was actually developed by a lot of other people."

Film credits are often bones of contention for actors as well. With the success of their careers dependent in part on their visibility, actors are always jockeying for their names to be in lights. Better means larger; the more prominent the credit, the more important the actor. The ideal is to have one's name before the name of the picture itself. Barring that possibility, actors at least want to be in a position to ensure that their name comes before any other actor's, even if their name would naturally fall second due to alphabetical order.

All sorts of compromises for title credits will be suggested; some actors, realizing that they are not yet big enough stars, will settle for their names to be placed alongside their co-star's, in typeface "no less than one hundred percent the size" of the other's. Or an actor may demand that a box be drawn around his name, or that various phrases be attached to it that would presumably give their credit more stature, such as "starring," "special guest star," or "starring John Doe as Jesus."

Actor's contracts, as is true for all employment contracts, first and foremost are concerned with financial compensation. In addition to adequate salary levels, other negotiating points include the schedule under which salaries will be paid: Will any of the money come as soon as the contract is signed, or will it be necessary to wait for the start of the shooting? Will salaries be paid on a weekly or bi-weekly basis? Producers, for their own financial benefit, often want to defer some or all of an actor's salary for weeks or, ideally, until the film finally makes a profit. In exchange for an agreement to defer some of the money an actor may demand the receipt of some percentage of the film's profits.

Actors also expect to be treated royally when shooting a film. Employment agreements regularly include stipulations that, in addition to salary, the actor will receive several free first-class round-trip tickets to the shooting location for himself and his family or friends, a limousine or rental car, a first-class Winnebago dressing room, and a first-class hotel suite (with an ocean view, of course).

Concerned about their public image, actors may demand that they be allowed to approve all publicity photographs of themselves before they are distributed to the press. And if they agree to do a nude scene, they may have a clause in their contract stating that no still photographs of the scene will be taken and that only key production personnel will be allowed on the set during that time.

Gruber was once called in by an independent studio to negotiate a contract on their behalf with an actor who was to be paid $800,000 for his work on a picture. "We went through four drafts on that contract. The actor's attorney would send over comments, we'd negotiate them, I'd do a redraft and then he'd come back with new comments. It was incredible. And it involved ridiculous things. My favorite comment was that he disagreed with the clause that stated that the actor would not fly on a nonscheduled airline during the production without the consent of the producer. That's an insurance clause; if the actors won't agree to that, then the insurance company won't insure the production [against losses due to actors' injuries or death]. For the same reasons, actors have to agree not to drive motorcycles during the film. I've been doing these contracts for years, and it's the first time I ever got a comment on that clause. It was ridiculous. This attorney had his ego involved in the negotiation."

It is this constant jockeying back and forth between attorneys that helps contribute to the enormous amount of time (and money, with attorney's fees typically reaching $150 per hour) that can be spent putting a project together. Add to that mix overworked film-studio executives, ever-changing management personnel, and a tendency never to want to say no to a project, and it's easy to see why one is often in it for the long haul.

"Projects always take longer to negotiate than you would expect," says Gruber. "It not only takes longer than you would expect, it takes longer than you can possibly imagine in ninety-five percent of the cases. These packages have to be put together ad hoc. You don't have people in a roster who are employed fifty-two weeks of the year who you can just assign to something, so you have to fit everybody's schedules together. But that's even after the deal has been made, after the picture has been financed.

"The reason it takes so long before that, during development, is that there are so many cooks. It's not a matter of spoiling the batter, it's a matter of putting the ingredients together to make the batter."

And a hefty chunk of those ingredients includes the many contracts that must be negotiated by and between various players in the production. Typically, a director will be contracted to the producer if it's an independent production, or to the studio if it's not. The producer will also have a contract with the studio and/or the distributor of the film.

Each actor will have a written agreement; the more principal the role, the more involved the deal. The writers will have spelled out their terms in a written deal memo or formal contract with the producer or studio, as will the major technical people: the director of photography, editor, and occasionally the gaffer.

In addition to contracts for talent, the producer or studio will employ an attorney to perform a title search to ensure that there are no restrictions on using a particular name for a film; that same attorney may also do a chain-of-copyright search, a procedure designed to ensure that the rights to an underlying book that may have been used as the basis for a screenplay is either in the public domain or is indeed owned by the party from whom a license to exploit the property has been obtained.

Other attorneys will be utilized by the producer to review the underlying documents between the producer and the studio that will distribute the film, and between the producer and a completion bond company that has agreed to provide money to complete the picture in case the project unexpectedly runs out of funds.

"Nobody has any authority [during negotiations]. These pictures cost a tremendous amount of money to make, and to get somebody to commit that kind of money means that there's a whole hierarchy involved that is just astounding. It just takes forever to get a development deal going. Then once a project is in development it takes a long time to write the script and months for people to read the thing.

"That's why it's a golden age for the independent producer, people like Ron Howard and Brian Grazer who've set up Imagine Pictures and have gone public with the company, and can make $15 million pictures without all the bureaucracy."

That lack of bureaucracy was apparent to Gruber when he represented the individuals who produced the horror film *Critters*. The producers optioned the script from the writer in December 1985. Only three months later a deal to produce the film was in place. It was all put together at the American Film Market in Los Angeles, an annual midwinter gathering for motion picture executives looking to buy and sell completed films.

"The people from New Line Cinema were there," Gruber recalls. "They read the script during the first weekend of the market, and we made a deal then.

"Their lawyer was in New York, he and I were sending back telecopies and telexes and Zap Mail and all that kind of stuff. We had a short-form agreement, which has been the only agreement that we bothered to sign in the meantime, but it has no large amount of boilerplate.

"We had that deal done within a week. The picture was shooting within three months of that, and was released one year after we made the deal at the AFM, in the spring of 1986. The only reason that deal happened so quickly was because New Line Cinema has only two people involved in the decision-making."

Very often, filmmakers find exactly the opposite situation when projects are brought to studios. If *Critters* is every producer's ideal fantasy situation, then *Ruthless People* is the nightmare. Gruber represented the writer, and the producers, Dale Lawner, Richard Wagner and Joanna Lancaster, of this comedy project, which eventually starred Bette Midler and Danny DeVito.

"The project just languished at Columbia," says Gruber.

"For five months they couldn't get anyone to read it. As soon as it went into turnaround it was picked up by Disney and immediately was set up.

"Disney was in a completely different situation at that point than Columbia was. This was the start of the new Disney regime and they needed projects in development, they needed to show people they could make deals. It was 'Go, go, go, do it.'"

To be successful in the legal field, Gruber believes one needs to possess two essential qualities: the ability to read and write. "Law schools do not select for very many things, but to a degree they do select for being able to read and communicate, to understand contracts and their implications. It's just a fact that business has gotten so complicated that lawyers have a leg up because they're somewhat trained in unraveling complicated business dealings.

"The problem with film studios is that there are very few people in them who work in development who have actually produced films. My producer clients are hands-on producers who are always frustrated by dealing with executives who don't know anything about making movies."

But that doesn't mean that hands-on producers should head studio operations. Filmmaking is first and foremost a business. To think that an artistically oriented individual would make a better studio executive than a businessperson "just shows the naïveté about the industry," Gruber believes.

"Is the head of Mattel a toy designer? Or is the head of General Motors an engineer? If you look at those industries that rely on creative people for their lifeblood, I think that the entertainment industry, the motion picture industry, actually puts its creative people fairly high up. I don't think that you could expect anything other than the fact that an attorney like Tom Pollock would be picked to be the head of Universal Studios, rather than someone like the director Francis Coppola. And I think that's probably a good thing, too."

Screenwriter
▬ Walter Newman

In no other area of filmmaking is the thought that "I can do it as well as that" as prevalent as in screenwriting. After seeing scores of truly trite films many an avid moviegoer has decided that the process of writing a screenplay clearly must be a snap.

An involvement in the business offers the hope of quickly obtaining a glamorous, lucrative job; the concept of getting paid for penning one's deepest thoughts is not the reward—the prospect of early retirement is. Los Angeles is a magnet for people who, having written one or two screenplays, spend their days sojourning at outdoor cafés, reading *Variety*, and fantasizing about the huge amounts of money that they're about to make.

The simplicity of the screenplay form fallaciously convinces neophytes that they will be able to master the task and quickly call themselves writers—and even artists—though they may have no interest in the written word or the visual world.

For many writers who have been earning a living on a regular basis from screenwriting, those illusions have long vanished; screenwriting, like every other profession in the film business, becomes a matter-of-fact occupation, albeit an often lucrative one. For Walter Newman, writer of *Cat Ballou, The Magnificent*

Seven, and *Blood Brothers,* among other works, there is no attraction to hobnobbing with stars, eating in certain restaurants, or hanging around the set during the shoot. The writing's the thing for Newman, and that's where his job ends.

"Once I've written a screenplay and it says 'Fade out'; I'm finished with it," Newman says. "I don't even really remember every film I've written. I don't dwell on these things."

What Newman does dwell on is his craft, the craft of writing a story that will be cinematic, one that will move an audience toward some emotional state. "A movie should make an audience feel something: laughter, tears, hate, pleasure. Which is the criticism I have about ninety-five percent of the movies I see. They don't make me feel a damn thing. Not a thing. These people [who make these films] have no feelings whatsoever. They simply saw a lot of old movies and decide, 'Gee, I think anybody can do that.' I don't feel that way about it."

Newman has written both original screenplays and adaptations of others' works. His preference is to write his own material, to consequently avoid that other individual constantly looking over his shoulder to see how he's doing. "When I have a final screenplay, I put it out, that's it. Take it or leave it. That's my little can of salmon. You buy it or you don't."

No two writers work the same way. The writer/director Paul Schrader (*Taxi Driver, Hardcore, Mishima*), used to tell his UCLA writing classes that, by thinking about an issue that is central to one's concerns, the writer can then determine a story that will serve as a metaphor for that issue. Hence, one "can even write an interesting screenplay about a bowl of fruit."

"I would hate to have to attend that movie," Newman counters. "I don't write in metaphors. Specific, concrete images and lines . . . . that's all I'm interested in. You can ascribe any metaphor you like to what I do, it has nothing to do with me. What you see up there [on the screen] is what you get. That's it."

For Newman, the intricate analysis that one may subject his or any screenwriter's work to is an exercise that he does not care to engage in, either before or after he's written a script. Newman becomes interested in ideas, not in theories; if he decides to write a particular story, it's because certain elements of that story—scenes, historical events, personalities—interest him, not because he is entranced by the meaning behind them.

That's why Newman can always be found in public either reading a book or carrying around a blank pad to jot down things that he thinks might be useful later on in his writing. "You should really look at people. Most people don't look and listen. But really make yourself receptive, and life is never boring. It's like being at a show at all times. Everything I meet or see or read is grist for me. If young writers were more open, they would find it easier to find workable characters."

One of Newman's most cherished screenplays, one that, twenty years after its completion, is yet to be produced, was written because elements of its story refused to leave Newman's consciousness.

That script, *Harrow Alley*, was written on "spec," that is, without any prior interest on the part of a producer or studio to purchase the screenplay. After completing several films at Columbia over three years, Newman decided that he wanted to take a year off and just write what he was interested in, not what he was assigned to do.

His thoughts turned to the Black Plague in Britain in the seventeenth century, an idea that had been haunting him since high school; he assumed that if the idea kept on returning to him, then there must be something to it. He went to the library to see if there were any eyewitness accounts of the period.

What he did not do was screen other films about the same subject to get a sense of how other filmmakers may have treated the material. "Sam Spiegel [a producer] once wanted me to write about typhoons. He suggested that I come to the studio and watch other films about the subject, but I declined. I told him that I wasn't interested in what other writers had to say on the subject; they may have missed something which is very significant to me. 'Get me eyewitness reports of people who have gone through typhoons and I'll be interested.'"

After digging in the local libraries, Newman discovered two interesting facts: there was not that much material on the subject, and after reading what there was, he was still interested in the topic. "Somebody once said that our first job in writing is to make sure that we're not boring ourselves," Newman says, "and this did not bore me. There's something here that keeps me excited and interested."

Newman organizes every screenplay he writes by jotting down all his ideas on five-by-eight index cards; each card contains a thought, a scene, a snippet of dialogue, a characterization, whatever is germane in one way or another to the script.

"With *Harrow Alley* I finally had seven to eight hundred cards. Then I said, let's see if I can put this in some sort of story line. You may get an idea, you don't see how the hell it fits into anything at all, but be patient. Put it down, stay with it. Sooner or later, you'll see the connection between that and the other stuff.

"Think of a screenplay in terms of decisions being made by your lead character. At the beginning, just before we fade in or as we fade in, life presents the character with a situation, a life-affecting situation about which he or she has to make a decision. The character makes that decision and acts upon it. But this calls forth a response, which means another decision. About the time of the first act curtain, about forty to forty-five pages in, there's a great big decision to be made. There's an even bigger one for the second act, which is going to change everything. And then there's a final one which is your climax."

One of the things that Newman came across in his research was the fact that out of the 137 aldermen in London, virtually all of them stayed in the city when the Plague hit, while the King and his court took off for Oxford. "I still can't think of such people without my eyes getting wet. These (aldermen) are wonderful people; so I decided that an alderman would be my lead character."

After that came Newman's decision to make the alderman married; as people married early at that time, he made the alderman's wife fifteen years old; to add to the couple's anguish he thought of making her pregnant during the Plague; the question then becomes, does the alderman follow his scruples and stay in London, or flee with his young family to the safety of the countryside?

Other characters developed: Newman learned through his research that the government could not get enough people to cart off the dead, fearful as the populace was of contracting the disease. Consequently, convicts scheduled for hanging were given a chance of freedom if they took the job and survived. Taking a name from one of Ben Jonson's plays, he named his character Gamaliel Ratsy; he made Ratsy's hidden motivation the fact that he had once had the plague, and wrongfully thought that he wouldn't be able to get it again. Later in the story, a doctor tells him that he's wrong, a revelation that completely changes his life.

"It came to me that what I was saying really was that life is a rather serious business. Death is always close. We tend to shove it under the rug and pay no attention to it, but any one of us can pop off in the next five minutes. It makes life better if you keep that in mind."

But this realization was never Newman's motivation for working on the screenplay; only his interest in the actual story was. "I never know where I'm going to be taken with the story. Unless it's an adaptation, and even then I'm not sure where I'm going. [Hidden meanings] are an abstraction, cerebral stuff. Specific, concrete things excite me. Things that you can hear and see up there on the screen. That's what matters. This is the way movies are. You don't put down abstractions in movies. You put down specific, concrete pictures up there. I'm not interested in any abstraction of any kind at any time."

Newman does not engage in extensive rewrites of his scripts; when he's finished with the cards, he has in essence constructed his first draft. After he has assembled all of his index cards, he begins to organize the story and construct scenes for the characters and situations he's devised.

That process Newman compares to solving a jigsaw puzzle.

Periodically stepping back from the story, he'll decide that he needs "something" here or there to fill out the story, characterizations, and structure. "This is no different if you've ever looked at Beethoven's notebooks: 'I need something here—the sound of a big bass drum, for instance.' And it's the same thing for me."

Harrow Alley, to this day, remains unproduced, but not for lack of interest. Finished in 1963, Newman assumed that it would be produced in 1965, in time for the 300th anniversary of the Plague. Newman brought it to his then agent, Ingo Preminger, who sent the script to John Huston's agent, who in turn sent it to Huston.

Huston contacted Newman, told him of his excitement with the project, and arranged a meeting at Universal Studios. At the meeting Newman was introduced to Huston's son and the young actor, George C. Scott.

Huston was unable to raise the necessary $2 million to make the picture at that time; despite continued rave reviews of the screenplay, it sat idle for another ten years, as Newman went on to write *Cat Ballou* and other works.

He finally got a telephone call from George C. Scott, who had been given a copy of the screenplay to read from Huston. "I could never get the screenplay out of my mind," Scott told Newman, and he arranged a deal with Newman to purchase outright, rather than through an option, the rights to the script. Scott continues to attempt to fund the picture, with himself as director.

But even if the picture had gone into production, Newman would not have been much more involved in the project. He had finished the screenplay, and as far as he was concerned, his job was basically over. Newman regards himself as the writer of screenplays, not the writer of movies. And for him, there's a big difference between the two.

If an actor needs some help in rewriting dialogue during the shooting of a film, then it'll be up to the actor to make it up himself. Newman won't be there to help him, not because he doesn't feel attached to the project, but because he won't be getting paid for his work at that point. And in the end, regardless of the fact that he gave birth to the story, nourished it and watched it grow, at some point he has to turn it over to others, to remove himself emotionally from its development.

"My involvement has ended when I write 'fade out.' That's it. I don't even bother to look at reviews. And if I can help it, I don't go to the movies. I can't afford to feel bad. It knocks me out for two to four weeks. I can't afford that. I have to work. I didn't inherit anything. [The talent] comes out of these ten fingers and this head."

Newman has attended the premiere of one his recent films, but in the end regretted doing so. "The lead actor made up his own dialogue. The lines didn't work. Nobody on the spur of the moment can make up a line. I spent five months on something, I know why every line is in there and how long that line is, and why the words are there, and in what order. Nobody can say to me, 'I'll tell you what we're going to do here.' "

But the fact of the matter is that others do make those decisions. Once a film is in production, the script becomes in essence community property, with directors, actors, and even producers feeling that it is their right to alter it as they see fit.

"I wrote a screenplay," says Newman. "I didn't write a movie. What others do with it [in production] is up to them. I can't exist otherwise, and I can't afford to be crushed by it. So I don't go to see the things and I don't read my reviews and I don't give a damn."

But while Newman strongly objects to the notion that anyone can successfully alter a screenplay on the spur of the moment to fit his or her taste, he has no objection to the concept of gearing a screenplay for a particular actor, of creating characters and dialogue that will appeal to a particular star.

"I pride myself on being a craftsman. I don't even know what the word 'artist' means. Do you think that Shakespeare didn't shape his lines for his troupe? Christ, you can see the lines that he wrote for Willie Temple or Dick Burbage.

"They call Shakespeare an artist. He was just a hack who

stole stories wherever he could get them and wrote them to fit the troupe he belonged to. He was not writing in a void. When he found out that the audience liked war plays, he wrote scenes about war.

"A hack is somebody who delivers the customer to the place where he wants to go, like a hackney horse. I'm a hack, and I'm proud of being a good one. My job is to be excited first so that I can excite others, beginning with a [studio] front-office guy . . . the hardest people of all to excite . . . and then on to directors, producers, and so on. My first responsibility is to make money for the studio, because if the studios go down, none of us work. That makes great sense to me."

Production

Director
▬▬▬ John Carpenter

The centuries-old battle between management and labor does not bypass the film industry; the only thing that's different are the terms used to describe the dynamic.

With enormous amounts of money at stake in the production of virtually every studio feature film, there is, almost by necessity, a continuing divergence of interests between the so-called "creative people" (the workers) and the studio executives (the bosses).

Those actually making the film would like to spend as much money as possible, to take as much time as needed to ensure that their carefully crafted vision is correctly translated onto the screen. But the businesspeople are burdened with the knowledge that the failure of a film, however artistic, can even bankrupt a company. They're constantly forced to minimize expenditures, to cut corners, to rein in the free spirits.

Perhaps nowhere is the conflict played out more than in the relationship between the **director** and the studio executives. As the guiding light in the production of a feature film, it is the director who is responsible for interpreting the original work of the writer, for promoting his own styles of lighting, sound, and camera work, of sets, costumes and music, into a symphony of experiences that will enrich and enhance the actual story.

A good director "is someone who can express a point of view of the world on film and hopefully move people," says director John Carpenter (*Halloween, Escape from New York*, and *Starman*). "Directors need to be technically oriented, to be theatrical, to be writers, graphic artists, and sometimes poets, philosophers, and mechanics."

Directors do not need to be well-read. "They don't necessarily have to have seen another movie, either. Or maybe all they've ever seen are movies. It really comes from within. You need to have certain charisma and power, to be able to lead people and control them, to be able to get people to do what you want to do and have them like, not hate you.

"You have to be able to say, 'Let's go over the hill and blow up the helicopter,' and not have a mutiny on your hands. They need to respect you, they need to feel you're in control and know what you're doing."

In the constant battle between the needs of art and the needs of the pocketbook, there is no simple solution. Studio executives know that pictures can always be shot in fewer days, with less expensive sets in back lots rather than on exotic locations; with lesser-known and hence cheaper actors, with modest sets and modest special effects. The question is not if a production can be done on the cheap, but if the results will, in the end, be as artistically worthy (and financially successful) as those of a film that was given more of a free hand.

Unfortunately, the major motion picture studios have become increasingly wary about spending money. Partially due to the financial debacle of the film *Heaven's Gate*, studio executives have felt a strong incentive to play their part in keeping costs down; even more than ever, they need to play it safe. Just as it is said that no corporate computer purchasing agent was ever fired for buying IBM, it often seems that some executives live by the belief that no one has ever been fired for saying "no" to a proposed project.

For Carpenter, the notion of playing it safe has serious hidden implications; he wonders what will happen to a motion picture if it is shot in less time, if it receives less money, than it deserves.

"You could shoot *Wizard of Oz* in the San Fernando Valley in five days," Carpenter says. "It would still be the same story. But it would look very different from the picture that MGM had made. Because they had set decoration, they had special effects, they had Judy Garland. There's no way to objectively determine the price of a film. It has much more to do with the style of the director."

Directors, as producers and screenwriters, can enter a production at one of several stages of development. The director may have written the original screenplay, either alone or in collaboration with a writer; the two of them may have taken the project directly to a studio, or to a producer with clout at a studio.

On the other hand, the project may have been developed without a director; a studio that holds the right to make the film may decide that it will go ahead with the project only if it can attract one of several directors that the studio executives believe will bring the right tone to the film, and bring it in at the budget that the studio believes is appropriate for the picture.

That's how Carpenter got involved in his 1986 film, *Big Trouble in Little China*. The screenplay was sent to Carpenter for his consideration by one of its writers, W. D. Richter. At that time, the project was in development at 20th Century-Fox, and Richter was looking for a director.

"It was my kind of film," Carpenter says. "It was a fantasy, fast moving, had a lot of action, and a few scares. It was very unique and different, which is what I try to look for in movies. I try to do things that I haven't done before."

There was one problem with the draft of the script that Carpenter read: it was too expensive. "It was just too elaborate to do. It was a forty-million-dollar film. None of us wanted to do that. So we rewrote it."

Carpenter worked with Richter on the rewrite, changing scenes to bring down the cost. In one instance, the script called for a giant underground lake teeming with dragons. To cut the budget, it was rewritten to make it an underground cave, much like a sewer. The size of the cave appeared to be larger than it actually was by shooting with different camera angles, and by creating false perspectives through the use of shortened structures that seemed to indicate a depth that in reality wasn't there.

Carpenter wanted to do the project; but the first question the studio asked was whether he could make the film for the money they wanted to spend: about $16 million, according to Carpenter.

Carpenter and his long-time producer partner, Larry Franco, worked up their own budget and came to the conclusion that it could be made for $22 million. Without finalizing discussions on the budget figure, the studio agreed to hire Carpenter, with the understanding that they would come to a mutual agreement on the amount of money that would have to be spent.

"As a director you come in and this very strange waltz begins [with the studio]; the director wants as much time [to shoot] as possible. And so begins the endless confrontation between management and creativity. They want it great, but they want it cheap."

Carpenter was responsible for hiring the production's key people: the line producer (his friend, Larry Franco); the director of photography; the editor; the production designer; the casting director; and the cast.

Of course the studio, to ensure to the best of its ability that the film is progressing satisfactorily, is not silent on the choice of cast and crew. On *Big Trouble*, executives suggested that someone like Madonna be cast to play the lead, a thought which Carpenter strongly opposed as inappropriate.

Producers may side with the director's goals, but often are brought in by a studio partially to keep control on costs. The film's producer in these situations may either work for or against the director's interests, depending on who hired him in the first place. The producer is hence often in a very compromising position, as he or she both tries to keep the studio happy, while trying simultaneously to keep the director happy, even if both parties have different goals in mind.

On *Big Trouble*, Larry Franco received producer credit. Executive producer credit went to Keith Barisch and Paul Monasch, two men who, because of their strong movie-industry relationships, were able to present the project to a studio and get a development deal to pay for the expenses involved in writing the script. The project was originally written not by W. D. Richter, but by two young writers, Gary Goldman and David Weinstein. Richter was brought in later to do a rewrite.

But while Barisch and Monasch received executive producer credit on the film, Carpenter never met with Keith Barisch during the production of the picture; nor has he met him to this day. In reality, that may not have been such a detrimental fact; for those named as executive producers often receive the title for having brought a project to fruition, not for actually performing the tasks of day-to-day organization that are generally recognized as the producer's purvue.

On *Big Trouble*, Carpenter was able to rehearse the actors for two weeks prior to the start of the shooting. One reason that Carpenter wanted to have prior rehearsals for *Big Trouble* is because there was a particular tempo that he was looking for in the delivery of the lines. But as actor John Lithgow states (*see page 130*), rehearsing prior to the start of a picture is often a luxury that is not always available.

"Rehearsing costs money," says Carpenter. "You have to pay actors to rehearse. It's nothing like a stage play. You can judge a film by reading a script. Only when it's a very complex multi-character story do I need to hear everybody in conjunction. If you have time, you rehearse. If you don't, then you just go shoot."

Without rehearsal time, individual characterizations are developed on the spot, just before shooting. "The way it works," says Carpenter, "is you come in in the morning, it's early, you're tired, you've been shooting for three to four weeks, you don't want to do this anymore. You have a cup of coffee, the assistant director gets everybody together on the set, the actors stagger in, they're half in makeup, half out. They have a lot of questions about the dialogue, so we go through that. Then we physically stage a rehearsal. All you want to do at that point is get [the scene] on its feet, just say the lines, save the performance for later."

Carpenter's not concerned about the performance during rehearsals, because there are other matters to attend to. It's now time for the director of photography, in conjunction with the director, to suggest camera angles and appropriate lighting that will reflect the mood that the director is attempting to convey.

After the rehearsal, the crew is given several hours to set up the lighting, camera, and sound equipment for the shot. In the interim, Carpenter may be doing a range of things, from assisting actors with an interpretation of their lines, rewriting a scene to make it easier for an actor to perform, or to help it flow in the structure of the film, running over to another building on the lot to look at some dailies or edited footage, or as sometimes happens, "just sitting and thinking, 'How can I make it through the day because I'm so exhausted?' "

While the concept and rewards of being a successful director are indeed glamorous, the day-to-day responsibilities and tasks are indeed draining. During the shooting of a picture, "You get up at five in the morning, you go to work at six-thirty or maybe earlier. You work all day, your lunch break is either dailies or it's a meeting. After work, you see dailies or see cut footage. You go into [script] rewrites, you go home, you fall into bed, sleep a couple of hours and get back up again. You're constantly going, even on weekends. I have never experienced not working seven days a week."

Once the camera and lighting equipment is in place, Carpenter returns to the set, running the actors through their paces once again to ensure that the camera operators; the dolly grips, those men and women who must push the dolly holding the camera at the appropriate moments; as well as the **focus puller**, that person charged with refocusing the lens as the actor moves closer to or further from the cameras, are all in synchronization with the actor's actions.

The fact that the actors may not yet have truly given their all to the scene does not concern Carpenter. The magic often happens only once the cameras start to roll.

"I've discovered that nothing really major takes place, no one commits, until film is running through the camera," Carpenter notes. "Then they commit. But until then, it's gobbledygook. Once that film is rolling through there, the actors feel like, 'Uh-oh, he may use this, I'd better be here. This may show up in a thousand theaters across America.'"

After that first filmed take, Carpenter can then start to explore the scene. First, he'll get it on camera just as it's written in the script. Then he'll try varying things slightly: change a line, have one character say the line before the other, alter a bit of action. "All of a sudden, you may have something good."

Not that Carpenter is ready to extensively rewrite the script at the actor's behest. While some actors are known to make drastic changes in scenes just prior to shooting, Carpenter finds that style of working abhorrent. "I haven't spent six months or a year of my life, or even two weeks of my life, writing something down to have it changed by somebody else. This is the way I want it done. At that point in the process, it's too late. When we're shooting, we're shooting, we're not rehearsing or writing."

This tendency to perform quick rehearsals just prior to shooting, the development of camera angles and lighting strategies only on the day of the shoot, looks to outsiders as a bad way to do business. Surely, it seems, film productions can be better planned; with a little advance work, the mania that seems to pervade so many productions could be lessened.

But the fact is that much of the process of shooting a picture cannot be worked out in advance. "To sit down with a cameraman and say, 'Okay, here's what you're going to do in this scene,' two weeks before he's there and we don't know what the problems are, is silly."

Prior to the shooting date, all Carpenter feels comfortable doing is talking in general concepts with his key technical people. "This is a dark film, this is a light film. This is a film that should be shot backlit and moody. This is a film that should have a lyrical feel to it, or we should light from inside of everything, so everybody's soft and airy. You talk about feelings, and visual ideas, but you don't talk specifics until you get on the set."

In *Big Trouble*, Carpenter told his people that he wanted a sense of fun, of excitement to the picture. He saw it "as a sort of Chinese *Wizard of Oz*." But the actual placement of cameras, the actual angles at which various actors would be shot, will not be discussed until the day of the shoot.

The inevitable rush of work, the literal chaos, that accompanies that type of last-minute planning is hence unavoidable. "In my experience," says Carpenter, "as soon as I have split the power [on the film] with anyone else, it becomes enormously chaotic, by necessity. As soon as the screenplay or the idea has come from someone other than myself, as soon as there is more than one person in charge of, or thinking they're in charge of, the destiny of the project, it becomes a nightmare."

Conversely, the more Carpenter is able to retain control of a film the easier it is. "Mostly I've done that by saying, 'Listen guys, I know how to make scary movies, I know how to make thrillers, okay? So let me do this.' But as soon as someone else is looking over your shoulder and they think they have the destiny of the film in their hands and they begin to tell you what they think of the dailies, and they begin to force you into certain situations, it becomes terribly chaotic.

"The chairman of the board's wife reads the script and doesn't like the scene with the girl at the dinner table. So all of a sudden, a command comes down to rewrite the scene. And then the director has to call the writer, and the writer's angry; he doesn't want to rewrite the scene, it's a perfect scene. And the director says 'we have to.' So it's rewritten and then the actor and actress say 'I don't want to say this, this is stupid.' So you call up the management and say 'I can't do this, it's ruining the film.' And they say 'you'd better do it.' There's always the threat that they'll pull the plug, on you or the picture."

That threat did not exist on *Big Trouble*, partially, Carpenter believes, because the picture was "so strange and bizarre. I don't think the studio ever figured it out. They didn't know what they were getting, they didn't know what I was doing, but they thought, 'He knows how to do it.'"

Carpenter's doing it continued beyond shooting, into the postproduction process. While the editor was in charge of constructing the footage into a cogent structure, Carpenter was by his side virtually every day, offering his opinions, ensuring that his vision of the film would be realized.

The look of the completed film, as it turns out, surprised studio management; but their reaction was no surprise to Carpenter. Creative work usually looks different from what an outside observer expects it to look like; the difference between one's fantasized expectations and the final product often produces disappointment.

The version delivered by Carpenter to the studio came in at 99 minutes. He found the studio's reaction to be "strange. They were strange about it, as if they expected another movie. They sort of reacted in a way like, 'Boy, there's a lot of Chinese people in this film.'"

It's not as if the studio executives had not seen any parts of the film before the final cut. They had seen all of the dailies; and while they were viewing them, their reaction had been "'We love it, keep going,'" says Carpenter. "What they came up with was the first confrontation with reality, and no one likes that. Everybody wants to dream."

The studio asked for a list of changes in the film; they wanted certain clarifications, voice overs, they wanted to cut down on certain performances that they didn't think worked. "It was a big fight," Carpenter says.

He made certain changes and readied the film for an audience preview, a special screening for an invited group of people, who would then be handed out cards at the end of the screening for their comments. The studio had given some strong thoughts about what would work and what wouldn't in the film. But after the preview, the audience reacted "so positively," according to Carpenter, that the studio executives were "all very shocked at the way the audience responded."

"We were all very nervous and one of the executives was sitting with me. As the audience was laughing and clapping, I turned to him and said, 'Goddamn it, look at 'em, what do you want from this audience? They love it.' And he said, 'Yeah, you're right.'"

While Carpenter sees the usefulness of audience previews, he doubts if a reaction from a group of people who have been able to see a film for free is any barometer of the film's success across the country, when people will pay to attend a film based only on word of mouth and the film's advertising campaign.

The ad campaign for *Big Trouble* was one of the reasons that the film essentially bombed, Carpenter believes, playing for no more than a month and a half in the nation's theaters.

"They positioned it absurdly," Carpenter says. "They tried to sell the picture like *Raiders of the Lost Ark*; and they tried to deemphasize the Chinese element. The film's about the Chinese. It's about Chinese mysticism, and that's what you have to put up there.

"Their (advertising) illustration was a lot like the illustration from *Raiders of the Lost Ark*. In fact, the same artist did it. Which gave it this idea of a pulp movie. But the problem was that that had been done before. *Raiders* had been done, *Raiders II* had been done. So we just looked like another one. And that wasn't going to do it. This was a unique film. The entire job of advertising is to tell you that a movie is playing. It's to make an impression in your mind that it exists, that it's there."

It's clearly distressing to spend several years of one's life working on a project, only to see it disappear from the public's consciousness in a matter of weeks. And it's even more troubling when one believes that certain decisions were made by others that may have hurt the film's success. The various machinations that Carpenter has been a part of over the years have now caused him to eschew the major studio system, to attempt to make films as an independent, working with a group of private investors that will give him complete control.

At the same time, Carpenter knows that the lack of investment from a major studio means that it will be very difficult for his future pictures to make a major impact on the marketplace. "You can't have a breakaway film, a film that really goes to the moon, unless you have a studio behind you. They are so strong and powerful, they have so many films that they release, that the theater owners are looking to them. The studios can keep a film in a theater, they can nourish it, they can make it grow.

"Directors have gone way over budget so many times in the past," notes Carpenter, "that the attitude in Hollywood now is very anticreative and very promanagement: 'We'll show these guys, we're not gonna give them that.' They assume that every director is like your clichéd idea of the director who just goes way over budget. Well, we're not all that way. I think most directors try to be responsible. But it's assumed immediately that we're not."

Production Designer, Art Director, Set Decorator
■ John Muto

Film students interested in learning how to write screenplays are often advised to examine the classic scripts of the past. By studying the greats of American film, they're told, they'll learn how it's done.

So many go off to the film library and carefully pore over the likes of *Casablanca*, *The Maltese Falcon*, and other noteworthy screenplays. They then mimic what they've seen in their own first scripts—and are shaken when they're criticized for doing so.

One problem with that approach is that script standards have changed over the years. For example, it was commonplace, rather than unusual, for scripts of the 1940s and 1950s not only to give accurate portrayals of the characters along with evocative dialogue, but also to include most camera angles and elaborate descriptions of sets. Terms such as "quick cut," "reaction shot," "dolly back," and "crane shot" were often included in a screenplay, along with carefully worked-out locations, listing colors, decorations, and sizes.

But screenplays today are not written as they were just a

few decades ago. An attempt to learn style by copying the style of the past only leads one down the wrong path.

Where screenwriters once carried the responsibility of director, production designer, and director of photography, today he or she is expected to stick to his own expertise, and leave the other aspects of filmmaking to the various specialists. Today's screenplays only hint at the way sets should look; and they leave virtually all of the camera angles to the imagination of the director of photography, who works them out in conjunction with the director (*see pages 105–115* for a more complete discussion about camera work).

Many screenwriters may have little or no idea how a location should look; they may know only how they would *like* it to look. The director-screenwriter Paul Schrader *(Taxi Driver, Mishima)* often finds elaborate research into locations superfluous. When writing *Blue Collar,* he sketched a description of the film's location into his narrative just by chatting via telephone with a friend familiar with the area in which the film took place.

Today, the actual design of a set, the realization of a location that may exist only in the minds of the screenwriter and director, comes to life through the work of the **production designer.** It is the production designer who, working in conjunction with the director, actually designs the sets, picking out their colors and deciding on their materials and overall look. The production designer is, in essence, an architect; but rather than being lauded for creating a new structure to serve the needs of a contemporary, changing society, the production designer is rewarded for bringing to light what has existed only in the imagination of the writer and director—for reconstructing an idealized version of a structure that will, through its shapes, size, and colors, embody the message or feeling of the motion picture.

If a production designer is doing his job well, then his job goes virtually unnoticed. Like a violinist in an orchestra, the production designer's work is not meant to stand out, to be admired. Rather, his true success comes when virtually no one sees the effort that went into the design, or even the design itself.

The production must be created in such a way that an audience unconsciously senses the appropriate feeling or mood of the story, without realizing that they are being manipulated into doing so. Like the violinist, the production designer, through the virtuosity of his performance, must add to the mood of the entire piece, without ever actually being heard.

An incorrect set, one that in retrospect seems out of keeping with the mood of the film, can destroy a picture. If a director is trying to create a particular world, and the set implies that it's another one, then the emotions of the audience may wind up being led down a completely inappropriate path.

It's that control, that ability to literally "set the scene" that first attracted John Muto to the idea of what he later came to know as the field of production design. "I always thought that the movie director was the guy who built the sets," says Muto, the production designer on such films as *Jaws 3-D* and *River's Edge*. "That's what I thought because that's what interested me most about movies: the way they looked, where the camera was, the shots."

Muto took an unconventional approach to his career; growing up in the 1960s, he originally had little motivation or drive. Majoring in English at UC Berkeley, he learned that while he wanted to be a writer, "I could hardly read, let alone write. The only stuff I read when I got out of college was comic books." That interest in comics led Muto to think that he could actually even draw them. While in San Francisco, he landed a job drawing cells, the individual frames which make up an animated film, "one of the great hippie jobs in San Francisco at that time." After a film crew came down to shoot a dance group that he had joined, he suddenly found himself interested in filmmaking. He became enamored with the medium, and started carrying lights for the crew; when they got a contract to do an animated film, he successfully convinced the people that he could draw the animation cells, even though he had never done it before.

Drifting in and out of jobs, Muto eventually landed a position at Harcourt Brace, working on educational films and filmstrips. He eventually gave up drawing to become a producer-director of those projects.

In 1979, Muto was asked to develop some animation for a film to be shot with the Los Angeles rock group Oingo-Boingo. "Once I finished it, I was suddenly known all over town," Muto recalls. He began working as a special-effects man, but began to feel after a few pictures that "effects was a dead end. Most guys in effects would really rather spend all their time watching movies or reading comic books. They're tinkerers. As a guy who understands special effects but really wants to be a production designer or art director, I have a skill that hardly anybody has. Most production designers in the last twenty years have come out of art direction, or interior design. But I was coming from much more of a pure film approach."

That approach allowed Muto to understand a picture from the filmic point of view. He knows not only what an art director needs, but also how those needs integrate or clash with the needs of a director or a director of photography. "I don't build a set and then walk away. I think about the kind of shot that the [director] needs, then build the set to fit the shots—that's my special-effects approach."

When Muto is called in to design a picture, the first thing he does is read the script; not just to learn what the story is about, but to help him understand what the picture is about: its themes, its point of view, its images. And once Muto understands that, "then the design sort of becomes obvious to me. The colors become obvious, the sources of the necessary locations become obvious."

That sense of the obvious does not just develop from thin air. Rather, it is a skill whose workings have become automatic; a skill developed by forcing oneself to perceive the world in a particular way. "I developed a critical facility, a personal sense of aesthetics and style, and now I apply it. I've got a million books, but I tend not to look at books. I just look at everything. Everything interests me—the way things are made and how they look. I put the TV on once a day and look at all the channels. I look at magazines. I look at all kinds of stuff. I just see as much as I can. And I keep everything. I'm a compulsive hoarder."

The production designer's job may start even before the script is finished. Muto often receives calls from screenwriter friends asking for his advice on how to translate a theme or idea into something that will work visually, rather than just on paper. On the 1987 Hemdale picture, *River's Edge*, director Tim Hunter asked Muto for his opinion of the script; Muto thought it "brilliant" but also felt that his expertise wasn't needed.

"The script was written like a documentary. I told the director he didn't need me to design the film, because it's what we call a 'director's movie.' You just go out and find a couple of locations and decorate them."

Director Hunter was interested in more than that quick brush-off. Pressing him, Hunter learned that Muto saw the picture as "a medieval film. It's about the breakdown of civilization." But in order for that feeling to be portrayed, it was necessary for the filmmakers to find an image that reflected that theme; otherwise the picture would look like just one more adventure film.

The story called for the lower-middle-class characters to live in a nondescript stucco home, but the script's description of the location was nothing more than "tract home in Pasadena." Hardly a useful tool in helping the actors, director, or even production designer in understanding the feel that the writer was trying to impart through his story. Muto cautioned against placing them in such a building unless a tract could be found where nature had begun to take over. He wanted foliage everywhere, "the way people lived after the fall of the Roman Empire, where the trees start coming in and crack the pavement and grow everywhere."

Muto got his idea from the character of Seck. As played by Dennis Hopper, he reminded Muto of "the guy who survived

Easy Rider after all," a man who spent all his time in this house with his inflatable "girlfriend," Ellie. "He's like a crazy knight; he fought the dragon and the dragon bit his leg off. He's like Don Quixote. Don Quixote has this girlfriend, Dulcinea, who's fake. Ellie is Dulcinea."

To find the right locations, Muto drove hundreds of miles around California, looking for places that fit his images. In the end, he discovered a ruined stone house, one with a sense of being a castle in decay. He also found, in Tujunga, a rural desertlike area near Los Angeles, an old school with a Romanesque flavor. And the more he worked, the more he looked, the more Muto realized that he was evolving his concept toward a religious image, a Catholic image.

Not that Muto suddenly expected that a film audience would look at the sets and say "Aha! This film has a religious flavor!" Nor did Muto consciously try to find "religious" images for the design. "It just meant pushing in that direction."

Ideas for a set design can come either through meticulous, carefully thought-out preproduction work, or may appear somewhat more haphazardly, as the film starts to take shape. On *River's Edge*, the director wasn't interested in looking at sketches of how the various sets would look, according to Muto. But for another recent release, *Flowers in the Attic*, Muto produced a multitude of design drawings prior to the shooting of the film. The attic itself was borrowed from literature, in the sense that Muto attempted to make it feel like Miss Haversham's attic in Dickens's famed novel *Great Expectations*. "I was modeling it on an English movie, a David Lean picture." The attic was designed with sharp converging lines, to give the set a sense that it was deeper that it really was. Cobwebs, clutter, and a large amount of muted brown tones added to the sense of decay, solitude, and warmth that family attics often evoke in people.

It's not just structures that are important emotional tools for an audience. Color plays an important part as well. In *Night of the Comet*, Muto not only collaborated with the costume designer, assisting in picking the clothes for the actors, but also made sure that the tones of the costumes, lighting, and sets made emotional sense.

Those required moods may change from scene to scene. While reading a script, Muto will break the action down into acts, learning the dramatic transitions, which will then be reflected in the scenic transitions. In *Comet*, Muto understood that the entire tone of the picture changed after the arrival of the comet on earth. That change was effected by changing the tone of the film to a red-orange color, achieved with the use of various lights and filters.

After the production designer decides on the overall look of the set, he will have the **art director**, who is concerned about the way the set looks, actually supervise the construction. The production designer, on the other hand, is concerned with the way the film looks.

The art director might suggest to the director of photography that a set be built without a ceiling or particular walls, if those parts of the room will never be shown in the film. (By eliminating parts of sets, time can be saved and costs be reduced. With fewer physical structures to contend with, the director of photography's flexibility will be increased as he will be able to place his camera and lights in a larger number of spots for more varied camera angles.)

Reporting to the art director will be the **construction coordinator**, the individual who oversees the construction of the set, the actual work of which is handled by a number of **carpenters** and **carpenter's assistants.**

That's the ideal. On lower-budget and nonunion films, it's not unusual to find one or more of these professionals fulfilling several roles: the production designer may also be the art director, the art director can also be the construction coordinator, etc.

In addition to the construction needs of the film, the set must also be "dressed," that is, made to feel that it is lived in, that it is a real house. Again, in the ideal situation, that dressing is done by a **set decorator,** an individual often with interior design experience employed to carry out the themes of the set as expressed by the production designer.

"I'll say, 'This is what this person is all about,'" Muto notes. "'The person who lives [in this set] has these sorts of ambitions, or comes from this kind of family.' I'll explain to the set decorator that we want to work in this color or this edge of the spectrum. Ideally, the decorator collaborates with me, coming up with his own suggestions."

The set decorator has his or her own assistant, the assistant set decorator or **lead man,** so named because that individual takes the "lead," literally running around town, looking for various objects, various artifacts with which to decorate the set. Those objects are decided on in advance in collaboration with the production designer and set decorator. Photos may be taken of objects that it is thought will fit into the design, then shown to the production designer and the director for approval. In the meantime, those items that have been photographed have already been put on reserve by the lead man in case they are needed for the production.

In case of a large production with requirements for a lot of objects, a **swing gang,** which reports to the lead man, will be sent out to actually bring all the objects needed for the production back to the set. Once the objects arrive on the set, a **set dresser** will be employed to arrange everything for shooting.

It's important to remember that these titles are not hewn in stone. "They're more honored in the breach," according to Muto. They represent the ideal crew, the one that exists when money is relatively plentiful and everyone can be hired that needs to be hired.

Other times, credits may be traded for money, not just in the production design arena, but in all aspects of the film process. "Sometimes you get a person for fifty dollars less per week because you promise to give them a set dresser, rather than a lead man credit," Muto points out. "They don't want to be called 'lead man' because nobody knows what a lead man is, but 'dresser' sounds important."

The actual dressing of a set is an art; it is not, as many film school students think, a simple act of throwing a couple of objects into a scene to represent a particular lifestyle or economic class. It is easy to overlook the fact that new homes do not instantly look lived-in; they become "decorated" over years of steady accumulation of objects. In order to create a "lived-in" sense, enough objects need to be placed in a scene not only to be seen, but also to be "felt." The set decorator and production designer understand that the placement of certain objects enhances the richness of the space, even if most people never consciously notice them.

That fact has not escaped the set decorators at Disneyland and Disney World. In the theme parks' famous "Pirates of the Caribbean" ride, many of the treasure-filled caves that one views are filled with objects in the outer reaches that few if any people will actually see; but their presence adds to the sense that one is indeed in what could actually be a pirate's cave.

This dictum can, of course, be carried to an inappropriate extreme. Some production designers get caught up in their own visions, in their own sense of how well they can decorate, while ignoring the actual needs of the production they're working on. During the shooting of *River's Edge*, Muto had "to spend a lot of time yanking stuff off the set that was put there by clever art department people who thought it was amusing, the trash that poor people have in their homes. I had to yank a lot of little cutesy-pie chotchkies off the set. There's an area of art direction which is so incredibly patronizing. There are these people that work in art departments and they all have the same stuff . . . they all have these little dinosaur notebooks, all that junk that you buy in little design stores, all those clever things. There are always these little [art department] in-jokes on the set."

For Muto, the perfect example of that was *The Trip to Bountiful*. "I'm watching the movie; it's about a crazy old woman and they're living in this apartment, and I'm saying to myself, 'What are they complaining about? They have a nice place.' Then I realized that what was going on from an art director's point of view was the opposite of what the film was supposed to say.

"Part of the conflict of that film was that the characters were supposed to be poor. But that apartment looked like some wealthy West Hollywood guy lived there, who had painstakingly collected a lot of beautiful 1940s crockery. I think the art director fell so in love with the subject that he forgot what the film was about."

Too often, Muto feels, art directors get wrapped up in the concept of "texture," in creating a space that will define the character by adding every type of object that, singly, might fit the personality of that individual, but that collectively are totally inappropriate. "You've seen those films where it's just junk everywhere—it's like kids' rooms and attics are full of stuff, but with no general sense of what the frame [of reference] is. It's for the lack of ideas that art directors will over-texturize and over-detail spaces.

"But that kind of stuff kills a movie. Because if you notice it, it draws you away from the film, the story. Instead you think, 'Isn't the art director witty?' That's the antithesis of filmmaking."

What Muto would rather do is have people perceive ideas, moods, characterizations, on a subconscious level, in a way that does not intrude with the simple storytelling itself. In *Night of the Comet*, for instance, Muto worked with colors to evoke and emphasize certain personalities. Muto saw the picture as a comic book: it had a hyper-real sense, and, like a comic book, it stripped out all the unnecessary elements from reality. He assigned a different color to each character and a characteristic color to each set. The "bad guys" were dressed in blues and grays, while the two female protagonists were in bright colors. The older girl, the more intellectual of the two, was in deep colors to emphasize her intelligence. "The other girl, who was kind of wacky, I did her all in tints.

"I decided to make up a cheerleader costume for her that no one would ever see [in real life]. So I made one of magenta and turquoise. Nobody realizes what we did, but you get a cheerleader that you really notice. You don't know why she looks so special, but you really notice her."

The actual amount of freedom that a production designer has in designing the space depends on how many preconceived ideas the director brings to the film. With the director being the ultimate authority on the picture, the designer must make suggestions in such a way as not to interfere with whatever notions the director already has.

"You make suggestions very innocuously," Muto says. "You suggest something to a director or a director of photography in such a way that they think it's their own idea. Because ultimately it's more important that the idea be on the screen, than that you get credit."

Often, one can wind up getting credit for something anyway. On more than one occasion Muto has seen "something on the screen that I had nothing to do with, but everyone will give me credit for it. Or I'll hear someone praising the director for some aspect of a film, and I'll realize that the director had nothing to do with it, it was all my doing."

The important thing in working with a director, or any member of a film crew, is learning how to represent one's ideas so that they are accepted, or at least heard. "That's why people often aren't successful until they're in their thirties," Muto believes. "Because you have to learn how to give your ideas, and if people don't accept them, you can't allow yourself to get too freaked out about it. Sometimes directors can start going off on a tangent that doesn't make any sense at all. You can sit around and be annoyed, or you can say, well, it's their movie, let's see where it goes. All the wonderful ideas in your head can't be used. You have to come to grips with that reality.

"But people who don't have enough emotional maturity will come up with an idea, and they won't get off of the idea, they won't take no for an answer. Finally they have to be told, 'Listen, this is the way I want to do it. You'll get your chance when *you* direct a film.'"

There are always insidious methods for getting one's own way. In the world of production design and art direction, high-powered individuals may force directors to shoot a scene in a particular fashion by presenting them with a fait accompli, a set that has been designed so that a shot can be had from only one particular angle, the angle that the production designer has unilaterally decided is appropriate. That's a tricky game to play, one that will work only with a weak-willed director, or a powerful designer who has worked long enough to achieve the clout necessary to pull off such a stunt.

Often, the process of design itself winds up forcing the shot into the mold that the designer wants. "At the end of *Flowers in the Attic*, I looked back at the sketches I had made before the shooting," Muto recalls, "and the scenes really looked the way they ultimately came out. And you realize that by making a little choice here and a little choice there, somehow, at the other end, the director or the director of photography is forced into shooting something the way you want it, even though it looks like it was their idea."

When the job of production design is over, the job of the production designer often isn't. For people like Muto, the responsibilities continue. Each day's screening of "dailies," the film footage shot the day before, is attended by Muto. If problems in lighting, set coloring, or decoration show up, he can make quick corrections to the set while it's still in use. "I'm the kind of person who even appears on the set to straighten an actor's costume prior to the shoot."

But such ongoing participation cannot occur unless the captain of the production team, the director, feels certain that the designer is there to help him achieve his vision of the film, not to interfere or attempt to sabotage his work artistically. "Once a director trusts you, he understands you're on his side. Being a director is basically a lonely position. And basically, all creative people are paranoid, including the people I work with.

My people have to convince me that they're on my side and not against me. And I usually try to convince a director that I'm in his corner, that I can help him.

"But if you don't go to dailies, if you don't try to get along with the director of photography, and you don't try to make sure the director knows you're with him, then you're just fooling yourself.

"I don't want lint where I don't want lint. I don't want the angle to be wrong and I don't want to see what I don't want to see.

"I want an image that's exactly what I and the director and the director of photography want it to be. When I create a film as a production designer, I want to create perfection."

Director of Photography
■ Haskell Wexler

The finished film reflects the director's image of what the picture should look like. But it's an image greatly tempered by the reality of the photographic process: its techniques, its limitations, its ability to transform a story on a printed page into something different, a world that at once looks real but in actuality is totally false.

Once a director is contracted to a particular film, one of the first people he hires and consults with is his **director of photography,** for it is the "DP" who—armed with the knowledge of how a camera works, how a camera "sees" a scene, and the various properties of different film emulsions—takes the needs of the director, his desire to evoke certain emotions, to explore certain facets of the actors, and attempts to translate them into a visual form.

Other aspects of the production process, such as lighting, costume design, and set decoration, exist only to serve what will ultimately be captured on film. Hence, the relationship between the director and his DP must, of necessity, be primary.

It is to the DP—not the producer, the actors, or anyone else—that the director imparts his inner secrets, his vision of the motion picture. If the director of a picture is a god—and to many, including himself, he often is—then the DP is his angel, his messenger among men. For the DP must not only help the director realize his own vision; he also must convey, interpret, and explain that vision to the production people on the crew, while the director does the same for the actors.

Such a lofty and respected position does not come without trade-offs. The responsibilities of the job also mean that it is the DP who is often held accountable for technical problems, regardless of whether the DP had anything to do with them. The DP, then, is not only the person who "shoots" the film, but often, as the bearer of bad news, is the one who gets "shot" himself.

"Sometimes directors have a love/hate relationship with DPs," said Haskell Wexler, one of the film industry's veteran directors of photography. "Some directors feel a kind of veiled threat from the DP because they're the tool through which a director's thoughts, ideas, and abstractions get changed into the material of the film. Directors depend on DPs, but they also want to feel that the film is theirs . . . and it's up to the DP to do that for them. As some say, DPs are not friends of directors, they're their servants."

Wexler has served as DP on a number of this country's most seminal films, including Elia Kazan's *America, America; One Flew Over the Cuckoo's Nest; Bound for Glory; Medium Cool;* and *Latino* (the latter two of which Wexler also directed).

The role of director of photography includes much more than a thorough knowledge of the motion picture camera. It just as importantly involves a thorough knowledge of the film business; the DP must understand, for instance, that if he works his crew harder and gets certain shots before 11:40 P.M., then he'll save the production a bundle of money by not forcing the shoot into double time, when crews get paid considerably more.

The third skill of the DP is nothing less than political savvy—an ability to work well with the producer, the production manager, and the director as part of a team; to know when to make suggestions and when to back off; to know how to elicit the support he or she needs from a crew to make the job easier, the production cheaper, and, ultimately, the film better.

The director of photography's involvement in the picture begins several months before the shoot. And as with every role in the film production business, his responsibilities vary from project to project. When a production is short of money or time, very often a film will be shot in a "formulaic" method; everyone's seen those pictures that, for one reason or another, look like "standard" fare: they're usually described as "looking like TV movies."

That's an adequate solution for films that have little ambition other than to entertain an audience at the most basic, escapist level. One wouldn't expect to see "artistic" photography, for instance, in standard exploitation films such as *Friday the 13th* or *Animal House*. By employing standard shooting angles, with no fancy crane shots or lighting, the producer can keep costs down by hiring a DP who is proficient in the basics, such as how to light a scene, how to shoot close-ups, reaction shots, wide angles, etc.

By contrast, photography can also be used to impart a mood, to enhance the characterization, to emphasize certain parts of the story, to allow a film to rise above the norm. For this to occur the DP needs to understand the picture and what the director is trying to impart emotionally and intellectually through the film. Preparing for the shoot in this type of situation means more than just studying the script to find out how many close-ups or exterior shots there are; it often means extended conversations with the director and a thorough understanding of the story and the period in which it is being shot. Just as an actor must immerse him- or herself in a role, so too the DP needs to feel fully a part of the picture, to reach the point where he and the director are so in synch that verbal communication between the two can be kept to a minimum.

Haskell Wexler is in the fortunate position of being able to turn down pictures that he does not want to shoot. After thirty years as a director of photography, working his way up from documentaries and cigarette commercials to become one of the most sought-after camera artists in the U.S., Wexler can often pick a project based in large part on artistic, not economic, reasons.

This was the situation with regard to Wexler's work *Matewan*, written and directed by John Sayles, starring James Earl Jones, and released in the summer of 1987. The picture tells the story of a coal strike in a West Virginia town at the turn of the century, when many miners were killed after the company brought in professional strike breakers to divide the black and Italian miners from the native West Virginia workers and, by so doing, to break the strike. Wexler heard about the picture and called Sayles to express his interest in shooting it. Sayles was pleased, but told Wexler that, as a film director used to shooting on low budgets (this picture cost in the $3 million to $4 million range, a very small amount of money for films today), he couldn't afford to pay him. Wexler agreed to take a salary considerably lower than the fee he normally commands.

The two began working together one month before the shoot. Besides reading the script, Wexler read extensively about the period and about West Virginia and the coal industry, and looked at multitudes of still pictures taken during that time.

Wexler quickly realized that the still pictures reflected exactly the kind of photography that he did *not* want to recreate for the film. In the last decade, filmmakers have attempted to evoke a particular era by shooting films not so they reflect how the world looked, but to reflect how we *view* that past world when we look at now-aged photographs of that era. Color photographs did not look washed-out when they were originally shot in the 1950s; yet that washed-out appearance often shows up in World War II–era motion pictures to give us the sense that we are watching something old. And while photographs taken in the nineteenth century show most people with somber faces in front of soft-focused backgrounds, that was a product of the contemporary photographic art, not of the culture as it truly existed.

"I had to say, when looking at those photographs, that this

was not the way people dressed normally," Wexler recalls. "It's not like candid pictures. We assume that pictures capture people, and most of the pictures I was looking at from that era were shots that were taken posed. I wanted to do something different. I wanted to do a period picture different from *Bound for Glory* or *Days of Heaven*. I was getting tired of a lot of diffusion [of light] and a lot of induced colors, and things that have become a cliché for period movies."

While Wexler was tiring of the now-clichéd techniques, he was also in large part responsible for having popularized them. In *Bound for Glory*, for instance, he placed a woman's stocking in front of lens to soften the image and give it the "feel" we associate with a 1930s scene.

"Somehow our view of the past, based on photographs, is soft, diffused. So I tried to go against that for this film, because I thought that a little more brittle look might fit the story better."

At the same time, Eastman Kodak, the principal supplier of motion picture film in the United States, was experimenting with a new "fast" (highly light-sensitive) film called 5297. Unlike other stocks, the film did not sacrifice a sharp image quality for its higher-than-normal sensitivity to light. Consequently, a greater depth of field could be achieved in low light conditions, while still providing an image that did not look excessively grainy, as is usually the case with regular emulsions.

This turned out to be just what was needed for *Matewan*. For shooting in dark coal mines, Wexler would welcome the opportunity to cut down on the number of lights that he would have to use. Wexler contacted Kodak, and they agreed to provide him with a special test run of the new film, even though it was not yet available on the market.

Some directors have very little visual sense. They may know how they want the actors to behave, they may have a vague idea of how the film should look, but after that, the actual camera angles are often left up to the director of photography. But John Sayles works very differently. Having spent several years trying to raise enough money to make the film, Sayles had enough time to figure out exactly how every shot should look. He created a "sto-ryboard" for the film, a collection of small drawings depicting every camera angle. But the DP cannot just follow the boards, shooting everything that the director envisions; for while the boards are a good basis for the look of the film, what works on paper may not always work on film.

"Certain conditions at the location are never anticipated," Wexler points out. "Fog, for instance; or a child's swing that would make a nice foreground piece in a scene. Sometimes, an actor will have a way of walking up a flight of stairs that will be much more interesting if the camera starts on their feet and moves up their body as they climb."

With Sayles, it was a situation with a fair amount of give and take. Suggestions made by Wexler different from the story-boarded concept were often accepted by Sayles. At other times, "he would say, 'This is the way I imagined it and this is the way we're going to shoot it.'"

Wexler's extensive reading about the period in which the film took place allowed him to feel "the tremendous hardship that these people lived under. These people had horrible condi-tions: not enough food, working in company towns where they were in debt, where they were under physical threat if they tried to do things to better their condition. I was always saying 'dirty up [the actors] more.' Here were these people who were dying at young ages with respiratory ailments. Miners were treated like disposables; there was no electricity. I tried to bear all that in mind while shooting the film."

But besides making the DP feel closer to the material, is there any tangible, material benefit to having all this knowledge? The problem is, according to Wexler, that we all continue to pan-der to contemporary tastes, regardless of how much we know about the period in which the story takes place. "If you really wanted to make a period film you should study the language, you should be aware of where people went to the bathroom, what foods they ate and didn't eat, what they told their kids. Even in my lifetime I remember commonly held attitudes which, if expressed today, would seem weird. I remember that when I was young if you saw a woman smoking, that was a loose woman."

While photography has a lot to do with the look of the picture, the camera can only capture, or exploit to its fullest extent, what is presented to it. Consequently, art direction, wardrobe, and makeup play a key role in defining the look of the image that will be recorded onscreen. And, as the director of photography is shaping the look of the picture, he is often integrally involved in the choices of costumes and production design.

In *Bound for Glory*, the film that portrayed the life of singer and American folk hero Woody Guthrie, Wexler was intimately involved in the art and costume design processes. He wanted as black-and-white a look as possible for the first three-quarters of the film. To achieve that, he made sure that all the costumes had nothing more than earth tones. Once Guthrie arrived in Los Angeles, the characters began wearing costumes with tones that would appear colorful.

Nor does an experienced director of photography just accept the dictates of a production designer; it is the DP who decides which walls of a set are to be left open to allow for large lighting units to be put into place, or how far away to place a large window from the center of a room to allow the placement of lighting units that will simulate daylight.

But things don't always work out the way one expects them to; it is not a clear-cut decision-making process. Directors of photography do not dictate their demands to production designers, and directors do not dictate their desires to DPs. Above all else, filmmaking is a business of compromises; actions are often taken more for economic than artistic reasons. A director or DP may want fifty costumed extras riding across one scene—but if the project can't afford it, then the scene will be scuttled or reduced in size. If a DP thinks a particular color of costume material would look perfect next to a brick building in Toronto, he may have to abandon his idea if the costume designer was able to get a terrific deal on fabric in another color from a local supplier.

It is a mistake to think that big-budget, $40 million movies are immune from compromises. All directors, all DPs, all production and costume designers, want to do more than they sometimes can. The question is not whether compromises have to be made. The question is, as Haskell Wexler says, "From what point do we have to compromise? I would have loved to have had a small crane on *Matewan* to make some little moves, but we couldn't afford one."

Similarly, a lack of funds often demands unique solutions to production problems. "You go back to ways of doing things you did in the early days," says Wexler.

On *Matewan*, a number of scenes take place in a coal mine. Since the company couldn't afford to build its own coal mine set, they had to work in a real one. While that, at first glance, might sound like a good, not a bad, idea, the fact is that actual locations often are worse than artificial ones. Real locations cannot be controlled; one must accept them basically as they are. If a wall is too close to allow good camera placement for an ideal shot, that's too bad. If a corridor is too narrow to permit a dolly for an ideal tracking shot, that also must be accepted.

When the actors had to crawl through dark, dank areas in *Matewan*, Wexler shot those scenes by putting the camera on a tube attached to a skateboard. As the actor crawled, the crew pulled on the skateboard to pull the camera along in front of him. To light the actor's face, a ring of small halo lights was attached to the circumference of the lens. The lights were on a dimmer switch that could raise or lower the light level as the actor got closer to or further from the camera. "When you don't have the tools you would like, you create other tools," Wexler says.

While the director and director of photography confer over the visual look of the film, it is the director, not the DP, who consults with the actors. The hierarchy of communication must be followed, even if the DP, as one of the individuals closest to the onscreen action, sees problems with the performance. For it is the director in whom the actors must place trust. No one can afford—for the sake of the picture or his or her own career—to undermine that trust.

In the same way, the DP must be careful about what he says to those below him in the hierarchical chain. For example, a change in the wind could affect the look of a particular shot if a tree branch suddenly obscures an actor's face. It's the **gaffer's** job *(see pages 151–162)* to ensure that the branch is out of the way. A good gaffer will know the problem without even being told.

"You've got to give the people you're working with the benefit of the doubt. I make an effort to notice what people are doing and thank them . . . it only helps my photography (although I also *want* to thank them). If someone has the attitude, 'I'll just do my job and the hell with him,' then you're in trouble as a cameraman. Because then you have to be on your toes every second. There's no one out there on your side."

The director of photography does not actually operate the camera; that's the job of the **camera operator.** By not actually looking through the viewfinder during the shooting, the DP can concentrate on the framing, lighting, acting, and composition. The DP watches the scene play out on the set and via the video assist's monitor. A relatively new invention, the video assist is a small television camera attached to the motion picture camera lens, offering a simultaneous image of the scene on the video monitor as it is being shot. While video images do not come close to the quality available on 35-millimeter film, they do give a good instantaneous approximation of how the shot will look.

But the camera operator does more than just push the button of the camera. He or she is balancing a number of critical concerns during the shooting of the scene. For example, it is the camera operator who, while shooting a "dolly shot" (a scene shot from a four-wheeled platform moved slowly through the set), must notice that it will be necessary to duck one's head as the camera is dollied through a doorway. It is the camera operator, not the DP, who must remember that if the dolly turns to the right once through the door, it can go only so far before bumping into the lighting stands. It is the camera operator, not the director of photography, who must remember that, as an actor approaches the camera, the camera can be tilted up only so far before the boom holding the microphone appears in the frame.

"If I, as a DP, were to do all those things," Wexler notes, "I couldn't look at lighting as carefully, I couldn't watch the performance in the dispassionate way I need to."

Just as the job of the production designer does not end with the start of shooting, so the role of the DP does not end with the completion of shooting. Directors of photography are often involved in the editing process, offering their suggestions to the editor as to which shots, from a cinematographic point of view, are the best. The process can be a painful one for DPs, as they often watch what they consider to be some of their best, most thoughtful, and most creative work wind up "on the cutting-room floor."

What often happens, according to Haskell Wexler, is that the interesting shots are crane shots, shots that "look through things and pass around with people going in and out of frame. With today's modern [i.e., fast] tempo, filmmakers don't want to take time with people coming through doors—they want to get right to it." So those shots often get discarded.

On the other hand, shots not destined for the film sometimes inexplicably wind up in it. On one occasion, during the production of *The Thomas Crown Affair*, Wexler had nothing to do; to kill time, he shot some grass blowing in the wind, just because he liked the way it looked. "Lo and behold, it was used by the editor."

In the end, the process, the orientation, the vision, all are the director's. The director of photography, as first mate, must take orders—or jump ship. "Sometimes the director will want you to shoot an angle which you feel is just plain stupid. In that situation, you have to ask yourself if he just might know more than you do. There's seldom only one way—and depending on your relationship with him, you can discuss it."

But one thing that is beyond discussion for Wexler is the

use to which his skills are being put. For Wexler, it is not enough just to do a good job. "What we're doing as DPs is important. The end product is important. There's a lot of emphasis on 'I'm just doing my job and if I don't do it, someone else will.' That psychology amongst privileged professionals in film and TV has to be challenged. You do have responsibility for how you use your art, your thoughts, your profession. All artists have to think about that."

Otherwise, "Once they determine that you're a whore, then the next question is 'What's the price?'"

Stuntperson
Conrad Palmisano

Filmmakers learned at the dawn of the medium that the camera was more than a recorder of reality: it overwhelmingly was a shaper of reality. Through positioning, camera angles, lighting, and framing, the cameraperson, working in conjunction with the director, could selectively record and reshape the world as they saw it.

In some ways, the film industry may have done too good a job. After seeing the umpteenth person disappear after having a magic wand waved at him, after seeing thousands of automobile near-misses in virtually every silent Keystone Kops comedy, the public has come to believe that it is all indeed a result of "trick photography." Of course the real trick is how filmmakers from the beginning of the art form have been able to make the most difficult physical feat look like a piece of cake on camera, truly like a trick.

While some of them clearly were "tricks"—Harold Lloyd actually hung just a few feet above a platform when he was swinging from that clock in *Safety Last*, for instance—other filmic activities have always entailed great potential physical harm to the performer. The reason it doesn't look that way is not because it's so easy, but because the people who carry out the stunts are so good.

With today's emphasis on technologically sophisticated and action-oriented films, stunt work has taken on an increasingly important part of the production. With the passing of "small" pictures in America, those that concentrated on telling a simple story, American film studios have instead looked for visually exciting projects, movies that will keep an audience on the edge of their seats not for psychological reasons, but because they're wondering if the hero is going to get pushed off a five-hundred-foot cliff or not.

The fact of physical endangerment has always been a part of the cinema. Buster Keaton was famed for performing most of his own feats—and suffered a broken neck because of it. But today, with rising liability insurance premiums and the very high expense of making any picture, it no longer makes sense for an actor to do his own stunt work.

Having professional stuntpeople fill in for feats of derring-do is "really just for the sake of good business," says Conrad Palmisano, a stuntman for the last fifteen years, and current president of the Stuntman's Association, the largest professional grouping of stuntmen in the United States (stuntwomen have their own organizations). Palmisano has performed stunt work in *Heartbeeps, Breaking Away, Whose Life Is It, Anyway?, The Jerk, Airplane,* and *One from the Heart,* among other films. In addition, he has served as second-unit director for *First Blood, Uncommon Valor,* and *Heart Like a Wheel.* "With movies being shot out of sequence, if an actor does his own fight scene and gets a fat lip in Scene 54, what can we do with him in Scene 6, which may not have been shot yet? Films are too expensive to allow an actor to do his own stunts."

The nature of those stunts can range from a simple fight scene, to a truly harrowing fall from a cliff, to a powerful collision with an oncoming truck. Danger is minimized through careful practice; stuntpeople learn the best ways to fall, how to survive car crashes, and how to reduce danger to themselves through the proper use of appropriate camera angles.

For all of the film industry's technological emphasis, stunts today are actually less dangerous than they were forty years ago. "Talk about danger," says Palmisano. "Try to fall from a saddle of a horse that's running thirty miles per hour down a hill with thirty cowboys following behind you. And with all the dust clouds obscuring the action, you have to fall in front of everything, while also making sure that you don't get run over by a covered wagon, cowboys, or Indians.

"The danger of turning over in a Conestoga wagon is a lot more severe than turning over in a 1994 Camaro with roll cages and a puncture-proof gas tank. It was more dangerous to fall twenty-five feet in the old days into cardboard boxes or sawhorses, than it is today to fall one hundred feet onto an inflatable air mattress."

Camera angles have always allowed the viewer to think that someone was getting hit square on the jaw, when the punch had actually completely missed his face. But today, not only do large air-bag type mattresses greet the stuntman at the bottom of a cliff from which he's just jumped, but harnesses, roll bars, and cages hold in a driver through a sequence of car crashes, while selective film editing reduces, but does not eliminate, the risks involved in high-speed car chases.

Stuntpeople either substitute for an actual actor, performing a physical act that would be too dangerous for an actor to risk, or they become actors themselves, posing as background extras—**utility stuntpeople**, they're called—playing anonymous pedestrians or other "atmosphere" characters—available to be hit by a car careening down a sidewalk when required.

The actual decision as to when to employ a stuntperson is made by the director, in conjunction with the **stunt coordinator**, whose job it is to map out all the places in a film where stunts will need to be performed. Typically, a director, the first assistant director, and often the production manager comb through a script, picking out all the obvious places in which a stuntperson will be needed. The stunt coordinator then covers the loose ends, often spotting sequences that, in and of themselves, initially didn't look dangerous. For example, if an actor is asked to fall down on a set of railroad tracks, and the location manager mentions that the tracks to be used will be covered in broken glass, then a stuntman will be called in to replace the actor.

The best stuntpeople know more than how to perform physically. The best of them combine the necessary physical talents with a knowledge of camera angles, editing, and direction, all of which come into play to make a stunt look like "reality." In a typical chase sequence down a mountain road, for example, what looks like a continuous attempt by one car to smash into and knock off another is often actually composed of up to sixty separate start and stop sequences. There's nothing that says that the scene couldn't have been shot in one long take—in fact, that's probably the way the director and the cinematographer would like it to be filmed—it saves time and, most importantly, money. It's the stuntperson or stunt coordinator who will point out that doing so will unnecessarily jeopardize the stuntperson's life, by forcing him or her to concentrate simultaneously on getting hit and on driving the car off the road in the proper sequence that will prevent any fatal injury. Instead, the sequence will be set up so that some shots are made with the two cars colliding, other shots with just the two cars coming toward each other, and then a final sequence in which the car does indeed fly off the cliff.

And "fly" is the proper word, for a car that just drove off a cliff would more than likely dive straight down, not up into the air as usually occurs in films. To promote the initial leap, a small, inconspicuous ramp is placed on the edge of the precipice, to give the vehicle that bit of extra lift needed to ensure that the car will soar, rather than sour.

The cameraman will use a telephoto lens to compress the shooting distance, giving the illusion of greater speed. Then a car can bypass another but look as if it's about to actually hit it. "But I'm still getting hit, I'm still going over the cliff, and my life is still in jeopardy," notes Palmisano. "We're not using camera tricks, but camera techniques to help ourselves."

Those specialized techniques are not taught in any school, but are picked up through experience. Nor have many stuntpeople learned their skills in any formal way. For Conrad Palmisano, life originally held out the hope of little more than manual work. Having come from a family of "common laborers," Palmisano left the marines after serving in Vietnam and got a job laying carpet for Sears. "I didn't know how to break out [of my mold]," he recalls.

Palmisano eventually met an extra working in movies, who invited him to watch a film being shot. In a story more typical of the earliest days of Hollywood, when studio carpenters might be enlisted as makeshift directors, Palmisano was asked if he would like to be an actor's **stand-in**, taking the place of someone who had just quit. The position requires little skill, as a stand-in does just that—he *stands in* for the actor while the lights and camera angles are adjusted in preparation for the photographing of the scene.

Suddenly, Palmisano found himself as a movie extra. Attracted to the whole idea of stunts, he began working out with other stuntmen on weekends, spending time "leaping out of Eucalyptus trees" and landing on mattresses in an attempt to learn how to do pratfalls.

"Working as a film extra was a tremendous tool," Palmisano says. "Because you get used to behavior on the set, you find out who does what, what's required. And if you pay attention, you learn a lot about cameras and lighting. And all those things help you, because you need to use film technique in order to survive as a stuntman."

Survival—not avoiding pain—is the key here. According to Palmisano, pain is unavoidable in stunt work; it's just part of the job description. "How can you do a fall without getting hurt? You can't. You just have to hope that you won't get severely injured."

Injuries can be minimized by knowing one's craft, knowing the filmmaking process, and by not giving up authority to others on the crew. For the fact is that it is the director's (and producer's) job to get the film shot as quickly as possible with the least amount of money spent. But that requirement may often be in opposition to the physical safety of the stuntmen and stuntwomen employed on the production.

It's not enough to be aware of dangers in the filmmaking process, says Palmisano. A stuntman must always be ready to alter the sequence or refuse to do something that might endanger his life.

Palmisano has seen the process from both sides of the fence. As a second-unit director, he has had to push his crew to get a stunt, when to delay it one more day could vastly increase the cost of production, or cancel the possibility of getting it altogether. For stunts involve more than just a daredevil feat performed by one person. Often, that feat occurs in a visually exciting locale that itself may be difficult to reach, or difficult to shoot in.

During the filming of *First Blood* for Orion in Canada, the company had spent two weeks clearing the rights to use a particular bridge for a crash sequence. (By law, upcoming road closings must be advertised in the local press for several weeks, thereby allowing travelers to find alternative routes.) But by the time the sun was about to go down, the shot had still not been successful—every time the army vehicle attempted to start its engine for its eventual high-speed run into a blockade, its motor would stall.

Palmisano was serving as second-unit director for the picture. He knew that if he didn't pull off the shot soon, there would be no scene at all. But as a stuntman, he also was well aware of the fatigue setting in for the entire crew, and the consequent increased risk of a dangerous mishap. As the light grew dimmer, the cameraman continued to change to wider-angle lenses to allow more light to pass onto the film. "Meanwhile I've got two technicians working on the trucks [to get them started] and the stunt guy keeps on pulling his helmet off and going crazy, because we would get ready to do something and then it never happened.

"I wanted that stunt, and I wanted it that day," Palmisano recalls. He knew he had only one chance to get it—just controlling the crowds of people that had parked a mile away and walked to see the filming had turned into an "astronomical" task. In the end, Palmisano got the idea of not starting the trucks—rather than take the risk of the engines stalling again as they approached the roadblock, he had them pushed up to the starting point, and told the drivers to start the engines only if they were confident that, after they were pushed up to speed, they wouldn't stall.

In the end, the stunt succeeded, and proved to be one of the most spectacular of the film. As the truck approached the roadblock at the end of the bridge, a small wooden ramp under one side gave the truck sufficient lift to propel it slightly up and over the roadblock, causing a tremendous explosion. "It was one of the hardest days I ever spent in the motion picture business," Palmisano recalls.

A cardinal rule in filmmaking is that no matter what anyone's job is, everyone really just wants to direct. Screenwriters often get their chance after several produced scripts; several cinematographers, such as Haskell Wexler, have had opportunities as well. But according to Palmisano, stunt work theoretically provides an even better route to directing, one that prepares an individual to work with actors, one that helps the fledgling director understand the necessary interactive processes between all aspects of filmmaking. "Being a stuntman gives me a lot more hands-on experience than an actor receives. I work with cameramen and talent. As a stunt coordinator I have to tell a stuntman the kind of character that he's doubling for. Oftentimes an actor has the least idea of where things should be headed.

"I see actors turned directors trying to control four actors all going off in four different directions; it's harder for them to control actors because of their empathy for them, whereas I'll talk to actors just like I do to my children: I say 'you must try it this way this time because I have asked you to, and I am in a position of authority.'"

According to Palmisano, he never encounters any resistance among actors to taking his direction, either in his capacity as a second-unit director, or as a stunt coordinator. "Actors are a little bit in awe of us, because they don't know much about us. Being a stuntman carries a certain charisma with it, because we can do things everybody can't do. We're treated with a tremendous amount of respect.

"Talent listens to stunt coordinators, from the littlest talent to the biggest. In *Tough Guys*, with Burt Lancaster and Kirk Douglas, both of them already knew how to throw punches in their close-ups, but if there was an action involving other actors I'd say 'Listen, this is the way I have it choreographed, does it work for you?' And they'd listen to me."

Taking responsibility for directing action is never a problem with directors, according to Palmisano, despite their big egos. "Most directors want you to take responsibility. It takes the pressure off of them. You can have as much authority on a picture as you're willing to assume. Directors can't wait to give you more.

"Stunt work is an ego-oriented business. When you do Superman-like things, it's hard to believe you're not Superman. But when you're out there to do your moment, all stuntpeople are united with you. There's a camaraderie there like when you're in combat. If a stunt guy's in trouble other stunt guys will go through hellfire and brimstone to get to him. And that's part of what's wonderful about our profession."

Actor

■■■ John Lithgow

In a sense, all of the work involved in putting together a motion picture rides on the actor and his or her performance. With the exception of a Steven Spielberg, George Lucas, or Francis Coppola, most writers or directors are virtually unknown outside the movie business. Unless there is already good "word of mouth" about a picture, most people will make their decision to buy a ticket to a film based on who's in it, not on who directed or wrote it. It is the actor who, more than anything else, helps people decide if a picture is worth seeing.

Consequently, producers often try to get an early performance commitment from an actor, one who is generally perceived as "bankable." It is hoped that the inclusion of an actor or actress in the project will serve as a form of insurance, a tenuous guarantee that a producing entity will in fact be willing to spend often upward of $10 million to finance a picture.

That approach, while tried by any number of fledgling producers, can often prove fruitless. Like any other part of the film production community, the well-known successful actor also wishes to play it safe, preferring to get involved in a film that's fully financed and ready to go, rather than with one that, no matter how promising, is little more than a hope and a dream. Successful actors are constantly besieged with scripts—either through their agents or even while walking down the street. But the ones thrust into an actor's hands while he's out trying to buy a banana are, virtually out of necessity, also the first ones to be discarded.

"I try to be attentive to people who've taken the pains to get scripts to me, who write me cover letters," says actor John Lithgow. "But there are so many people who need the enthusiasm of an actor to get their project going, so they try to make me part of what's impressive about a script. That's the cart before the horse, as far as I'm concerned."

Lithgow has earned the right to be choosy about the material he selects to become involved in. Hailing from a theater family in Rochester, New York, Lithgow slugged it out on the New York stage until he began to become known through his roles in such pictures as *Rich Kids* and *Buckaroo Banzai*. He played the crazed passenger convinced that someone was trying to destroy the engine of his jet plane in *Twilight Zone—The Movie*. He was the conservative businessman who carried on an affair with Debra Winger in *Terms of Endearment*. And perhaps his most famous role to date is his portrayal of the transsexual, Roberta Muldoon, in *The World According to Garp*, starring Robin Williams.

Lithgow has been approached with scripts in the most unlikely of situations. "I can't wait at a bus stop too long," he says. After leaving a Seattle bar late one night, he went walking down a dark street. A car drove by and screeched to a halt; the driver leapt out, not to rob him, but to hand him a screenplay.

But Lithgow shuns unsolicited material. "It's much easier for me if the project is already underway, if it's financed, if there's a clear offer made to me, a fixed start date, and then the script's presented to me through my **agent**. That's how bona fide projects arrive."

An agent serves a dual role for an actor: he acts as a script screener, reading material submitted to the agency by writers or

writers' agents from the same or other companies; and he negotiates the terms of the contract for his client once he is offered a
job on a film (for more details on what that contract includes, *see
pages 66–69*).

While he no longer needs to worry where his next job will
come from, Lithgow still finds that weeks go by without his receiving an offer. Mostly, that's due to his agent, Rick Nicita of
Creative Artists' Agency, honing down submissions to the ones
that he believes best suit Lithgow's career needs. "I'll get a phone
call from Rick recommending a script, or telling me that he's got
one that he doesn't think is very good, but he'll send it over if I
like," Lithgow says.

One of the major factors in determining if Lithgow will be
interested in a role is the same consideration that every other
participant in a film thinks about: who else is involved. In order
to think seriously about a part, Lithgow will want to know who's
written the script and who will direct it, who's producing it, and
what studio will release it.

"I look for the same things reading a script that anyone
would look for when seeing a movie: how compelling is the story,
how interesting is the character, what kind of [psychological]
journey does he travel, does the character change throughout
the story, does it move me to laughter or tears? Is the story
interesting?"

Lithgow's agent told him about the casting of Roberta Muldoon in *The World According to Garp*, a book that he had read
and enjoyed years before without ever then thinking about himself in the role of the transsexual. "The first time I ever conceived
of playing Roberta was when they told me over the phone that
they were interested in considering me for the role." Lithgow
was one of the first people to be seen by the director, George Roy
Hill, for the role. He was selected by the producer and director
who, working in concert with Marion Dougherty, the **casting director**, drew up a list of actors that they thought might be right
for the part. Lithgow was selected to be interviewed by Dougherty. He did no preparation for the meeting, at which both

Dougherty and director Hill were present. That's because he discovered early on in his career that directors want actors who don't seem to need the job at all, those who are most relaxed about themselves and the entire selection process.

"An audition is not a place to impress someone with your acting talents, it's merely to show what your own aura is. The whole process of casting is putting people together in a kind of logical combination. So all you can do is just say, 'Well, this is me. This is me at my most relaxed.'

"I don't have to prove anything in an audition or meeting situation. When I meet with directors, it's absolutely nothing more than a conversation. I went in to meet James Ivory a couple of weeks ago for a new film he's directing. I just marveled at his film, *A Room with a View*, and I loved the idea of working for him. But I didn't go in there nervous and trying to impress him. I went in there to meet a man I respect and would like to work with. 'Hire me if you see fit; but if not, I know you have plenty of reasons, and find somebody better.'"

Lithgow did not dress for the *Garp* interview in a way that would fit the role of Roberta Muldoon; he did not show up in a dress or high heels and a wig. He came in casual clothes, read from the script, and talked to the director. The conversation began with a little small talk, with Lithgow knowing that he was being evaluated all the while. But as far as he was concerned, he was evaluating Hill as well, trying to get a sense of whether he would be comfortable working with the director.

"I felt that I was a shoo-in for the role. I thought that I had this unique combination of qualities. I was a big person, big and reasonably athletic so I can portray an athlete. And yet I have a kind of softness, a funny combination of big and soft. So that playing a woman would come a little more easily to me. I just felt that there was some certain chemical combination that made me good for the role of Roberta Muldoon."

But regardless of Lithgow's strong belief that he brought major strengths to the part, things did not turn out the way he had hoped. "I was rejected out of hand. The director thought I was great for it, but way too tall. They thought the combination of me and Robin Williams would be too bizarre. I accepted it a little ruefully, and hoped that he'd come around."

Lithgow was actually one of literally hundreds of people who were seen for the part. Other contenders included Kevin Kline (*The Pirates of Penzance*), Jeff Daniels (*Terms of Endearment*), tall actresses, professional athletes, and actual transsexuals. They tried every casting idea, because they knew this was going to be the hardest character to make plausible and sympathetic.

"I wanted very, very badly to do the role, but I had to accept the fact that I was not in the running. After that, I pretty much forgot about it."

Several months later, having heard nothing definitive about the outcome of the casting, he asked his agent what was going on. Rumor had it, said Nicita, that Kevin Kline was favored to win the role, a fact that Nicita would know since he was Kline's agent as well.

Lithgow pretty much gave up his expectations, until several months later when he was asked to come in for a screen test.

"That's when I thought I had a pretty good shot. If I could really put the characterization of Roberta together and do it on film, then I thought that I could outdo anybody for the role."

Despite his enthusiasm, Lithgow did not do anything particular to prepare for this second meeting; he did not think about the character, read the script again, or think about the part. In fact, he felt that it would be bad to be prepared, as that would take away any of the spontaneity that the director would like to see. "In my early days of theater, there was a time when I would learn every word and rehearse before an audition. I did that with Bob Fosse when I tried out for a musical of his. Goodness knows, Fosse was impressed. But he didn't hire me. He hired somebody who was just much more right for the part.

"Directors don't want an actor all that prepared in an audition because it doesn't leave anything for them to do. If you present a fait accompli, then you're taking away the director's role from him. You have to walk right in and sit in the chair like a lump of clay and say, 'I'm here. I'm good clay. Mold me.'"

The screen test turned out to be marvelous. This time, all of the actors trying out were expected to wear women's clothing. The audition was held in a studio on the West Side of Manhattan. The actors came in at one-hour intervals; when Lithgow entered, Jeff Daniels was already in the makeup chair. Then Richard Jordan came in. As Lithgow left, Victor Garber entered. So each actor was seeing the others in various stages of cross-dressing.

"I just changed into a brassiere, a wig, and a skirt right in front of George Roy Hill. Just as relaxed and businesslike as I could be. That's not even a choice. I just can't stand being nervous in those situations."

Lithgow was due to read a scene with Robin Williams, but Williams's commitment to the television show *Mork & Mindy* prevented him from being there. So Lithgow read a scene with another actor, the scene in the film where Roberta is sitting on the back porch reading letters, and she tells Garp that she feels that something terrible is going to happen, that she knows because of her woman's intuition.

"It was a very kind of funny and very melancholy scene, one with great foreboding. A scene with a lot of colors. And I did a nice job."

Then director Hill had Lithgow play a game of football in drag. Lithgow took the quarterback position; hunched over center, he took the snap, faded back and passed the ball out of camera range to a grip in the back of the room. And when the grip caught it, Lithgow leapt up and down and clapped his hands like a young woman. "I always thought that that was the moment when I got the role," Lithgow says.

The last thing he did was to sit down with Hill and improvise a conversation with him as if he really was the character Roberta. Hill asked Lithgow, playing Roberta, to tell him about the first feelings, the first time he felt he wanted to have a sex change. Lithgow hadn't prepared for this kind of discussion; but years before, he had read *Conundrum,* the story of Jan Morris's decision to become a woman. That book stuck in his mind, and it came out during the conversation. "I even told anecdotes from Morris's book as if it was Roberta telling stories about her own experiences. Hill was captivated and thought this was pretty ingenious."

A few days later, Lithgow received a phone call, a wrong number; it was casting agent Marion Dougherty meaning to dial Rick Nicita to tell him that Lithgow had the role; but she dialed Lithgow by mistake. She gave him the news then and there.

His agent negotiated the contract within a couple of days. Less negotiation than statement, it was more a case of the producers presenting Lithgow's agent with an offer; being a relatively unknown actor, he had little room to deal. "I was dying to play the part. I was not a known actor. It was an unbelievable break to be offered it and I would take anything they offered me. It's only when you begin to accumulate a little bit of background and renown and clout that you begin to call a few of the contract shots."

Then an unusual thing happened—director George Roy Hill held two weeks of rehearsals prior to the start of shooting. In the fourteen films in which Lithgow has worked, he has had only three in which there was any rehearsal time before shooting: *Garp, Twilight Zone,* and *Buckaroo Banzai;* that is, rehearsal the way stage actors think of it, with blocking and working on stages where the actual places to stand are marked on the floor with tape.

In addition to the rehearsal with the director, Lithgow was also able to get a sense of character through the extensive costume-fitting sessions that were necessitated by Lithgow's character, by his transformation into a woman.

His whole body had to be reconstructed. A foundation girdle with a three-inch circlet around his stomach was made; hip padding was designed, and a strong dance belt was built to flatten his male organs. He and the costume designer jointly decided on the size of his breasts, constructing them from prosthetic devices purchased at a salon for mastectomy patients.

There were wig fittings and hairstyling sessions. In fact, every garment that he wore as Roberta had to be built from scratch.

While the process took hours and hours, the time and the work helped give Lithgow a strong sense of his body as a female—a necessity, as George Roy Hill was very concerned with this one character and making her believable.

The actual rehearsals were just like stage rehearsals. They were held in a gymnasium in the Foreign Students' Center in Manhattan, where Hill actually rehearsed every scene as if it were part of a play.

The director of photography was brought in and camera angles began to be devised. That in itself was unexpected. Often directors enter the production process without any idea of the kind of angles that they want, making them up as they go along, a process that wastes an incredible amount of time. But Hill, as a meticulous man, did just the opposite. He tried to have every-thing as prepared as possible before going into the shoot.

"I'm tempted to use the word *incompetent,* but some direc-tors simply have no clue how to direct a scene," says Lithgow. "I've worked with one director who said that he wouldn't know what to do with the four weeks that a theater director has to rehearse; he would have no idea. On the other extreme is a direc-tor like Herb Ross who is not only a stage director but comes from choreography. He wants to have everything adjusted and addressed before shooting has begun."

The run-through was a real luxury in more ways than one. When a film is actually shot, it isn't filmed in the order of its scenes. Depending on economies of scale, weather, and set avail-abilities, the final scene of the film might be shot before the first. In order to keep the sense of the film within one's head, the actor must continue to think through the story in his own mind, to keep track of the action, even though it is not progressing in a linear fashion during filming.

"You have to have a sense about the rhythm of the story, what pitch it's at and how much punch it should have," Lithgow says. "At the best of times the director is reminding you of this constantly. If he's not reminding me, I tend to ask him questions: 'This is a scene where we really have to have a breakdown, right? This is a scene where we really do have to plant the seeds for what happens four scenes from now, right?'

"I always put it that way so as not to overstep my place as an actor. But it so often comes to the director as the first time he's thought of it, I feel I'm performing an essential function as kind of an outgrowth of his own thought processes, or the thought processes he damn well ought to be having."

Upon entering the set of *Garp* the first day, Lithgow did a very unusual thing: he said hello to the entire crew. He studied people's faces and learned who they were. Within a few days, to their great shock, he was calling everybody by name. "The crew was so surprised that any actor had taken the time to do that. Actors breeze through a two-and-a-half-month-long shooting period and they don't know most people's names. I find that incredible. Getting to know them immediately created a bond that's tremendously important for me. The more you can make the crew into your collaborators, the better off you are. They're not only your collaborators, they're the closest thing you have to an audience of warm bodies while you're acting."

His attention to crew runs the gamut, from the DP to the gaffer. Being friendly to everyone breaks down the distinction between cast and crew; it makes everyone feel more a part of a process wherein everyone is equally important in making a film happen. In fact, Lithgow gets so friendly with everyone working on the film that he immediately knows when a stranger is in their midst. "I will know when one person walks onto a soundstage that I don't know, that I've never met. There are fifty people wandering around. One stranger comes on, I will know that immediately and feel a little twinge of tension. It's not paranoia; I have to feel that this is my home in which I can operate comfortably and all these people working with me are my family. So I can go wild in front of everybody and they'll know. I can trust them with wherever [my acting] goes."

His friendliness with cast and crew also allows Lithgow to

take a more active role in the production process than do many of his fellow actors. Without asking for the director's permission, Lithgow will regularly talk to the **dolly grip**, the individual responsible for pushing the four-wheeled cart holding the camera, to the proper positions at the proper times. He'll tell the grip what his next scene entails, where he'll be moving, and when. This is an unusual thing to do. Most grips, according to Lithgow, are accustomed to just picking up that information as people rehearse, not from a direct conversation with the actor.

During shooting, Lithgow will keep on checking with the sound mixer to make sure that everything is being recorded properly, that the microphone can get as close as it needs to be. And then he'll do the same thing with the camera operator, carrying out little shorthand rehearsals without telling the director about them, telling the operator where he'll be moving, checking out the framing in the camera to ensure that it will be able to cover him in time as he walks through the scene.

"This is not typical of what actors do," said Lithgow. "Movie actors are not nearly as exhaustive in rehearsing as I am. Maybe it's a certain rigidity in me, but I don't think so. I feel like the more in control and predictable I am for all the other crew people, and for myself, the further I can go."

Lithgow's approach was typified in his portrayal of the hysterical plane passenger in *Twilight Zone—The Movie.* Here was a man who was convinced that he was seeing a creature on the wing of the aircraft trying to cause it to crash. This was a character with hysterical flight fear. Lithgow developed the role into a man who flung his whole body across the aisle of the plane, necessitating eight people having to hold him down, as he shook and babbled like crazy.

"I did that and hit my [floor] mark within a quarter of an inch every time in take after take. This is something that I pride myself on, and I think it comes out of a theater actor's training when, night after night, you hit your mark, you deliver your cues in the same way. Yet, in the course of that very kind of rigid structure, you can really fly."

Through the process of rehearsing the scene, the actors and director come to a consensus of how it will play, and how it will be **covered**. In order for a scene to be edited to include different camera angles, it is necessary for that scene to be performed several times, at least once for each new angle. When one sees a conversation on film between two people, and the camera cuts back and forth between them, that scene has actually been shot two separate times, with each actor carefully reciting his lines in as similar a fashion as possible. The first time, the camera shoots one person's face; the next time, it will record the other actor.

If there are delays in the shooting process, one of the angles may wind up being shot hours or even days later. To ensure that, when those two separate "takes" are edited together, they will form what appears to be a continuous scene, actors must take careful pains to remember exactly what words they were saying, and exactly how they were moving their hands, faces, and bodies.

They are aided in this work by the **script supervisor** or **continuity person**, an individual or individuals whose job it is to record any changes in the written dialogue as eventually spoken by the actor, and to keep track of exactly where an actor moves, where he has his hand, between which fingers he is holding a cigarette, in what order food is placed on a tray, and so on.

The first angle to be shot of an individual scene will be the "master," the shot that will include all of the actors and all of the action within the frame of the camera. It is called the master because it includes the entire scene as it should play dramatically. After that, the camera moves in and shoots a close-up of every actor within that scene, saying the same lines and moving in the same way as he or she has just done in the master.

The number of close-ups filmed depends on how important certain actions are within that scene. It is possible that one character, even though reciting some lines, may not be central to the action; a close-up may not be needed. On the other hand, another character may have only one word to say within a scene, but it could be one that completely changes the course of action, or the interpretation of events. In that case, the director may decide to do one or more close-ups of that character, as he is speaking, as he is reacting to someone else's speech or actions, or even as his hands are just fidgeting with a cigarette.

"It's very good for an actor to be aware of how the coverage of a scene is going. Because if it's a very strenuous scene, one needs to make sure that, by the end of the day, you still have your energy left when the camera comes in for your close-up; that's the most important acting you can do."

According to Lithgow, many actors mark time in the long shots; they think that the editor will then be almost forced to use their close-ups, where the acting will be better and they'll be seen better. "My own philosophy is, 'Do the best you can and act the fullest you can at every single moment, no matter where the camera is, on you or off you.'"

In fact, Lithgow often likes to work even harder in the master shots. That way, if it is an emotionally draining scene, by the end of the day when the director is ready for his close-ups, he's already drained from the work itself, and his emotions will fit right into the role. "I love it when, if the scene calls for it, I'm reduced to being bleary-eyed by the actual process of acting. Then you don't have to worry about tomorrow. You give it all you've got, you destroy yourself, and then it's over with."

Lithgow also uses emotional tricks to get into the roles he's playing. If he needs to be particularly sad or distraught, he'll take a few minutes to himself and think in as focused and concentrated a way as he can, usually about his kids. He'll meditate on his children, even thinking about terribly sad things happening to them, about them getting injured; he'll think about things that are most difficult for him to deal with emotionally.

"Something bad happening to your children. I can't think of anything harder than that. It reduces you to emotional jelly and you just become ragged emotionally, so vulnerable. It makes you into a tabula rasa for a scene."

Lithgow used that device in *Twilight Zone*, as well as in

Garp's mourning scene, as he sobs and sobs and sobs over the death of the character Jenny Fields. "The day we shot the funeral scene in *Garp* where I cried so much, I actually cried all day long. I was just shaking with tears by the end of the day. It is a kind of agony, but there was another feeling there that you're thrilled that the scene has gone so well.

"And that's another thing that comes in handy in getting to know the crew. They are the people that allow you to do that. There's a completely unspoken understanding you have with them that we are friends, we're collaborating, anything is allowed. It just frees you to do all that."

That friendship extends off the set for Lithgow. During the production of a film, he finds that he becomes close not only to two or three of the actors, but also to the makeup, hair, and wardrobe people. "They are the first people you see in the day, they are the people you have your most constant tactile contact with, and it's ongoing. They are the people that are dealing with the things that we are the most vulnerable about: the way we look, 'how will I look in front of the camera a year from now magnified on a movie screen?' The makeup, costume, and hair people are exquisitely sensitive to these issues. Before you know it, they become your shrink. They are hearing all the gossip, all the dirt, all the deepest fears, things you wouldn't even tell your wife. And that becomes a terrific friendship."

While that friendship cannot always last after the film is finished, as actors and crew move on to their next project, Lithgow always tries to remember the occasion by drawing a caricature of the entire crew, presenting each member with a copy of it, each one personally signed with his thanks. When he did this on *Garp*, members of the crew were flabbergasted. "They'd never been given such a thing. I did it because I really meant it. It was a really sincere gesture to these people. Crew people are so often taken for granted. By actors, by everybody."

After shooting is over, Lithgow, like any film actor, must make himself available for a "looping" session, a time when it may become necessary to go into a sound stage and rerecord dialogue that had been garbled or muffled during the actual shooting process. At this time, he'll drop by the editing room just to say hello and see how the process is going. And this will be the first time that he'll have seen any film of his own work during the production.

Lithgow is an actor who will not go to **dailies**, those screenings of each scene the day after it is shot. He believes that the viewing of dailies is a dangerous business while one is still involved in acting the role. "Either I am crazy about what I see, which puts me in a great mood until I find out that the editor does not use what I like the most. Or I'm horrified by what I see of myself and it freaks me out and makes me very self-conscious the next day when I have to go back and play the part.

"You start worrying about the sibilance of your s, you worry about the moles on your face, the camera angles, and the lighting. Suddenly you're paranoid about the cinematographer whether he's lighting you correctly."

When the film is finished, its advertising campaign finalized and a release date set, Lithgow has one more job to do: promote the film. "The only thing I do is talk, talk, talk, talk, to the press when it's time to release the film," Lithgow says. The obligation to do so is not in his contract, but Lithgow feels that if he has decided to act in a project, he should also be prepared to promote it. That usually means journeying to some central location to meet the nation's "consumer" press, those individuals who write for daily and weekly newspapers and popular-interest magazines such as *TV Guide* and *People*. On a regular basis, reporters will take press junkets to major cities to meet the stars and see the upcoming motion picture releases. The trips are paid for by the studios, who see the gatherings as a good way to get the publicity that they'll need to entice that initial crowd into the movie theaters to see their film. Then those people will tell their friends about the picture, thereby generating positive "word of mouth."

Lithgow will sit in a hotel room as one reporter after another enters with an audio cassette recorder or a TV cameraman to record an interview. That interview will then be edited and played back on a local news show in the reporter's hometown, thereby giving viewers the impression that Lithgow had actually been interviewed locally.

Other promotional activities include guest appearances on talk shows, which exist in part to allow performers to appear and promote their latest ventures, be they books, films, or plays. For *Garp*, Lithgow got up early to make a 5:00 A.M. appearance on the *Today* show, an interview that was less than fulfilling, as it was clear to Lithgow that the interviewer, Bryant Gumbel, had not seen the film. Other appearances included *The Tonight Show*, once with Johnny Carson and once with Joan Rivers. With Carson, "I came on right after Buddy Hackett, and I was kind of moribund. I was totally unfunny and felt this terrible compulsion to try. It was just a nightmare. It helps a lot when you become better known and don't have to crank out a lot of credentials. It's much easier when you feel this giant audience of millions already knows you."

What Lithgow wants the audience to know him for are the kind of roles typified by such films as *Garp* and *Buckaroo Banzai*, roles that test him as an actor, in films that have something to say, either as serious works of art or respectable entertainment. "The really satisfying thing is to take what is my equipment and my talent, and indeed my standards as an actor, and apply them to a gigantic popular entertainment, and end up with something that I'm very proud of.

"I have all these feelings running around naked. Somehow or other this superego marshals them and organizes them into some kind of dramatic structure—in order to unleash other people's feelings. Which is the closest I can come to a definition of what acting is for."

Sound Mixer, Boom Operator, Third Man
██ Jeff Wexler

Of all the elements that go into making a motion picture, it is the sound track that is the least noticed. In our visual world, sound can be easily forgotten, overlooked, and taken for granted. Being invisible, it is often not regarded by film crews and actors as germane to the medium. Its recording is an afterthought, an element of filmmaking that many regard as being simple to capture. And if the sound is not accurate, all one has to do, it is said, is "fix it in the mix," after the shoot is over.

If it were only that simple. Like every other aspect of filmmaking, sound needs to be as perfectly performed and recorded during the production process as possible. But the goal of a perfect recording is not a simple one to achieve. It is helped to some degree by today's technology, by the relatively new ability to alter voices, to make people actually sound better than they do in real life, to change reality in just the way that the screenplay, the cinematographer, and the entire photographic process do.

"People are less sensitive to sound in motion pictures than they are to other film elements," notes veteran sound man Jeff Wexler. "People say either 'I heard it,' or 'I didn't.' But people are, unbeknownst to them, profoundly affected by a soundtrack. If I didn't believe that, I wouldn't continue in this business."

Wexler has recorded sound for such films as *An Officer and a Gentleman, Against All Odds, Being There, Coming Home, Bound for Glory, Foul Play, Staying Alive,* and Mel Brooks's 1987 work, the science-fiction spoof *Spaceballs.*

Wexler is the on-the-set sound person, recording the sound as it occurs. After the film is shot and "in the can," a **sound-effects editor** will reconstruct, edit, and embellish that sound during the postproduction process in an attempt to improve its quality, to make it sound more real and more dramatic, to construct a symphony of sounds that will parallel the development of the story itself.

Most feature-film sound crews consist of three individuals. Wexler, as head of the sound team, generally takes the credit **production sound mixer,** or **sound mixer**. His other colleagues receive the titles **boom operator** and **third man.**

The sound mixer is often brought onto a picture several months before a film is due to go into production. Literally hired by either the production manager or producer, he is usually asked to join the project by the director. With *Spaceballs,* Brooks contacted Wexler based on the recommendation of another soundman whom Brooks had originally wanted, but who was not available.

"In the past," says Wexler, "I've worked for the same people over and over again, like Taylor Hackford [*An Officer and a Gentleman*] and Hal Ashby [*Being There*]. The director chose me, and then we put pressure on the studio and the producer to make sure I was on the job. We had to do that because there are often problems with studios that want you to use their people, and don't want somebody from the outside there."

Brooks hired Wexler over the telephone just in time to give him two weeks of preparation before starting to shoot. But before he was willing to accept the job, Wexler wanted to read the script; he wanted to know, among other things, that the script was "makeable," that it could be translated into film; that the project was the kind of story that appealed to him; and that he wouldn't have any trouble working with the director.

Once Wexler decides to work on a film, he'll perform a script breakdown, which for the sound mixer entails carefully reviewing the screenplay scene-by-scene to determine what special sound requirements there are.

Spaceballs had two particular problems: since it was a science-fiction film with special effects, the sound would be complicated to record. In addition, Brooks made it clear that he wanted the sound that was recorded live on the set to be used as much as possible in the final film. That meant that whatever effects were performed on the set would have to be done in such a way as not to interfere with the sound recording.

Many film directors take the opposite tack: they do not expect most, if any, of the sound recorded during the shooting of the film to be used in the actual film. Rather, the live sound is used only as a "guide track," a road map of the dialogue that will then be added to the picture during the postproduction process, when the actors will be called into a rerecording stage to rerecord their voices in a controlled atmosphere. The advantages of this approach are that the sound can be controlled, manipulated within what is virtually a laboratory setting, where complex electronic instruments can raise and lower, speed up and slow down sounds to make them "perfect." What one gains in raw quality, however, one often loses in terms of performance. No matter how hard the performers try, voices recorded later can never match the spontaneity of those recorded when the scene was actually shot.

"In all the *Star Wars* movies, ninety-nine percent of the dialogue is replaced," Wexler points out. "They know that they'll do that going in. That's why I don't do those kinds of movies. A monkey can record that kind of sound. All that's required from the production sound person is a guide track to later replace the dialogue. The guide track does have to be pretty good to make it easier to replace. But on that guide track will also be all those noisy effects and the other things that have made it impossible to get usable dialogue.

"In those situations, you'll hear a plate fall during the shooting, or even the director talking to the actors while the scene is being shot. It doesn't matter because you know that all that sound will be replaced during the postproduction process.

"But when I did *Spaceballs*, Mel Brooks made it very clear that he didn't want to do that. He said 'This is a comedy. I don't like to loop [replace the sound in] comedies because timing is very important. I want usable good production dialogue, and everybody on the production knows that.' He said that we would tailor all our effects and all other things as much as possible to preserve the dialogue."

Wexler is opposed to the replacement of dialogue on principle—he just doesn't think that replaced, or "dubbed," dialogue ever sounds as good as the original. "You've changed the whole feel of the movie. No matter how well you replace the dialogue on a film, even a film like *Apocalypse Now*, or the *Star Wars* movies, there's always a distance that's created between what they're saying and watching them say it."

According to Wexler, a study was done that showed that people who saw films in which the dialogue was slightly out of synchronization with the picture by just one frame (one twenty-fourth of a second) thought that the film they were watching didn't "ring true." They didn't "know" the sound was out of synch with the picture. They just didn't believe what the characters were saying. "What this means to me is that there is something that's viewed by us as 'inauthentic,' because in real life there's no such thing as 'out of synch.'"

Wexler got together with director Brooks two weeks before the shooting start date. His major concern was that everybody in addition to Brooks would understand the need to obtain usable dialogue. "I was concerned because I read in the script about some pretty noisy special effects, such as wind machines, explosions, laser fire." Wexler needed to make sure that the effects people knew that they would have to do their work carefully.

In that first meeting with Brooks, which lasted no more than ten minutes, Wexler asked him what his feeling would be if it looked like a losing battle, if some visual effect could not be done without losing dialogue. "I want to do whatever I can to preserve dialogue," Brooks told Wexler. "I don't want to replace a lot of it."

"We also talked a lot about several creature-type characters in the film—from a reading of the script, I didn't know if these were going to be characters who were in very exotic costumes that would make it impossible for them to even talk. For instance, I didn't know if one character, named Dorothy, or Dot Matrix, would be so covered up, just as C-3PO was in *Star Wars*, that it would make it impossible to record her dialogue. Brooks told me not to worry, because all of her dialogue would be replaced by Joan Rivers's voice.

Wexler and Brooks also discussed how Brooks felt about **wild lines.** In production sound recording, if all the lines have been well recorded except for one or two words, then some directors like to get those words "wild," that is, without the camera rolling, to avoid having to bring in the actor after the picture is finished to record them.

Mel Brooks likes to get wild lines, but each director has his own feeling about them. Some directors hate them. They'd prefer to replace dialogue three months later in the studio, rather than hold up the pace of the shooting. Other directors are fanatics for wild lines. Even if a scene has been shot perfectly, they'll want to record the whole scene wild. And they'll get the actors in a group and have them do the entire scene without the camera.

Wexler sees no secret to recording sound during a production. "Directors come over to me, complaining that they can't understand what an actor is saying. They want to know what kind of microphone I'm using. I say, 'We've got all the microphones we need. That's not the problem. Go over and listen to the actor—you can't understand what he's saying. I'm a sound director, not a magician. I can't record something that's not there.' "

And that is the basic dilemma facing the sound recordist. With the world's increased reliance on high technology to solve problems, it is naturally assumed by many that any poorly recorded sound can be fixed, can be made right, by the various recording and postproduction sound equipment available. "Believe it or not, motion picture sound, particularly dialogue recording, has been getting worse and worse over the years, even though everyone says it's getting better and better, with stereo television and all that. But it's definitely getting worse, and for one reason: there is almost no voice training whatsoever for American actors these days. The effects are getting bigger, the music is getting bigger, but the actual clarity of speaking is getting worse and worse and worse.

"In the old days, there was only one way to record sound. You didn't have wireless microphones, you had one microphone on a boom. The actors had to be under that microphone speaking clearly, otherwise you got nothing. Now actors wear wireless microphones under their clothing and the quality of the recording is godawful, but everyone is so excited that the sound can be recorded at all. With wireless mikes, you can record a person speaking as they walk down a New York City street. But they sound terrible—a woman's voice may not even sound like a woman. But that's the style of film."

All of this elaborate sound recording equipment does increase the options available to the postproduction sound engineer. To a limited extent, poor diction can be covered up, and even poor acting techniques can be doctored. Wexler recalls that, when he was recording sound on the Hal Ashby film, *Slugger's Wife*, producer Ray Stark asked him why one of the actors sounded so screechy in the recording made during the shooting.

Wexler understood what the problem was, and he knew that it had nothing to do with his recording technique. "I said to Stark, 'Listen to him, he has speech problems. He has real problems with meter—if there's a sentence that's said one way by ninety-nine percent of the population, he'll say it the other way, he'll say it in some way that no one has ever said it before.'"

Stark told Wexler that he just couldn't understand what the problem was; in fact, the actor even sounded completely different from how Stark remembered him to be on another picture. Intrigued, Wexler decided to call up the editor from that film and ask him why he thought this might be so.

"The editor told me that it was a constant battle" to get this actor to sound right, Wexler recalled. "He had to construct entire sentences from words stolen from this tape and that tape. He had to replace parts of his voice with other people's voices.

"Half of what the audience heard was not this actor's voice. It was a processed voice—tremendous amounts of equalization, changing the actual pitch of the voice during the editing process.

"People think that technology will solve the problem of poor recording. What will solve the problem is good acting, good diction, good discipline with the director, and a strong knowledge of what it takes to record sound."

On *Spaceballs*, most of the shooting was **interiors,** that is, it was done indoors. Wexler, as head of the sound crew, always stations himself off to the side of the film set hovering over a Nagra tape recorder, a small Swiss-made machine that has become the standard of the film recording industry.

The actual handling of the microphone used to record each scene is done by the **boom operator**. It is his or her job to ensure that the microphone, attached to the boom, or fishpole, is correctly positioned to record the actors. That essentially means pointing it at the actor who's talking, anticipating when the next actor will speak, and swiveling it over to him. This must be done soon enough to pick up all the second actor's lines, but not so soon as to miss any of the dialogue delivered by the first speaker.

It is also the boom operator's responsibility to ensure that the microphone does not move down into the viewing frame of the camera. All too often this is not carefully watched, especially for films that are transmitted over television after having been shot for an initial theatrical release. With the different **aspect ratio**, or proportional dimensions, of a television screen, boom operators often seem to misjudge the greater height at which they must hold the microphone for a television framing. Consequently, if the camera operator is not vigilant, it is all too common to see the microphone sticking into the top of the frame when watching a film on TV.

To know how one has to place the microphone to remain out of the shot requires a knowledge of camera lenses, and the viewing angle that each different type of lens covers. This information is obtainable through various tables or from the camera operator, but with so little time to set up a shot the sound crew increases its efficiency if it has that data memorized.

The boom operator also needs to understand lighting, to know immediately that, even though the microphone may not show up in the frame of the shot, its placement may still cast an unwanted shadow over the scene.

Boom operators are also responsible for placing **planted** microphones in a scene, for being able to hide a microphone when a boom "mike" would be too far away to record the sound adequately. In this case, the operator must know the recording capabilities of the microphone in question and know how to hide the mike in a vase or plant so it will not be seen, but will still pick up dialogue without losing tonal quality.

If the actors in a scene are standing far apart then a second microphone may be needed; that one will be handled by the **third man** or **cable person**. The third man is also responsible for handling all sound cables during a shot: if the camera is dollying, then it is up to the third man to follow alongside that dolly, making sure that the sound cable attached to the microphone flows smoothly and uninterruptedly along with the boom.

In addition, the third man is in charge of "noise abatement": discovering the extraneous noises that might intrude onto a soundtrack during the recording of a scene, and eliminating or minimizing them. These sounds exist in virtually every environment; in real life, we all "tune them out," unconsciously training ourselves to ignore door squeaks, refrigerator motors, and creaks in wooden beams as we carry on our conversations or other daily activities. The sound recording device, unfortunately, does not have that sophistication. Tiny noises that are usually unobtrusive become magnified in one's perception once they are recorded on tape. Hence, it is essential for the third man to quash them as best he can before the scene is shot.

Over several years' time, the third man, like all members of the sound crew, develops his own bag of tricks, his own kit of materials that have proven useful in lessening the sound ills of a shoot. The third man works his cures by paying particular attention to room or exterior noises during the rehearsal period. Wearing headphones, he can pick up sounds caused by clothing rustling over microphones, extraneous motor noises, airplanes, birds, and static electricity, among other things—sounds that would not be audible to the casual observer listening with just his ears.

Thanks to Mel Brooks's insistence on the primacy of the location sound recordist, Jeff Wexler's and his crew's jobs were relatively easy. But it is not always true that sound is king on a motion picture.

Wexler's most difficult sound-recording challenge came when he worked on Hal Ashby's *Bound for Glory*. "It was so challenging because there was so much live music. Every scene involved David Carradine playing the guitar, singing a song, going into a big dialogue scene, and then breaking into a fight with somebody. Every scene had every possible thing you have to deal with in recording sound.

"But Hal Ashby was such a good director that he would design things that would actually allow us to get good sound. Sound that would cut together properly."

That is the other necessity in recording sound: movies are edited. A scene does not just happen once; as discussed previously, it is repeated over and over again, for the master shot, then for a single shot, a close-up, and an over-the-shoulder shot. One of the most important jobs of the production sound mixer is to make sure that the film will come together aurally, just as a cinematographer shoots scenes with a parallel visual goal in mind.

"The fact of life is that movies are cut together. If the audience is suddenly experiencing a close-up shot but they don't even know how they got there, then you've done your job as a sound or film editor."

One problem that results in extra work for the sound editor is the tendency by new sound mixers to place the microphone too close to the action—its placement will be so proximate to the actors that, when the editor cuts to a "long shot," a shot with the camera far away from the action, the sound resulting from these drastic changes in recording distance will just not match up. While the visual cuts may look seamless and motivated, the differences in the sound recording will be just too dramatic.

"When the editor switches angles," says Wexler, "all of a sudden your track sounds like it was recorded on another day, on another planet. Since it doesn't sound good, it gives away the cut."

These are the kinds of considerations that sound recordists are expected to decide on, without any kind of assistance, on a daily basis. Directors often assume that experienced sound people can be relied upon for all sorts of creative judgments on how the scene's playing, "Because they know that I'm listening to the scene probably more carefully than anyone else who's in a position to listen to it. So often I'll go to a director and, as carefully as possible, suggest that there's a serious problem with a particular actor's performance. A lot of directors do not want to hear that from a sound person. They say, 'You want it louder?' I say, 'No, I don't want it louder. It's just that on this take, the performance has changed so drastically that when you cut those together it's going to be like you put somebody else in the scene.'

"'If you don't want it louder, then shut up,' directors will sometimes say. At other times, a director has become so familiar with the script after rehearsing it many times, that he's memorized the lines. He's consequently lost the ability to tell if the

The various stages of a dinosaur's creation. *Bottom left:* the wire frame model used to create the 3-D creature. *Top right:* Skin is added to the wire frame model. *Bottom right:* the dinosaur with the addition of a ground shadow. *Photo used with permission of Industrial Light + Magic.*

Computer sketches of different angles of the Tyrannosaurus Rex. *Above and below: Photos used with permission of Industrial Light + Magic.*

Creation of the kitchen sequence from *Jurassic Park*. *Top left:* the empty kitchen. *Top right:* the computer wire frame models of the Raptors. *Bottom left:* the frames are placed in the scene. *Bottom right:* the final result, with the Raptors now covered with skin and shading.

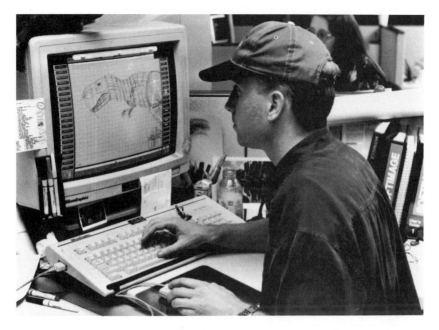

Industrial Light + Magic's graphic artist Geoff Campbell uses a Silicon Graphics computer to create a preliminary wire frame rendering of one of the *Jurassic Park* dinosaurs. *Above and below: Photos used with permission of Industrial Light + Magic.*

Several renderings of the T. Rex in combination with the Ford Ranger.

The three stages involved in placing a dinosaur in a scene. *Copyright © by Universal City Studios, Inc. Courtesy of MCA Publishing Rights, a Division of MCA Inc.*

Star Jeff Goldblum is photographed reacting to the nonexistent T. Rex.

The computer-generated frame of the T. Rex is placed in the scene. *Photo used with permission of Industrial Light + Magic.*

The completed rendering of the dinosaur is composited into the scene.
Copyright © by Universal City Studios, Inc. Courtesy of MCA Publishing Rights, a Division of MCA Inc.

Sam Neill runs from the nonexistent dinosaurs in a scene from the opening portion of *Jurassic Park. Copyright © by Universal City Studios, Inc. Courtesy of MCA Publishing Rights, a Division of MCA Inc.*

The final version of that scene, with the dinosaurs composited into the picture. *Copyright © by Universal City Studios, Inc. Courtesy of MCA Publishing Rights, a Division of MCA Inc.*

© 1991 by Carolco Pictures, Inc./A TriStar Release. Terminator is a trademark of Carolco Pictures, Inc.

Individual shot of Schwarzenegger. *Photo by Aaron Rapoport. Copyright © 1991 by Carolco Pictures, Inc.*

Schwarzenegger composited into the background. © *1991 by Carolco Pictures, Inc. / A TriStar Release. Terminator is a trademark of Carolco Pictures, Inc.*

Individual shot of Linda Hamilton. *Photo by Aaron Rapoport. Copyright © 1991 by Carolco Pictures, Inc.*

Ad concept composed of three separate shots. © *1991 by Carolco Pictures, Inc. / A TriStar Release. Terminator is a trademark of Carolco Pictures, Inc.*

delivery is good. I've got to explain that a take that he thought was good was actually delivered incoherently. I can do that because I've trained myself to hear those lines for the first time every time they say them, whether we do one take or forty."

Wexler recalled the time when Taylor Hackford spent hours getting the right performance for a scene in *An Officer and a Gentleman*. After the tenth take, Hackford finally decided that he had it right—until soundman Wexler let him know that there had been CB radio interference on the sound track, and that he'd have to do the scene again.

"You can't tell me this," Wexler recalls Hackford saying to him. "That was it, that was the performance. We can't do another one, the actors will never be able to replicate it."

"I said to Hackford, 'They're going to have to do it again in four months, on a sound rerecording stage. The sound is just not usable. Do you think that they'll perform better in four months than they will now?'

"So he did one more take, and that's the one that got into the film. And it was actually better than the other performances. There's no such thing as a perfect performance, and there's no such thing as a perfect performance if the vocal performance is not good."

Monitoring the entire sound "look" of a film has become the purview of a new class of film technician: the **sound designer**. Unlike sound mixers or postproduction sound editors, the sound designer functions much like a production manager: he oversees all of the audio elements of a film, much as a **production designer** does for the visual portion of the project.

"*Sound designer* is a very pretentious term," says Wexler. "A lot of people who call themselves sound designers have not had enough experience in any of the areas of rerecording, sound effects, and film editing to preside over them. Sound designers are often brought in to a movie after it's already in production. And the sound designers are often sound-effects oriented. The question becomes 'What are all the great things I can do to build sound montages after the film is finished? How many different layered levels of chirping birds can I put in there?' And that bothers me, because a lot of those effects end up intruding on dialogue which is otherwise well recorded and which should predominate."

For Wexler, the ability to construct symphonies of sounds for their own sake does not make for a good soundtrack. All too often, the triumph of the symphony is celebrated, while the appropriateness of the track to the film's overall goals is overlooked.

Wexler has been able to supervise one film's sound from start to finish. And the final track of that picture, *Being There*, reflected Wexler's belief that "the measure of a good soundtrack is being able to close your eyes and almost construct the scene, not just visually but emotionally as well.

"Very few films ever approach that. But what I would like to do is to be able to go and watch the daily takes in the screening room, to close my eyes and say 'All right, what's happening in this scene is we're in a big shot, the guy comes to the door and he's angry, he sits down on the couch and has a conversation with his girlfriend.' I want to be able to visualize that perfectly just from the soundtrack. And that's my responsibility, the responsibility of the sound mixer. The problem is, a lot of other people working on a picture don't understand that.

"A director will often say after a take, 'Well, the soundman's not going to like that one.' I'll say 'Hey, it's not my movie, it's yours, and *you're* not going to like it. I'm there to make Mel Brooks's movie, not to stroke my own ego or get a paycheck.'

"Sound is often overlooked because the one thing that separates us from every other department is that our work can be redone later on. You can replace the entire soundtrack, but you can't replace the entire picture visually. You can't replace the lights. You can't replace the costumes. But you can replace the whole soundtrack.

"If there's a commitment to the value of the shooting soundtrack on the part of the production team, then that's when I'm happiest. Because that's when my work actually has some bearing on the making of the film."

Gaffer, Grip, Electrician, Best Boy, Rigger, Nursery Man, Standby Painter

■ Gary Holt

A motion picture succeeds on a technical level when it can convince audiences that the action it presents is a depiction of reality. A character in a film who is seen sitting across a room and then suddenly appears very close to the camera cannot have suddenly leapt up in space. But if the editor has done his job well, an audience will perceive that sudden jump as "natural."

Similarly, it is necessary to ensure that the interior and exterior locations shown in a film are also perceived as natural, as looking just as they would in real life. But for something to photograph as "real" paradoxically often requires a major transformation of that environment into something that, in real life, would look completely artificial.

That is the result of the medium used to record the motion picture's image. Film is not the same as the human eye and brain, which can process a scene, unconsciously adjusting to different light and contrast levels, correcting one's impression of colors that might objectively look washed out on a cloudy day but brilliant on a sunny one. As a passive recording medium, film can register only what is physically present or absent. In addition, the light sensitivity of motion picture film is considerably less than that of the human eye. Objects which a normally sighted individual could discern in a dimly lit environment would often not even register on film. It is consequently up to the production crew to adjust the environment, through the use of various camera angles and different light intensities, colors, and contrast levels, so that the physical space reflects the emotions that the director wishes to convey in a particular scene.

This is no easy job—with motion picture film considerably less sensitive to light than the eye, it is often necessary to utilize literally tons of lighting equipment to illuminate a scene. Furthermore, it is rare that a director will be able to find a location that exactly expresses what he hopes to convey filmically. More often than not, any set will require some sort of reworking, from a simple paint job to a massive rebuilding, before it begins to approach what the director has in mind.

The leader of the crew charged with the preparation of a location to fit the film's needs is the **gaffer**. Overseeing a crew that can often number in the dozens, the gaffer carries out the dictates of the director of photography as translated through the needs of the director, the ultimate definer of the film's point of view. The gaffer scouts out locations to learn what type of lighting equipment will be needed, ensures that the appropriate equipment is available and at hand, and generally helps make the technical aspects of the production run as smoothly as possible.

"The gaffer is a direct bridge between the director of photography and the working crew," says Gary Holt, gaffer on such picture as *The Right Stuff* and *Taps*. "That leaves the director of photography the time he needs to spend with the director and with his camera operator setting up shots, while I act as the go-between, the man who organizes and puts the labor together."

That labor consists of a variety of positions. On unionized productions, each of those various positions' responsibilities is clearly defined, and rarely overstepped. On nonunion shoots, however, it is much more common for various crew members to jump in and lend a hand to someone of another job category.

Crews can grow to as large as fifty people, depending on the amount of lighting work that is needed. Roughly speaking, those jobs are divided between electrical and nonelectrical tasks, with the electrically oriented workers coming under the gaffer's umbrella, and the nonelectrical people classified as some sort of **grip**.

As usual, things are never what they first seem to be in motion picturemaking. Film **electricians** are not really electricians; they're the people whose job is to find the source of the electricity on a location, to "patch in" to that source with the film crew's own fusebox so that its lighting equipment can run off a location's existing electrical source, or to set up independent electrical generators, and to rig and operate the actual lamps.

A **best boy** is not the "best" boy; and second-best would be a more accurate description. He's the assistant to the gaffer, his right-hand man. He's in charge of the lighting crews, and is also responsible for ordering all the necessary lighting equipment, canceling it if necessary, keeping track of employee time cards, and other basic paperwork.

"A lot of time you have to run errands between the production office and the set," Holt says, "and the best boy does that job. If a message comes down to me stating that I have to get in touch with someone, then it's the best boy who will relay that information to me. In general, they take care of a lot of business that I could not do."

There's one **electrical best boy** per film, and there's also one **grip best boy**. The grip best boy reports to the **key grip**. Among other things, the grip crew sets up the **scrims**, pieces of light-diffusing material placed in front of some lamps that will give the light a more pleasing, softer effect.

Here's where the confusion begins. On a union shoot, if diffusion is needed just in front of the light, held up by some sort of stand, then the material has to be positioned by the grip. But if that same diffusion is needed to be placed on the light, it's done so, according to union rules, by the electrician. Lights themselves are hung in place by the electricians, also known as **lamp oper-**

ators. Depending on how many lights are needed, there could be dozens of operators working on a union picture. The gaffer will ask the lamp operator for a particular lamp, and the operator then will put it into position, raise it or lower it, and wait for orders from the gaffer to turn it on, further adjusting the light by adding diffusing materials to the front of the unit, or shutting down the spread of the beam by using the unit's attached black metal shutters, called **barn doors**.

In addition to handling equipment stands, the grip crew is also in charge of the camera **dolly**, the four-wheeled platform on which the camera rests, allowing it to be easily swiveled from place to place, to follow the actors down a hall or out a door during a scene without any abrupt, jerky movements. A camera will also generally be kept on a dolly even if no elaborate moves are planned, because it's usually a lot easier to move the camera a few inches by swiveling a dolly than it is to pick up a camera sitting on top of **sticks**, also known as a **tripod**, those three wooden legs often seen holding cameras in the earlier part of this century. The dolly will be run by the **dolly grip**. It's his or her job to show up at the camera department with the dolly, each morning before shooting, to make sure that the camera is correctly and securely mounted, and then to bring it over to the area where the shooting is occurring.

Much of the dolly grip's job consists of waiting—waiting for something to happen. If there is no need for him to work with the dolly, he may assist other grips in the movement of various pieces of equipment, or he may be needed to run a **crane**. Resembling a cherry picker used by municipal utility companies, this device allows the camera to quickly rise high above the action of the scene.

If the crane needs to move only up and down, then the dolly grip will be in charge of that job. But if the crane also needs to move back and forth, then another grip will take on that responsibility from the device's **hot seat**, a chair that, on larger cranes, is next to the driver's, but in a reverse position.

While some of the lighting work is dictated by the director

of photography, a DP also expects his gaffer to act independently, to anticipate lighting and its related set-construction requirements without waiting for specific instructions from him.

"If you need something on the set darkened because it's reflecting too much light," Holt points out, "then you as the gaffer take the license to go out and find your **standby painter** who'll spray that white post down a bit. Similarly, you'll bring in the **nursery man** to cover up some object that shouldn't be seen in a shot. This way you're helping out the DP, giving him more time behind the camera."

The gaffer's job begins several weeks before the actual start of shooting. For Francis Ford Coppola's latest release, *Gardens of Stone*, a film shot on location in Washington, D.C. and Arlington National Cemetery, Holt was brought in six weeks before the start of actual production.

After negotiating a salary with the production manager, Holt then hired his own crew. Except for the other top positions, most technical crew members are hired at scale, being paid whatever salary has been agreed to in the location where they are shooting. The others negotiate their salaries either with the gaffer or the production manager.

Holt's first act was to accompany the director and the director of photography to Washington, D.C., to scout locations. They spent a week there, going over each place where a scene would be shot.

"You get an idea, just by walking through the set at the particular time of day that the scene will be photographed, what kind of physical problems you may have in setting up the scene. For instance, if the director and the DP decided to shoot a scene on the second or third story of a building during what is supposed to be a bright sunny day, then you may need a lot of lights to simulate that sunshine.

"So you have to make arrangements for that. I'll spend hours talking to the director of photography about the lighting requirements of the various scenes. I'll talk to the key grip and to the DP about building scaffolding outside the set to put lights on that will be able to shine through the windows. Perhaps we'll also discuss constructing some sort of overhead rigging on the set itself to hold additional lamps."

Holt will never tell a director or DP that a shot they want to do is impossible to accomplish. "Anything can be done. I will point out that certain shots may be difficult or expensive to accomplish, however."

For example, on the film *The Right Stuff,* it was decided to shoot one scene on the sixth floor of a hospital that was supposed to be in the New Mexico desert. The scene was actually being shot in San Francisco, so it was essential that when the camera was pointing toward a window, the city skyline would not be visible. To accomplish this, translucent paper was taped over the windows, material that is thin enough to allow light through, but too thick to enable one to perceive objects on the other side of it. Holt then had to build a seventy-five-foot scaffold on the exterior of the building that would reach the sixth floor. The scaffold would hold the large lights that would shine inside the room to give the impression that bright sunlight was pumping through the windows.

When the film was budgeted, the construction of a scaffold was not expected. Hence, it was necessary for Holt to mention the need for a scaffold to the DP before shooting started, so that the cost could be factored in.

Throughout the Washington trip, Holt was making written and mental notes about the kind of equipment he and his crew would need for the shoot. "It's something that I just predict; I have a certain style and a certain group of equipment that I normally work with. As I go through the potential film locations I'm talking to myself basically about: 'Will what I have on the equipment truck be suitable for those scenes?' If I think I'll need more equipment I'll make a mental note saying 'Instead of four 10-Ks [10,000-watt lamps] I'll need six.' And then that'll be put into notes.

"A lot of these notes are for my best boy, who at this point has still not been hired. These will help him keep track of what equipment will be needed at which particular times. In addition, I need to have an overall equipment list, because we'll be shooting a large part of this film three thousand miles from Los Angeles. L.A. is basically where all of the film equipment in the entire country can be found. So I have to consider what equipment I'll be able to find locally in the D.C. area, and what I'll need to take out of Los Angeles, package in trucks, and ship back to Washington."

In order to learn what will be available in the local area, Holt and/or the production manager will visit local rental houses to see what they have. "Often you call these rental places and they tell you they have a particular piece of equipment. But once you get there, they don't have anything."

It seems like it would be simple to just journey to New York and rent the necessary equipment, but when it comes to electrical requirements, it's not. The East Coast uses a different cabling system than Los Angeles: "trico" cable in New York, "pin cable" in Los Angeles. So Holt tries to deal with Florida- or Atlanta-based equipment companies when shooting in the East, because they stock West Coast equipment, or at least adapting pins for that equipment.

By this time, Holt has read the film script, more for his own pleasure than for technical reasons. "I don't find reading the script to be very helpful, because in the majority of cases the scripts change. They change scenes, and then we have to reconfigure different lighting requirements for different moods."

Instead of the script, the most important preproduction tool for Holt is a script breakdown, known as a **one-liner**. This breakdown spells out what will be accomplished each day: which scenes will be shot, what the scene numbers are, and what kind of action occurs in each shot. The one-liner is developed by the first assistant director or the production manager. "I put all my notes on this," says Holt. "It helps me because it's a more mechanical part of the script, not an artistic part. It tells me what I'm in charge of. It gives me the days, it gives me the mood of the shot, whether it takes place in the day, at night, or at the 'magic hour,' that time just before sunset."

It also makes the crew aware of anything that might be a necessity on that particular day. There will be notations on the bottom of the one-liner stating "Prop Department: Get phone," or "Grip Department: Tighten crane," or "Transportation Department: Get car." This way, the gaffer knows what equipment will be needed on each particular day, allowing him to order it, either from the motion picture studio's own stores or from an equipment rental house, without having to carry around tons of supplies before they're needed.

Once back in L.A., Holt set about hiring his crew, those grips, best boys, electricians, and lamp operators. Trucks were loaded with the necessary equipment and driven back to the location. At the shooting site, each truck was reconfigured from what is known as a "road load"—packing of equipment for safety during transportation—to a "practical working load," the repacking of that same equipment to allow for its easy accessibility during the shooting process.

When shooting begins, Holt will walk the set each morning with his best boy to discuss what will be needed for that day. That's especially true if they're shooting on location, where the hanging of lights becomes a considerable challenge. Nine times out of ten there are never any overhead areas to run electrical cable on a location, few places to hang the actual lamps. In such situations all of the lights have to be mounted on floor stands.

The sound department faces its own problems in these kinds of locations. While a sound stage back at a studio will be completely soundproofed, an exterior location or even someone's home being used for a scene will be subject to a variety of extraneous and unexpected noises. To prevent those sounds from interfering with the sound recording, it is often necessary for the soundman to hang **sound blankets**, thick, quilted pieces of material, up around the periphery of the action. While effective, these blankets interfere with the ability of the gaffer to place his lights appropriately.

If at all possible, Holt tries to take electricity from an existing source, be that on a sound stage or a distant location. Sometimes that doesn't work. For instance, AC current, the type normally used in residential buildings, will cause the filament of a large lighting unit to vibrate at sixty cycles per second. That vibration then is often transferred to the sound tape and recorded as a hum. To avoid this situation, a film may need to use its own DC generating equipment, even if a location's power supply is otherwise adequate.

The use of that generating equipment can often mean major logistical problems. If a scene is being shot high up in a building, it will not be unusual for a gaffer and his crew to have to string hundreds of yards of electrical cable up the sides of a building, through elevator shafts or along stairwells, to the actual place of shooting. At the same time, the actual electrical generators will have to be parked at a sufficient distance to ensure that the noise of their gasoline-powered engines does not wind up on the soundtrack.

There is no "standard" time required to prepare the lights for the filming of a scene; it can vary from half an hour to many times that, depending on the intricacies of the location, the shooting angles, and the availability and variation in natural light. For example, if a shot is to be made from just one angle, then the lighting of that scene will be easier than if the camera moves all around, rotating across, above, and below the action. The larger the physical space to be seen in a particular shot, the more difficult the job for the gaffer, who must be able not only to light that space, but also to hide the lights from the view of that moving camera.

During the filming of the press conference scene in *The Right Stuff,* Holt needed to design lighting that would impart an early-morning feel to a large building that housed the Gemini space capsule. The actual site of the location was a deserted airplane hangar north of San Francisco that had been occupied by nothing but pigeons and broken glass for the previous ten years. The art department came into the structure, cleaned it up, put glass back in the windows, and repainted the floor a high-gloss cement gray. Holt decided to hang fifty-by-fifty squares of silk taffeta over the windows so that when the sun shone through them in the early morning the interior of the building would have a "beautiful kind of whitish overexposed look that also had a wonderful kick in the floor. You could even see the windows in the floor."

To reduce the contrast between the actors in the hangar and the outside, Holt added some "fill" light by bringing in a few HMIs—high-intensity 4,000- to 6,000-watt carbon-arc lamps that run on AC current. Rather than direct those light sources directly on the actors, their light was bounced off muslin sheets to give a softer effect.

As the day progressed and the sun moved away from the windows, Holt supplemented what had been an intense sunlight with six carbon-arc lamps that had already been placed outside the windows, ready to be rolled in as needed. They ensured that if segments of scenes shot at various times throughout the day were edited together, there would be no discernible passage of time as far as the audience was concerned.

It is not unusual for a particularly ambitious shooting sequence to deploy a major film studio's entire supply of lighting equipment. That happened to Holt when he was working on the motion picture *Taps*, a film that presented him with the most difficult lighting challenge of his career.

For *Taps*, which centered on life within a military school, Holt was required to light the entire campus of Valley Forge Military Academy for several night scenes. To compound the problems, the school was in session at the time. That meant that lighting units had to be placed in as unobtrusive a place as possible. To make matters worse, all of the lighting had to be taken down each night to allow students unobstructed access to the school grounds the next morning, and then replaced and read-justed each afternoon.

The lighting requirements were so massive that the necessary equipment filled three forty-foot tractor-trailers sent from 20th Century-Fox studios in Los Angeles. "We literally cleaned out the Fox warehouse," says Holt.

Those trailers contained high-intensity carbon-arc lamps, similar in design to beacons used to advertise store openings. With the necessity of photographing the entire campus at once, only arcs could cast a bright enough light to even register on film. In addition to the six arcs used on the streets, Holt brought along fifty 5,000-watt and thirty 10,000-watt units.

The cabling needed to connect these lights to the generators was enormous. Generating units were parked on one end of the campus. The power drawn by these lamps required extremely thick cable, known as "0000" cable. Each foot of this wire weighs one pound, and the shoot required twenty-six 100-foot lengths, or 2,600 feet in all.

Another challenge was faced in the lighting of the campus chapel. With huge stained glass windows and a large central area of worship, Holt could hide lights only outside the windows. He required twenty-six high-intensity carbon arcs. "Churches are often the most difficult places in which to shoot," Holt says. "The windows are usually very dense, both in terms of thickness and color. It takes a lot of light to punch through those leaded panes."

This shoot was so massive that Holt needed entire crews working both ahead and behind him, setting up the next shots and pulling down the equipment from the last one. In addition to his best boy, Holt had ten lamp operators working under him, plus another crew with a rigging gaffer, a best boy rigging gaffer, and fifteen other people. At times, the entire gaffer/grip team reached fifty people.

The enormous amount of equipment took a long time to set up. The generators alone took hours to get into place, and then hours more to strike.

"That's when the director talks to me," Holt says. "I usually talk to him only on occasion, not too often." Most of Holt's discussions are usually with the director of photography. But at times like these, the director "will want to know what's taking so long.

"I think it's because he's impatient. He's got his actors warmed up and he's ready to bring them in to do the scene. But we're still doing lighting for a particular reason. It's just a nervous statement. I think the director understands that our job is important; I'm sure in the end he would just as soon have us take our time and do nice work."

Postproduction

Computer Graphics Supervisor, Visual Effects Supervisor, Visual Effects Producer

Mark Dippé
Janet Healey

Filmmaking, by its nature, is concerned with the creation of artificial worlds. But until recently, the places and people that populated those worlds have always been real. Whether or not Humphrey Bogart was photographed actually driving down a road or sitting in a car with a road projected behind him, everyone understood that the pieces that made up the scene had once actually existed.

Today, with the development of powerful, sophisticated, graphics-oriented computers, even the existence of the basic elements of life are, for the first time, called into question. Now used to create everything from the dinosaurs in *Jurassic Park* to a scene showing President Kennedy speaking words to the character of Forrest Gump that he never actually said, these new innovative techniques, while supremely entertaining, have major technical, financial, and moral implications for the film industry.

Computers can now create on film worlds that don't exist and can populate them with people who never lived, who say words that were never spoken. While still in the most preliminary stages of development, rapid technological progress ensures that within the next few years talented filmmakers skilled in the emerging art of **computer graphics (CG)** will be able to create other realities that seamlessly and transparently blend into our own.

In the most significant technological change to affect the film production industry in decades, scores of largely self-taught computer aficionados and filmmakers are rapidly carving out a place for themselves in this new area of production. Job categories and positions are being created and defined on the fly, much as in the early days of filmmaking. Special effects that once could be created only with standard optical equipment and frame-by-frame, stop-motion photography are regularly being developed without any mechanical devices, as computer craftspeople show producers that they can do the work of structuring realities faster, more cheaply, and with greater realism.

It was not much more than a decade ago that the Apple Macintosh first captured the imagination of designers and graphic artists. Until then, computers were of little use for anything except the manipulation of text and numbers; all commands were executed by typing often meaningless key combinations onto a black or orange screen. The Macintosh, an overpriced and very underpowered alternative, gave the user the ability to manipulate pictures as well as text; moving a "mouse" across a desk created a shape on the computer screen that corresponded to that mouse's movement. While the resulting image looked not much different from a sketch anyone could make on a pad, this electronic drawing did not really exist; it could not only be erased without a trace but could also be easily rotated, stretched, or compressed by the creator.

These new computer graphics techniques were out-growths of work being done with much more powerful machines in college labs throughout the world. That experimentation captivated Mark Dippé, a San Francisco Bay Area resident, who enrolled at the University of California at Berkeley in the 1970s to study under Jim Blinn and Alvy Ray Smith, two men doing pioneering CG work. Dippé wanted to create films with computers, and he was amazed at what the two were accomplishing at Berkeley's computer lab.

By the early 1990s, Dippé would emerge to head the team of computer engineers and designers responsible for creating many of the dinosaurs in Steven Spielberg's epic, *Jurassic Park*. Fifteen years earlier, such notions of otherworldly creation could not have been high in the consciousness of Dippé nor other industry pioneers. At the time, they were happy learning to harness the computer to recreate the likeness of a piece of fruit.

By the late 1970s, Blinn and Smith, using a Digital Equipment machine, were fashioning 3-D pictures of oranges on their computer screens, a simple task now but one that was daunting at the time. "It sounds like nothing today," Dippé says, "but back then, the concept of creating an object in space that didn't exist but looked like it had been created with a camera—that blew my mind!"

When Dippé put his hand to designing, he realized how difficult it was to make a digitized "object." Attempting to draw a vase on a computer in the late 1970s took over three months, because every angle of the shape had to be fed into the computer in a mathematical formula. "I could input a limited amount of information by using a drawing tablet to sketch the shape on the screen," Dippé recalls. "But then I'd have to use the keyboard to modify that information and properly translate it. The image could be rotated, but only very slowly. It was terrible. I almost quit, but then I realized its potential."

The potential was the promise of total filmic freedom. In film production, much depends on the condition of the physical elements: the angle of the sun, the season, the weather, the condition of the camera and the camera dolly, and the health of the technicians will all affect the look of the scene. If one sequence is shot over several days, then all the elements must be identical, so the action will fit together flawlessly. Any misguided element can halt production until the conditions necessary to produce the right look can be obtained.

Dippé and others realized that if scenes could somehow be created in a computer, then all of those elements could be controlled. For example, a person could be photographed with a real camera, standing in front of a blank wall. Then, that image could be superimposed over a shot of the Rocky Mountains that was drawn in the computer. If the scene was to take place at dusk, light and shading could be added to evoke the end of the day. If the mountains were drawn from a perspective that was not the same as the angle from which the person was shot, then the mountain could be rotated until the viewing angles coincided. If more birds were needed, animated ones could be added.

As all objects and sounds in a computer can be defined by a series of ones and zeros, it made sense that any object, no matter how complex, could be created if one could determine a particular algorithm, or series of equations, that would define the relationship of one line of that object to another, as it moved through space. Similarly, a real person's voice could be reproduced by the computer once the nuances of a particular person's speech patterns were broken down into their essential elements.

In 1979, George Lucas, the director of *Star Wars*, created the first commercial film group to use this primitive digital technology. Blinn, Smith, and Ed Catmull were hired to run the facility, but there was little call for the time-consuming and expensive processes they had developed. Dippé lost interest. He began to create performance art pieces in Los Angeles as well as a few TV commercials and moved to the woods to live. By the mid 1980s, Lucas's production facility was up and running in the Bay Area, but Dippé, despite several invitations, did not want to work there. He was first and foremost a visual artist and was not in love with computer technology for its own sake. Lucas's staff members continued to woo him to join the company, but he refused. The action-oriented, strong narrative films that Lucas was working on did not appeal to Dippé; he preferred to make creative art pieces. "I did not want to spend the rest of my life making movies I wasn't interested in," Dippé says.

But he never cut his ties to the people on the inside, and during a short visit to San Francisco he was asked once again to work for Lucas's operation. This time, his colleagues had something of interest to offer him. "We've got this movie, Mark; you really should check this out. This is the one." It was *The Abyss*.

The fact that James Cameron was to direct this underwater science fiction film meant nothing to Dippé, who hadn't seen any of Cameron's pictures, not *Terminator* nor *Aliens*, nor *Rambo: First Blood, Part II*.

"I rented some of his pictures, read the *Abyss* script, and was fascinated by these strange spaces and surreal worlds. Cameron was trying to do some technologically interesting work. I thought that this was my chance. He'll buy us a bunch of computers, they'll support us, and we'll get to do some very visually sophisticated work."

Dippé was brought in to create the "pseudopod," a seemingly benign snakelike creature formed from nothing but water. There was no concept of what the creature would look like, so Dippé set about visualizing what he thought it should be. He built an initial model that showed Cameron and the art director how the snake could move and appear. Once everyone agreed that the snake was a viable creature, the scenes in which it would be present were shot, with the actors reacting to the snake, which, of course, was not really there.

In order to understand how to move, the actors practiced delivering their lines to a water snake stand-in: Dippé held a large vacuum hose where the pseudopod would be; this way, the actors had something to relate to when they said their lines. The actors became used to speaking to an inanimate object, but it was more of a challenge for the cameraman to film the scene correctly: once the hose was removed, the cinematographer had to remember to leave room in his frame for the insertion of the snake.

Dippé and his team determined the look of the creature and then set about creating it within the computer. First, it needed to be animated. The sequence of movements was decided, and various **key frames,** or reference points in the action, were created. The computer, using animation software, filled in the interim changes in the movement of the creature, creating a smooth sequence of action.

Once the entire sequence had been generated by the computer, the shot was **rendered,** combined with all the elements such as lights, shadows, and texturing that make a graphic look like a real object.

The seventy-five-second sequence took Dippé and his four-person staff nine months to complete. No one had ever created a creature using computers before, and the available machines were unreliable and slow, having less than one hundredth the speed of those used today. Graphics information requires so much processing power that rendering one frame of film took more than two hours. Multiplied by the 1800 frames in a seventy-five-second sequence, the automated rendering process alone would have taken five months—assuming everything went without a hitch.

"We'd find bugs in our software and the machines would crash. Or we'd be working on a ten-frame sequence, everything would look fine, we'd go out to dinner and come back and realize, 'We screwed up. The shadows were overlapping.' So we'd have to stop and do the sequence again. Everything was just so fragile."

While Dippé was trying to figure out how to work in this new world, another employee at Lucas's Industrial Light and

Magic facility was trying to understand how to keep all the work by the very talented people there under control and on track. ILM was beginning to branch out and provide effects for films not associated with George Lucas. Janet Healey, a woman who had absolutely no interest in computers, had been working at the facility for several years as an **assistant production manager.** Her job was to schedule the various resources available to clients looking for certain special effects. As the facility began to take on more outside computer-based work, Healey realized that ILM needed to mirror the structure of any feature film production company. She created her own job of **visual effects producer,** a person who would be assigned to oversee the budgeting and progress of particular films, rather than all the work at the facility at large. As new film projects came to ILM, which was housed in a nondescript Marin County industrial building across from a beer distributor and labeled with a purposely misleading sign reading KERNER COMPANY, Healey assigned **visual effects supervisors** to each, overseeing them all. By the time Steven Spielberg approached George Lucas for help creating the dinosaur sequences for his new film *Jurassic Park,* the facility was properly structured to take part.

While Spielberg and his producer, Kathleen Kennedy, had decided to create the special effects using the ILM facility, the notion of computer-generated graphics played no part in the plan. They expected to create the dinosaurs using one or more of the three standard methods: for the giant dinosaurs, Stan Winston would create large animatronic animals, much like the robotic Abraham Lincoln character seen at Disneyland. When single normal-sized creatures would be shown, such as in the kitchen sequence at the end of the film, men in dinosaur "suits" would be used.

The smaller animals and those seen in herds would be created through go-motion photography. A variation of stop-motion photography, in which a static object is slightly altered and then shot, one frame at a time, go-motion allows the camera's shutter to remain open between each frame, imparting a small amount of blur to the action. This blur increases the realism of the movement and prevents the artificial, stilted "King Kong" look so prevalent in stop-motion work. This go-motion technique was so expensive that Spielberg had decided to create its look artificially, by shooting stop-motion, then adding the go-motion blur with the aid of a computer.

ILM's responsibilities under this plan were minimal: they would concentrate on compositing the various elements; that is, they would combine the creatures with various backgrounds so that the dinosaurs would appear to be walking across an appropriate terrain.

"We weren't thrilled about this," Healey admits. Yet there was no reason for Spielberg to get involved in a virtually untested, time-consuming technology that, until recently, had cost more than standard special effects techniques. The ILM people were frustrated because they were convinced they could create a better look than Spielberg thought possible.

"When I heard what they were going to do," Dippé says, "I immediately told visual effects supervisor Dennis Muren, 'Dennis, we can do this whole thing in computer graphics, for Christ's sake. It's a big opportunity.' For me, the animals in *Jurassic Park* were the stars. It would be silly to have them look caricatured and artificial by using go-motion and animatronic creatures. Not that that style isn't good, but that makes it a kid's movie, it becomes a Godzilla kind of thing."

Dippé bristled at the thought of what some of Spielberg's dinosaurs would look like if computers weren't used. "If you put a man in a suit, you'll see that he doesn't move the right way. A man doesn't move the way a gazelle or a crocodile moves. Even a man in a gorilla suit, the closest thing to human movement, is really tough to create. You can be drawn into the fantasy, but we wanted this to be dinosaurs. We wanted people to be totally drawn into the thought that that is what they were seeing."

Healey met with the Spielberg team to discuss how best

to create each dinosaur shot. It soon became apparent that one sequence in particular would prove very difficult to pull off with standard techniques. The idea was to show a herd of dinosaurs running across a plain and then passing behind and in front of several live characters. The sequence had to involve a large number of animals and create an epic sense. Healey knew that to do such a shot with go-motion would be very expensive. Another possibility would have been to shoot a herd of ostriches from a distance and then use men in dinosaur suits for the close-ups. But the dramatic, awe-inspiring sense that Spielberg was looking for would certainly not have been achieved.

If go-motion were to be used, each animal would have to be shot individually, then combined on film with the others. To complicate matters, the scene consisted of five to ten individual angles: the animals came across the hill, reversed direction, ran toward the camera, chased some of the live-action characters, jumped over a log, and ran away. While it would have been technically possible to shoot several animated animals at once and then duplicate that to create a larger group, the identical movements of some of the dinosaurs would have been apparent.

Healey did some calculations: each shot would have twenty-five or thirty animals, and each element in the shot would take a minimum of two days to create. (Assuming everything went according to plan; if it was decided that one animal was shot at too high an angle, then the camera would have to be moved and the sequence redone.) Therefore, each shot would take fifty days, or ten weeks. Multiply that by the five to ten angles that made up the scene, and it was clear that the entire twenty-second sequence would take from one to two years to complete, an inconceivable amount of time and money to spend. Healey and Mark Dippé began to discuss with Dennis Muren the possibility of using computer graphics techniques as a substitute.

Dippé seized the opportunity. Working with another colleague, he used late-night computer downtime to construct, without compensation, the skeletal outline of a Tyrannosaurus rex on an ILM computer. They were able to animate it so that it would "walk" and rotate it so it could be viewed from different angles. Healey brought in *Jurassic Park*'s producers, Frank Marshall and Kathleen Kennedy, to look at the creation, and the two were thrilled. Realizing the potential, Marshall and Kennedy gave ILM a small amount of research and development money to continue their work.

In November, 1991, Dippé began to work seriously at creating computerized dinosaurs. By the beginning of 1992, the work was going so well that he was sure they'd win the assignment to create a number of sequences using digital effects. In February, the ILM people showed Spielberg a Tyrannosaurus rex sequence, except this time the animal wasn't just a skeleton but possessed skin and muscle as well. "Spielberg loved it," Dippé recalls. "He said we're going to do a lot of shots computer-generated."

In just a few months, production techniques had been turned on their heads. While it was once assumed that all shots would be done with live-action characters or using go-motion animation techniques, it was now accepted that the herd shots and some of the T. rex scenes would be done on the computer. "By April or May of 1992, the idea of using go-motion had completely evaporated," Dippé recalls. "And some of the shots that were going to use Stan Winston's full-scale models also got transferred to us. But the honest truth is, they'd already spent millions of dollars on these full-scale objects, so they had to use them."

The switch to CG was tumultuous, upsetting the balance of responsibilities that, until that time, everyone had taken for granted. Established ways of working no longer applied, and it wasn't a happy time for everyone associated with the film. "Phil Tippett was very disappointed, because his shop did stop- and go-motion, so in essence his big plan was totally changed. He was going to leave the show, but we convinced him to stay as **animation director.** He was essential in helping us with the movement of the creatures."

With the exception of a few sequences that used the full-size models, the majority of the dinosaur shots would now be computer-generated. The mechanical dinosaurs were better adapted to one particular type of shot: whenever a creature needed to be seen physically interacting with an object—as when the T. rex rammed the Jeep on a rainy evening—it was better to use a mechanical model. In this situation, the momentum and force of the creature would literally be able to bend the Jeep's sheet metal and cause the car to jerk. But even that shot used not a full-scale dinosaur but a mechanical head attached to a ramming arm.

Here's how computerized dinosaurs would be created: a wire-frame drawing of an animal was made; it was then rotated within the computer using 3-D software, which allows an object to be viewed in perspective from a multitude of angles. Once the team was satisfied with the way the creature looked, skin was drawn over the skeleton; that skin was then colored and given surface texture. Movement was added by drawing beginning and ending positions and having animation software create the various interim frames that when played together would simulate a smooth action.

But movement is more than the shifting of an animal's extremities. For a creature to look real, it must also change its appearance as it travels. Facial expressions may alter depending on the pressure put on a particular leg. Muscles must ripple, expand, and contract as limbs are extended. Skin may shift as the creature bumps against an object. Changing shadows deepen or reduce the perceived thickness of a depression on the body. There are no computer programs that "automatically" make these compensations. Rather, it was up to the ILM team to write specific programming instructions that would say, "when the outside muscle on the T. rex's leg contracts so much, the opposing muscle will expand this much." That program had to cover a wide range of movement; if it didn't, another formula had to be written to expand the capabilities.

"It's not the computers that process information, it's the

artists sitting at the machine," Healey points out. "Every joint, every move, every nuance is something they consciously have to do on the computer. They create it, smooth it out, and make more impact where they need it. Those shots take many weeks of someone sitting at a computer animating. Then there's someone doing the secondary animation: the breathing and the muscles, for many weeks. Then you have someone who's figuring out what the surface looks like, how the rain hits, what the textures are, how much sheen it has, how the light matches the light on the set."

Spielberg understood the significance of the pioneering work that was being created. As the director of *Jurassic Park* and one of the most powerful people in Hollywood, Spielberg was kept away from the initial decision making. Only once the computer effects were ready did he get involved. As soon as he saw the experimental footage, he was amazed at its potential. "At one point, he made an analogy between what we were trying to do with the computer and the pioneering work that had been done on *Star Wars*," Healey recalls. "He understood the potential— that this ground-breaking technology was going to make the film special. Yet it took a leap of faith on his part to say, 'We'll trust this picture to an entirely new technology.'"

By February 1992, the three-person computer crew had grown to five. By July, the number had jumped to fifty, with up to ten newly minted job categories and responsibilities.

Meanwhile, Janet Healey was meeting with Dennis Muren, Phil Tippett, and Spielberg, as they tried to figure out which shots should be done in the computer, and which should be accomplished with models. Healey quickly told the producers that they could create only about sixty separate shots on the computer; it was immediately decided that the climactic kitchen scene, in which two raptors search out the children, would include live actors in raptor costumes and then switch to matching computerized animation. To cut down on production time of the other scenes, Tippett created and filmed sequences using stop-motion puppets that would give a clear, detailed view of how the shots in the Jeep and in the kitchen would look once put to film. As Spielberg actually shot the scene, he could first play a tape of the animated version that Tippett had made to get a sense of the pacing and scope of the scene.

Dippé, as co–visual effects supervisor, was, along with Dennis Muren, in charge of the operation. He was the creative leader and had the final say on the visual look of the creatures. "It's my job to make sure we're getting the right kind of feeling with the dinosaurs. If it's raining, I have to make sure there's the right amount of rain. If the animals are walking through the trees, I have to make sure the trees shake.

"The keys to filmmaking are all subliminal. If you put in all the details, and you see a dinosaur walk by a tree and the tree shakes, you believe it's there. If you put a beautifully made dinosaur in a scene, it walks by a tree, and the tree doesn't move, you don't believe it's there."

Working under Dippé and carrying out his instructions were the **computer graphics supervisors** and **animation supervisors.** Reporting to the graphics supervisor were the **digital cinematographers,** the individuals who altered the angles and the lighting that appeared on the creatures. The animation supervisor checked to ensure that the **computer animators** were actually manipulating the creatures' movements so that they would "walk" and "run" as expected.

Modelers actually constructed the dinosaurs in the computer, while the **2-D painter** was responsible for coloring the surface of the skin. **Digital rotoscopers** and **wire and rig removers** eliminated the masks and extraneous marks, wires, and underlying apparatus from the frames. The **match mover** ensured that the "camera" angle at which the dinosaurs were drawn in the computer matched the camera angle at which the surrounding scenery was photographed; if this did not occur, then the perspective of the animals as compared to the fore- and backgrounds in which they were traveling would be skewed.

It was the job of the **compositor** to create the illusion that the constructed dinosaurs were actually within the scene, be they chasing a car or stalking children in the kitchen. If the T. rex was to be shown running down a rain-slicked road, for instance, then the compositor had to combine several different filmic elements—the T. rex running, a shot of rain, the road itself, and close-ups of a hole with water splashing out—so that the resulting sequence would appear to show a dinosaur running in the rain, water splashing as his foot hit the rain-soaked surface.

Dippé knew that his team had little idea how dinosaurs, and animals in general, actually moved. Before they could construct movement on the computer, they would have to understand this basic element. He and Phil Tippett began to spend a lot of time at Marine World and the local zoo, observing the movement of elephants, rhinoceroses, alligators, giraffes, iguanas, and ostriches. Since nobody knows how dinosaurs actually moved, the ILM team decided that they would replicate the movement of living creatures that most approximated the shape, size, and bulk of the animal they were trying to create.

To supplement their knowledge, Dippé and the crew read about animal movement, attended lectures, and spoke to paleontologists about how they believed dinosaurs might have looked, both statically and traveling through space. Dippé realized it was essential for his people, as they sat in front of their computers drawing animals, to free themselves as much as possible from the sense of themselves as humans. He enrolled everyone in daily movement classes to practice animal pacing. Each computer artist had a mirror taped to the wall next to his or her monitor; as the artist sketched a particular angle, he or she could check to see if that pose made sense.

"We wanted to make sure everyone could communicate physically. You wanted to know that when you were speaking to someone about a movement, you weren't being too abstract. When you got into a pose, you needed to know that someone could say, 'Hold your head down a little lower.' "

Each creature they created was likened to an animal that existed. The Velociraptors, the vicious creatures that search out the children in the kitchen during the final sequence, were made to look like a combination of cat and reptile. The herd of animals seen in one of the earliest sequences were drawn to be ostrich-like, while the tree-eating brachiosaurus was thought of as an elephant with a giraffe's neck.

It was the Tyrannosaurus rex, *Jurassic Park*'s villainous dinosaur, that proved to be the most difficult creature to portray. "It was basically a six-ton *chicken;* it's got two legs, it's kind of birdlike, and it's got this massive jaw," Dippé says. "It's just a mouth with legs, it's this mouth that kills things, but it's six tons. If it falls down, it breaks its neck. If you have it move too slowly, it looks even bigger than it should. But if you move it too quickly, it loses its threatening, menacing attitude."

While the dinosaur sequences were being modeled, animated, and rendered, Dippé and others were on the set, acting as dinosaur stand-ins during filming. Since the creatures would never actually be next to the actors but would be **composited** in later on, it was important for the actors to have something to which they could react.

"We had sticks with cardboard monster heads on them, and we were running around in the scene, as Steven directed us, yelling 'Grrr!' " Dippé recalls. If it was known that a creature would run past a character, then one of the crew members would attach a wire to a tree or bush, so that the branch could be moved at the appropriate moment of passage. When the sequence was complete, the same shadowing and light as appeared in the live-action sequence was painted into the computer animation.

Once Spielberg saw what ILM was accomplishing, he decided to change the ending of the film, adding a sequence showing the T. rex in a fight with the Velociraptors. "There's no way Spielberg would have been able to show a full T. rex walking down the road without computers," Dippé says. "We could do the work quickly and easily. We could keep the pace going. With stop-motion photography, everything would have looked weird."

The daytime herd shot was one of the most difficult to create. With all the light present during the day, mistakes could not be easily masked. ILM's computer program had little trouble simulating light that seemed to emanate from a specific source, such as a streetlight. But once light appeared diffuse, like the bright Hawaiian sunshine in which they filmed, Dippé's crew had more difficulty. The unrelenting overhead light left no dim areas that could mask any imperfections or lack of detail that the animals might exhibit.

In addition, the fifty animals continually took different paths, running in several directions and over varying terrain, which meant that distinct movements had to be created for a large number of them. While most of the animals would be seen only in the background, three to four of the creatures became the shot's "heroes," ones that the audience would pay the most attention to; these would consequently require the most physical detail. "Steven saw the dailies, and he realized that what we were doing was amazing," Dippé recalls. "We were doing stuff he never even thought we could *try*."

It took the ILM crew nine months to create just eighteen minutes of dinosaur sequences in *Jurassic Park*. On March 21, 1994, the team responsible for creating those eighteen minutes won an Academy Award for best visual effects work of the preceding year. It's a measure of *Jurassic Park*'s structure, story, and editing qualities that while they appear in only one fifth of the film, the creatures seem to be prevalent throughout. "The strength of the images is so strong that there's never anything but suspended disbelief," Dippé says. "They're there."

And soon, they may be everywhere. Computer-generated worlds are coming to many new films. "In five years, we'll see the integration of the computer and the real worlds. We'll create amazing new characters, we'll have computerized leading men and women," Dippé believes. As the ability to control the subtleties of movement becomes more sophisticated, computer designers will be able to create not just grossly moving animals, but also the nuances of emotion expressed by the human race. According to Janet Healey, it's just a matter of time before someone devises a computerized individual who looks, walks, and sounds just like Humphrey Bogart (or President Kennedy, Zsa Zsa Gabor, or the pope), places him in a setting in which he never was, and has him say things he never said. And no one will be able to tell the difference.

"It's like anything else," Dippé says. "Initially, CG will be used as a gimmick. 'Hey, give me some more of that computer graphics.' In the end, it's always going to be, what's the movie you're trying to make? What's the story you're trying to tell? What's the point of view? That's going to make all the difference."

Film Editor, Assistant Editor, Apprentice Editor
▬ Mark Warner

If the director of a motion picture is a god, then the motion picture **editor** is his Moses. For it is the editor of the film who is charged with taking the director's beliefs, be they obscure or even subverbal, and translating them into a form that everyone can understand.

As with any disciple, it is possible for the editor to completely misinterpret the director's goals; through a simple miscalculation in the length of a scene or the use of the wrong take, an editor can so completely transform a film that its point of view will be the opposite of what the director intended. That is why it is the editor who, except for the producer and director, works more intensely for a longer period of time on a motion picture than anyone else. The editor holds the key to making that film a compelling, understandable, intelligent piece of art.

The editing process is really a kind of second writing of the film, a second direction of the film, a final formulation of what the structure of that film is. There is so much that one can do in editing, there is so much that one can change from what was intended in the original script, that it is essential that the director feel completely in harmony with the editor.

Director Norman Jewison (*Fiddler on the Roof*) needed to find out what Mark Warner thought about the script for his new film, *A Soldier's Story,* before he made a final decision about hiring Warner as his editor. Jewison contacted Warner after being told about him by the editor that he had originally hoped to use on the project, who turned out not to be available.

In fact, Jewison had no interest in talking to Warner at all until after he had read the script. The possibility of working with Jewison was a good opportunity for Warner. If he got the job, he'd get his first **supervising editor** credit. While he had done extensive work as an editor, Warner had never received top billing, having picked up co-editing credits on *Rocky III* (with Don Zimmerman), *48 Hours* (with Billy Weber and Freeman Davies), and *Staying Alive,* (again with Don Zimmerman, plus three other editors who received a lesser billing).

Jewison was interested in knowing how Warner felt about the story on both a conceptual and a thematic level. He wanted to be sure that he could communicate with Warner about the material, that he would be able to find out what Warner truly thought about it, rather than have Warner just tell him something that he may have believed Jewison wanted to hear.

"The editing process is so intimate and time-consuming and intense; it goes on for from six months to a year," Warner points out. "So you have to live with the material. If there's nothing that you can relate to about the material, then the process becomes very mechanical. The aspect of the material being a technical challenge wears thin very quickly."

Warner called Jewison at his home in Toronto after he had finished reading the script. "He asked what did I think—a fairly ambiguous question." Knowing Jewison's previous work, Warner understood that he had a sense of social consciousness, and that Jewison would probably want to converse with him on that level. So while he read the script, he had specifically looked for the themes of the picture.

"It was a script that was very solidly written and had few

structural problems. Its most negative aspect was that as the stage version consisted mostly of interiors, a translation to the screen would be difficult. The screenplay needed more exteriors, an opening up of the scope of the picture. This was a period piece, a film that would explore a whole era in the South, and interiors don't do much to illustrate that."

After the phone discussion, Jewison expressed interest in meeting Warner when Jewison came to Los Angeles, although he tempered expectations by letting Warner know that he had several others in mind for the job. An in-person discussion similar to the one on the telephone was held when Jewison came to town. A few days later, Warner was asked to come on the picture.

Warner negotiated his own salary, even though an increasing number of editors these days have agents. At that stage in his career, there were not many perks that Warner could ask for; for example, he didn't even broach the subject of getting a credit on print advertisements, knowing that it would have been inappropriate to raise the issue. (Credits on advertising become an important subject of negotiation for all top production people as well as on-screen talent. With enough clout, an individual involved in a film can demand that his or her name appear on every print ad, no matter the size; he can dictate the size of type used to print his name; and he can demand that his name be larger than other names listed in the credits.)

Warner was appointed supervising editor on *A Soldier's Story*. His credit read simply "editor," but it was at the top of the list of editors, before his colleague Carolyn Biggerstaff. She was brought on later in the cutting of the picture to ensure that it would be finished in time. Both received a listing in the **main title credits**, those credits that appear prior to the start of the film.

Warner's job began a week before the picture went into production. His work followed the routine necessary for all feature-film cutting: finding editing rooms, renting the editing equipment—the flatbed KEM or Steenbeck editing tables, and/or the upright Moviola editing machines—and purchasing all the little items needed for editing: grease pencils, editing tape to hold the spliced film together, white gloves worn when handling it, boxes to hold cut film pieces, etc.

Warner started his assignment, as he does all of his jobs, by attending the various logistical meetings held for the crew, in which the shooting schedule was discussed, the needs of each day's scenes were brought up, and various crew groups, such as the gaffers, grips, and set decorators, made their needs known. It's important for the editor to attend these sessions so that he will be generally familiar with the entire production process and its overall timetable, thereby giving him a clear understanding of when he can expect to receive film of various sequences to edit.

That was the last time that Warner saw Jewison until after he returned from his location shooting. They would talk daily on the phone, however; Jewison would ask Warner how the **dailies** had turned out. Dailies are nothing more than the film shot the day before. The director is typically not the first person to see them. Busy shooting other scenes, and far away from a processing lab, he relies on his editor to initially examine the footage and report back to him.

After a roll of film is shot, the unexposed film, which is actually a negative, just like the negative that one receives from the photo shop when picking up snapshots, is sent to Los Angeles to be processed. In the case of *A Soldier's Story,* the MGM lab was used. After the negative is developed, a positive print of that roll is made and sent back to the editor. The soundtrack, at this stage of the process, is transferred from standard reel-to-reel recording tape to magnetic film, which is basically nothing more than 35-millimeter film that has been coated with the brown ferrous oxide used on all sound tape. The editor then takes the print of that day's shots, the dailies, synchronizes it with the reel of sound film containing the sound that was recorded that same time, and views them together on his editing machine.

First, he'll look at the material for technical flaws. This is a job initially performed by the lab on a cursory level; after the editor receives it, he'll rerun it and give it a careful once-over. If he sees any problems, he'll call the lab and tell them the imprinted serial numbers closest to the frames that are in question so that they can look at the original copy and assess if there is any damage.

During this examination, Warner is looking for technical problems: scratches on the original negative; outside light leaking onto the film while it was in the camera and causing a red cast over the shots; poorly recorded sound, or no sound at all. If problems are found, Warner will immediately telephone the location crew to let them know so that they can see if they can correct it from their end, and prepare to reshoot the scene if necessary.

In the case of *A Soldier's Story* the film—also known as the **workprint,** because it is the copy of the film that will actually be worked on, cut up, and rearranged—was shipped back to Jewison. He had rented a special projector that could play back the film in synchronization with the magnetic sound track, just as Warner could do in his editing room. After viewing the dailies, Jewison either shipped the film back again to Warner the next day, or he decided to hold on to it. If the crew needed to shoot one scene over a period of several days, then they would keep the film at hand to ensure that the **continuity** was correct—that, for instance, a character who held a tray in his left hand during the master shot would continue to do so when that same scene was shot again in close-up. Otherwise, when the scene was cut together, a character might appear to be instantly switching the tray from hand to hand every time the scene cut from one angle to another.

Once the film is returned to Warner, it remains with him until the end of the editing process. With the aid of his assistant and apprentice, Warner begins to break down the film into small rolls. Each shot is recorded into a book along with its serial numbers, the number of the **take** (whether that is the first or second or tenth time that that scene has been shot), and perhaps a comment on the qualities of each take.

The rolls are organized by angles. For instance, all of the master shots of a sequence will be placed on one roll; on another roll, Warner will place a particular set of close-ups; on a third roll he will place some other angle of the same scene; and so forth. If a scene has been shot of a man and a woman facing each other talking, then the first roll will contain the master shot, i.e., one that shows the two of them at the same time. Another roll will contain an **over-the-shoulder** shot of the man facing the camera and talking to the woman. A third will contain the opposite: a shot of the woman facing the camera as she talks to the man.

The KEM editing machine with its multiple screens allows an editor to project those three different rolls at once. But if an editor brings in two or more machines, he can actually watch four or even six angles of the same scene simultaneously. Under this scenario, the editing space begins to resemble a television control room, with banks of editing machines running multiple angles of the same sequence. For *Rocky III*, Warner had eight screens projecting material simultaneously, while a ninth screen, actually a video monitor, was used to display slow-motion fight footage shot with a handheld camera to give the material a more active look.

Breaking the footage down into those rolls typically takes two entire days. If the film is shot on a Monday, it will be sent back to Los Angeles and processed that night; Warner and his assistants will screen the footage the next day. If any of the production crew are in town, they're shown the film that night.

Not until Wednesday morning will the editing assistants begin to break down the footage into the appropriate rolls. After the breakdown is completed, the film rolls are then **coded**, sent through a special machine that simultaneously adds the same tiny succession of serial numbers along both the picture and sound rolls. These numbers allow the editor to keep track of the bits and pieces once they have cut up the rolls into different configurations.

All of this work is handled by the editor's helpers—the **as-**

sistant and **apprentice editors**. Both of these individuals are hired by the supervising editor; generally Warner and other editors continue to use the same assistants from film to film; that way, the editor needn't worry that his new assistants may not be talented or experienced enough to do the job.

But the freedom for Warner to hire his own team, to begin to act more like an associate producer in that sense, also brings with it political problems; from time to time he'll be caught between the producer and director, trying to maneuver between the different egos and needs of each individual while not alienating either of them, and not losing his point of view about the film he has been hired to edit.

The assistant editor deals with most of the mechanics of the film editing process: taking the footage to the lab, picking it up, making sure there are no scratches on the negative. He or she also physically files all of the material into separate rolls, in the process categorizing, cataloging, and describing everything. If special optical effects—such as slow dissolves between scenes or the joining on screen of two images that were shot separately—are to be included in the final film, then it is the assistant who will arrange to have those effects made by the **optical house**.

The apprentice editor works with the material on a similar, but more mundane, elementary level. It is the apprentice who will synchronize the visuals of the dailies with their respective sound tracks; he or she will be in charge of coding the image so that individual pieces can be tracked after they're cut up. Depending on the editor, both the assistant and apprentice may also be given their chance at cutting some scenes, although the editor is under no obligation to allow this.

"I can't stress how important the assistant and apprentice editors are to the editing process," says Warner. "Without their manipulation of the film, getting it ready, categorizing it, and all the other work that goes along with that, it would be very difficult. The longer a relationship endures between yourself and your assistants, the less verbal communication one needs with them, and that streamlines the whole process."

If a scene has taken a long time to shoot, say two or three days, then the cutting and coding process cannot even begin until the entire scene is sent back to Los Angeles and developed. A film's early scenes often take several days to shoot, so what most people know as the actual editing process, the cutting of the film into some sort of logical order, often cannot begin for a good week after the shooting process has started.

Once the scenes on *A Soldier's Story* were assembled, Warner looked at the film to determine how it conformed to the intent of the script. Based on discussions he had with Jewison, he tried to understand what each scene was saying in the movie, and what it was supposed to say to the audience. When he didn't understand what it was trying to say, Warner didn't hesitate to call director Jewison to ask him.

The film was viewed not only on the flatbed editing machine; Warner constantly took it into a screening room to project it onto a large-sized screen as well, one approaching the size of most screens in typical movie theaters. This is a standard activity for film editors, because "watching a film on a large screen is distinctly different from viewing it on a small one," Warner points out. "Somebody like Jewison doesn't want to watch it on a small screen because he is shooting the film for a large-frame presentation."

Energies are different when one looks at them on a small screen. The nuances in certain performances show up more on a large screen because the image itself is magnified. And a sequence of cuts that appears to be appropriately timed on a small screen will often seem too slow on a large one. That's because the eye has more opportunity to explore an image projected on a large screen, thus increasing the sense of time that one perceives to be passing during that moment.

"Norman Jewison taught me profoundly," Warner says, "that you really do need to constantly project your cuts and your various versions of a film in a large-screen format. The film doesn't reveal itself until you see it that way."

Editing a motion picture often entails much more careful thought and attention to nuance than a typical television series. Due in part to time and budget constraints in the television business, the TV editor will often make the simplest, most obvious cuts possible; for example, in a dialogue scene, where two people are basically talking to each other and doing little else, the simplest way to cut is in synchronization with the dialogue: when one person speaks, you see his face, and perhaps the back of the listener's shoulder. When the other person begins to speak, you cut to his face.

But feature films often attempt to convey more subtle themes and feelings, and it is essential that the editor project those feelings through his cuts, rather than rely on what have become editing clichés. "You have to have a central idea about what the scene is supposed to be saying," Warner says. "The cuts should encompass that theme. In *A Soldier's Story*, a character's reaction was as important in communicating what was being said in that scene, as was the actual dialogue being spoken."

During the sequence when Howard Rollins, as the black lieutenant, has begun to interrogate various men in the platoon, he has very few lines to speak. He's basically trying to prompt the recruits to speak to him and to help him understand their recollections of the events leading up to the murder of the sergeant. "In a scene like that, the balance between Rollins sitting there responding or not responding and the information that's given to him by the person he's interviewing is very critical. It's very easy to stay off of him and stay on the person he's interrogating because that is the one telling you the story. The hard thing is to be able to constantly cut back to Rollins and show him just assimilating what's going on, responding to a particular plot point.

"There were few dramatic responses and very little dialogue from Rollins. Rollins prompted the soldiers to speak and then they did so. So that becomes a particularly difficult thing to cut because you have to decide what's important for him to hear. What's an important response? What are the important plot points in a scene, and are they better served by having the actor who is speaking be shown on camera, or to see his reaction? By cutting to Howard Rollins when his character perks up his eyes or changes his gesture, you're communicating to the audience that [what he just heard] means something."

Warner found *A Soldier's Story* particularly challenging to edit because of all of this subtlety of dialogue and meaning. "The cuts were barren. There was no place to hide. There were some action sequences within the film, but basically it was a dialogue movie."

In those situations, it may be necessary for the editor to add his own action, his own momentum, to cover up what is missing. In a scene that takes place in a mess hall after a baseball game, Warner found himself adding energy by constructing a series of cuts from one recruit to another at the time when the sergeant enters the room and begins to destroy the revelry the men had been enjoying amongst themselves after they had won the baseball game. If he had edited the scene based on the footage, he would have had little more than a static scene, a group of men standing around talking and reacting to the presence of the sergeant.

"I had to carry the momentum in a much more intellectual sense," Warner says. "It was an emotional intellectual sense, not a kinetic sense like what you get in action-type photography."

Cutting decisions become like notes in a symphony. There is an internal rhythm to them that, if violated, stands out for the viewer to see. Not that the average film patron will be able to verbalize what is wrong with a particular edit; but they will sense that something is "not right," is "out of synch" with the way they feel things should be.

"If you cut to somebody and it feels wrong, you don't want to be there. If you're having somebody else say something which is much more important, and you're not showing that person, the audience feels askew. They'll just feel like they're missing something."

Jewison did not stay in Los Angeles to watch the editing of the picture after his production work was finished. Extremely tired, he went on a long-planned ski vacation in Switzerland. But prior to his departure, he screened eight reels of what would turn out to be a fourteen-reel first cut of the film. He shared his comments with Warner, impressing upon him his feeling that the picture needed to get as much humor out of the footage as possible. Warner accomplished this by carefully choosing close-ups and reaction shots (shots that show a character's reaction to another's statement) for their humorous effect.

At one point in the film, Howard Rollins appeals to the commanding officer for permission to interrogate two white officers, a situation that was forbidden during the era of the 1940s. The officer finally agrees to his request, and Rollins is elated at this extraordinary situation. As he walks out of the commanding officer's house after receiving that permission, he is so excited that he does a soft-shoe routine to himself. Unknown to Rollins, the commanding officer's wife is outside gardening and watching him.

That scene could have been edited in any number of ways. Staying on the master long shot would have kept the audience distanced from both the action and the resulting emotional responses of Rollins and the commander's wife. Staying on a cut of the wife looking disdainfully at Rollins, or cutting quickly to Rollins as he notices the wife and then walks off, would both have showed Rollins to be little more than somber, basically still cautious of offending whites by his presence.

Instead, Warner chose to emphasize the glee that Rollins felt after he received permission to interrogate the white officers. "For Rollins it's one of the few areas where he really became unglued emotionally, he let himself open up to the audience and show that he had part of this character in him, because he was so staunch and stoical in the rest of the film," Warner says. "We stressed that by staying on Rollins long enough to the point where you really feel the scene, you start to get involved in it, and then you can deal with the fact that the commander's wife is watching him.

"We had a choice in his reactions; he could have become meek, withdrawing, pulling himself together and walking off. If he had done that, there would have been very little comedic element to the scene." Instead, Warner chose shots that showed Rollins pulling himself together (after he realizes the wife is watching him), "but we allowed him this little smile to indicate that he really kind of liked the fact that the wife caught him off guard."

The fact is that audience reactions can be dramatically altered through the editing process, effecting a change in the entire meaning of a sequence, and consequently of an entire film. By cutting to a shot of a particular character, holding on someone's face for a fraction of a second after he says a line, or just catching the slight rise of someone's eyebrow, the entire point of view of a film can be drastically altered.

When Warner was editing footage of the baseball game in *A Soldier's Story*, he found himself inundated with visual material. He proceeded to cut the sequence into a six-minute scene; but director Jewison's reaction to it was that Warner had failed to convey the scene's point of view.

Warner felt that this was not his fault; that there was no point of view in the sequence because the entire film was shot without a point of view. He did not share this view with Jewison, for fear of damaging the rapport that is essential for the editing process to continue smoothly. Instead he looked for a solution, which he found with his decision to distill the baseball-game footage into a **montage** of a game, a very fast impressionistic sense of the sport. The scene was recut to emphasize the energy while downplaying the actual game itself, a process that reduced the scene's length from six to two minutes.

The job of editing is never finished in the traditional sense; it is not suddenly completed and turned over to the director or producer for comments. Rather, various sections of the film are completed one at a time, and often not in chronological order.

Once the sections are done and locked in, they are turned over to the sound-effects editor in order that the various effects can begin to be put in place. But prior to that point, the sound editor will view the nearly completed picture during a session called a **spotting run**; while the mass of work is still in process, he gets a sense of the type of effects that he will have to construct.

In *A Soldier's Story* it was necessary to add effects that would give audiences a sense of the bayou. One scene was shot in the middle of the winter, but sound effects made it appear to be summer. The two actors were so cold as they stood inside a barracks in their T-shirts in the thirty-eight-degree weather that they had to suck ice cubes to mask their warm breaths. What sold audiences on the belief that it was really steamy hot was the addition of sweat spray, plus the sounds of summer: birds, locusts, and mosquitoes.

Warner also wanted to give audiences the impression of a bustling army base, so he instructed the sound people to add sounds of trucks, airplanes taking off, men jogging in formation down a road, and maneuvers. "So much of the film was inter-rogation [of characters] and dialogue, all shot in interior sets, that we wanted to create another level of experience for the eye," Warner says. "We couldn't do it visually, so we did it with sound."

There is no set number of editing revisions which Warner carried out for each scene; some scenes were easy to cut and were finalized in one or two passes. Others, such as the above-mentioned baseball scene, took twenty or twenty-five times until they finally looked right.

The final cut of the film is not the editor's prerogative; depending on the track record and consequent clout of the director, the final cut can reside with the director, the producer, the producing company, or the studio or financing entity that is paying for the film. All directors can be assured on only one fact: thanks to Directors Guild of America rules, they will auto-matically be entitled to edit the picture as they see fit for about ten weeks after the end of the production process. After that, the contract spells out with whom further editing decisions reside.

In Jewison's case, he has been successful enough to be able to demand and receive the right to the final cut. By the time the picture was released, it had shrunk in length from its original two hours and seventeen minutes to around one hour and forty minutes, a reduction of thirty-seven minutes.

This is not unusual by any means. The first cut of a film, like the first draft of a book or magazine article, is where the writer or editor feels the most freedom to include anything that he believes might fit the subject or the rhythm of the piece. Only by viewing and reviewing the material can he carefully examine the story, honing the scenes to the point where the picture "flows," where the cuts move imperceptibly from one to another, where the viewer does not notice the cutting or structure of the picture at all, but sees only the final product as a logical and continuous piece.

It is when editing is inappropriate, when it does not match the intention of the script or the demands of the acting, that the structure stands out for all to see. In those situations, the audience will begin to pay more attention to the framework than to the film; they will become distracted or bored, feeling that something is "wrong" with the picture, but not necessarily knowing what it is.

The job of the editor is not so much to impose a structure on a film, but to discover what the underlying, latent rhythm is. The excision of a single frame can often completely change the flow of a scene; the incorrect juxtaposition of angles can throw off a story.

"You don't impose your will on a film," Warner says. "You derive your patterns and editing patterns and structures from the film, not from the script."

Warner's point is that scenes in motion pictures are shot in such a way that they are meant to express only one thing. Good editors understand that and don't try to force a picture or a scene in a direction it doesn't want to go.

"My job is to render what the director is trying to say. I'm not there to say what I want to about the film. A film has a life of its own. My job is to try to find that life, and somehow depict it editorially."

Sound-Effects Editor

▬ Frank Warner

One of the problems with reality is that it can never be recorded.

Towering buildings that bowl us over with their power look like minor edifices when we look at their photographs. The majesty of a sunset seems like an array of little more than interesting colors when transferred to film. And the symphony of urban sounds that confronts the first-time visitor to New York or Paris resembles nothing but a cacophonous hodgepodge when put to tape.

The motion picture industry has tried to overcome the deficiencies of the recording process by making film more lifelike: by adding four-track stereo systems, 3-D, and even aromas in the theaters. But part of reality will never be present: it is only the brain that can add the psychological component that makes a crowd scene exciting, or that separates out certain sounds, emphasizing the ones that the listener finds most appealing, repulsive, or threatening.

Filmmakers lessen the distance between reality and its recorded depiction by altering a scene before it is shot. Actors are treated with makeup to look better before the lights; lights themselves are used to make a scene look more dramatic, to force a viewer to feel a particular emotion that would not be present unless he were personally involved in the events depicted.

Similarly, sounds that appear normal in real life would be incomprehensible or boring if directly transferred onto film. Due to the nature of the recording process—the sensitivities of equipment, the quality of the locations, and the psychological distance of the viewer—the raw sound material must be edited into a form that, in conjunction with the completed film itself, leads the viewer down the emotional path that the director wants the audience to travel.

That task is handled by the **sound-effects editor** (or simply **sound editor**). Utilizing the track recorded by the location sound man *(see pages 139–150)* the sound-effects editor reshapes the sound to conform to the emotional needs of each scene. He adds sound effects: from a simple squeaking door that wasn't recorded satisfactorily during shooting, to a spaceship landing that couldn't have been recorded at all. He also smoothes out the sound, ensuring that the audio transitions from cut to cut and scene to scene are accomplished without any jarring change in volume or background noise.

"Our main objective in working on a film," says sound-effects editor Frank Warner, "is to make the sound, the dialogue of the picture, comprehensible. The best compliment I can receive is to have someone look at a movie I've worked on and say 'What did you do on that film?'"

Warner has worked as a sound-effects editor on some of the most popular American movies of the past few years, including *Taxi Driver; Coming Home; Close Encounters of the Third Kind* (for which he won an Oscar); *Rocky II, III,* and *IV;* and *Over the Top.* In each film he has started from scratch, reconstructing his sound effects from a library of elements, rather than using ones from another film, even if the sounds are the same.

"I destroy all of the sounds that I have created at the end of each picture. I think that creativity, that design is a big part of the sound, a big part of the picture. I cherish the challenge. I've done it before, I've got to do it again, and it's got to be different."

Warner and his team of two assistants usually begin their work after a film has finished shooting and is several weeks into the visual editing process. Recommended for the job by the director and film editor, Warner negotiates his actual employment agreement with the producer.

As head of his team, Warner will devise all of the special sound effects, farming out their construction to his associates. But Warner's immediate attention is drawn not to special sounds, but to the sound that was recorded during the shooting to make sure that it is comprehensible.

Dialogue tracks are constantly becoming more difficult to understand, Warner believes, due to the fact that there is a great deal of sound *pollution* throughout the country. "There isn't one place in the nation that isn't polluted by sound today. If you're working on a period picture, it's almost impossible to get away from the sound of the environment."

When Warner was faced with recording the sounds of horses galloping, for instance, he found himself traveling all the way to Utah in order to find a location that would provide a place where the pure sound of the animals could be captured. At one point, he had even considered traveling to Russia just to record these sounds, and had gone so far as to write to Soviet officials seeking permission to do so.

It would seem at first glance that virtually any sound could easily be recorded without extraneous audio interference; all one would need to do is bring the desired sound source, be it a snorting horse or a ticking clock, into a film studio's "sound stage," a room specifically constructed to keep out any unwanted noises, and record it there.

And indeed that technique has been used many times. Pictures as diverse as the television series *The Lone Ranger* and the feature film *Casablanca* have recorded outdoor scenes within four walls of a building. But the results are always less than convincing. Watch an old episode of the famous television show and it will become immediately apparent that the Lone Ranger is galloping around inside a building. Rick and Captain Renault discuss their fate at the end of *Casablanca* in what is clearly a large dark room, not the local airport.

In order for sounds to be perceived as appropriate and natural, they must be recorded in the type of location in which the scene is meant to occur; that's because a sound's reality is judged partially by its context, by the combination of the sound and the **ambience,** the background noise, within which it is occurring.

That's why Warner, on his horse-recording trip to Utah, did more than just tape some animals. First he hired a wrangler who hired some horse workers and then recorded them. Next he went on to Montana and got a community of Crow Indians to construct a sort of Crow village, complete with teepees. Warner had the people walk throughout the village performing their everyday tasks, while he recorded the sounds.

All of this work was necessary because it was clear from the footage of the particular film that he was working on at that time that few of the background sounds so essential to establishing a sense of reality were recorded when the lead actors were filmed. That situation has become more prevalent with the increased use of radio microphones, wireless recording instruments that are so close to the actor that they can't pick up many of the essential external noises.

Those additional sounds are added to the film by Warner and his associates after the picture has been completely edited. The sound editor adds the sounds by constructing additional reels of sound effects on 35-millimeter sound tape, each one of which is identical in length to the edited version of the film. If the film reel is exactly two hundred feet and ten frames long, then so too will be the sound-effects reel. Within that reel, Warner places various effects so that when the visual and sound reels are played back on a special machine that allows both to run in synchronization, the sound will appear just at the appropriate moment in the picture. If Warner needs to add more than one new sound at the same time, then he and his assistants will construct a second, third, fourth, or even tenth sound reel of the same length in which to physically place those effects.

But Warner does not think about individual sounds in isolation. Rather, the sounds are to him like notes in music; the sum total of the sounds makes up a sort of musical composition.

This approach is what guided Warner's decision to develop the notion of *silence* as an important element in *Close Encounters*, an element as important as loud noises themselves.

"The lack of sound is minus sound, negative sound. Silence can of itself actually be a very strong note at the end of a symphony of sounds," he says. Consequently, Warner decided that, just prior to any event of a major nature in the picture, he would introduce absolute silence. The audience would be made aware of that, as Warner would increase whatever ambient or direct sound was occurring just prior to that period.

"And then everything would stop. Everything. At the beginning of *Close Encounters*, when there would be some sort of [extraterrestrial] happening overhead, we'd first increase the sounds of the crickets, and then all of a sudden just stop them. At the end of the silence, I pitched the sound up. First one, and then another and another one. Eventually a dog would bark, and we'd build all of the notes back up to the full ambience that had been going prior to that. Later on in the picture every time an occurrence happened, we did that."

Warner devises the overall sound "look" for a picture by first reading the script and then discussing his ideas with the director. With *Close Encounters*, director Steven Spielberg told Warner that it was "a very simple picture, really. It's a love story, with just a few people involved in the story. And he said that at the end there would be something magnificent happening, and he didn't even know what that would be yet."

Once he knew the gist of the final moment, Warner went ahead and began to construct sounds for it without waiting for the final model of the spaceship to be designed. To do so, he used the same design techniques used on all his films, including *Rocky II, III,* and *IV,* and *Taxi Driver.*

Rather than looking for specific sounds that are prime examples of a particular noise, such as the ideal door slam, or the ideal fist in the face, Warner designs sounds by taking a variety of unrelated noises, then adding them together in various combinations to create an effect. It doesn't resemble the sound as an audience would hear it in real life; rather, it approaches the audience's impression of how that sound *should* be perceived.

He achieves this sound recipe by the physical construction of loops of recording tape. During the playback of the film, Warner lets a number of tape decks run, each playing a particular sound in an endless cycle. At any moment in the film, he can raise and lower the volume of one or more of the tape players to achieve the appropriate mix.

Some of the most difficult sounds to capture in *Close Encounters* were not those of the mother ship, but of deceptively simple objects: a screw and a waving railroad sign.

When the extraterrestrial ships fly past a country road, the energy surrounding their passage causes a railroad crossing sign to wave wildly in the air. Warner could not figure out how to create its noise until he was sitting in a chair and noticed its squeak. He proceeded to record the chair squeak and then slow it down during the playback process, simply by putting his hand on the tape reel until the sound approached the frequency he needed.

During an early scene in the film, two screws holding down a floor grating are seen to unfasten themselves and rise into the air, after which the grating itself flies off. Warner spent considerable time working with his own screw, trying to capture the sound as it was turned out of its metal plate. But it never seemed to sound right.

"I had to free myself from the obvious," Warner says, "because it wasn't working." Finally, he used a combination of a number of objects, such as pieces of wood, string, and nails to create the sound. "I made a bigger sound from bigger objects with bigger circumferences, and that's what worked."

Similar techniques were used in the creation of the punching sounds in the *Rocky* films. None of those effects are created from actual punching noises, for two reasons: every punch in real life sounds similar—to hear the same sound over and over would quickly become boring. And even if an audience could accept that, they'd never accept the sound. True fist punches sound tinny and weak, possessing none of the strength, power, and bone-crunching anticipation that film punches have. For the *Rocky* films, the sound of each punch was constructed of from seven to eleven different individual sounds, generated from such actions as breaking glass, breaking wood, and punching raw meat. Warner divided the body into three parts, upper, middle, and lower, and constructed a different sound recipe for each section. Each section then was broken down further, into variations on individual punches. "With 120 different hits per round, if two or three punches in a row sounded alike, the monotony would be unbelievable."

At this point in his career, it is rare that Warner needs to go out in the field and actually record raw noises. Over the years, he has accumulated a library of over 1.5 million feet of audio tape containing thousands of individual sounds, to be used in various permutations for his effects. He supplements that material by asking the film crew to record various sounds during filming that he thinks he'll need during the editing process.

That kind of material can include anything from the wind rustling in the trees to birds chirping, cars passing, or the background conversations heard as people pass through a park where a scene takes place. It's always better to obtain those sound bites during the filming process for possible use, rather than be forced to return to the site later on.

Each of these sounds needs to be perceived as authentic. Not that many viewers will actually notice if a bird sounds like an East Coast rather than a West Coast bird, but an audience watching a scene that takes place in New York with background sounds recorded in Los Angeles may be able to perceive some unspecified inconsistency; "something" will appear to be wrong with the scene, even if most people won't be able to verbalize what that something is.

That kind of situation pops up often in television series. TV editors, due to time and budget constraints, will breeze through the sound-editing process, adding sounds of trucks with automatic transmissions when the heavy rigs used in the scenes have manual ones, dropping in the sound of a bell ringing as coins drop in pay telephones, which haven't made ringing sounds for the last fifteen years.

The sound-effects tasks are divided up between Warner and his assistants. One individual may be put in charge of all dialogue replacement; another may put together all of the punching noises in a fight scene. By assigning work by type of sound, Warner ensures that one point of view will prevail throughout a particular sequence.

One of the last tasks of the sound editor is to add any footsteps that may have been left out or poorly recorded during the actual shooting. The sounds themselves are produced on a **Foley stage**, a soundproof recording studio with what look like several small sandboxes facing a motion picture screen. In each of these boxes are various materials that people might normally walk on: sand, gravel, stone, cement, wood, etc. As the film is projected, one or more individuals will walk in the box that contains the same material as the actor was walking on in the scene being shown. A microphone then records those footsteps as the technician walks in time with the character on the screen.

The sound editor's final task is to be present during the motion picture's **mix** attended by the director and the film and sound editors. The mixing session allows the various sounds of the movie, including the dialogue recorded during shooting, Warner's added sound effects, and the musical score composed for the film, to be **equalized.** During this process, a **mixer,** seated at a large control panel, manipulates the volume and intensity of each group of frequencies that make up a particular sound to ensure that a particular effect sounds appropriate for its location and distance from the camera.

Bass tones will be removed at this time from one actor's off-camera dialogue to simulate the tinny speech heard through a telephone. If a scene cuts from an actor's close-up to another shot of him from far away, the mixer will decrease the volume in the long shot to preserve the sense of distance. If an airplane is faintly heard behind lines of dialogue, the mixer may try to identify the particular frequencies that make up that plane noise, and, if they're different from the frequencies of the speech, eliminate them.

All of these decisions are made only in consultation with the director, editor, and sound editor, although the mixer's opinions are strongly considered. Not only is he skilled at his work, but this is also the first time that he has seen the picture; his suggestions for sound changes therefore will presumably be based on a fresh perception of the film, a perception that probably no one else who has been involved in the production process has at this late stage.

For the two editors, the mixing process is also likely to be the first time that either of them has heard the film complete with the newly composed musical score. During their editing tasks they have worked with a picture that has been devoid of music, possessing only dialogue and, in the case of the sound editor, the sound effects that he is creating.

The theme of the music may have been heard before as a simple, sketchy melody line played on a piano. The recording of the final version of that score, played by all the appropriate instruments in the orchestra, takes place on another sound stage with a process similar to that used by the Foley technicians. The entire orchestra records the score while watching the film projected in front of them. As the final version of the picture is run several times, the composer, conducting the orchestra, makes sure that his composition runs the exact length of the scene over which it is being played. By watching the film, he can also raise or lower the volume of a particular segment to ensure that the music is appropriate and that dialogue is not pushed into the background and lost.

"Once the music comes on a picture, it's a whole different shot," says Warner. "When the music comes on, the picture blooms. It's like the difference between black-and-white and color. When we first heard the score for *Spartacus*, which I worked on, it was the first time I ever saw everybody working on the stage stand up and applaud."

While the sound editor is forbidden by union regulations from doing any of the physical mixing of a picture's sound, he does not withhold his opinions. The important thing for Warner is to look at the film as a story, to continually try to discern what the director is trying to say with the film, and to decide in his own mind if the dialogue, the sound effects, and the music are contributing to the director's message.

"I try to decide if the sound is right for the moment. If it isn't, I argue against it just as strongly as I can. Some people argue so hard in their little area of the film that they don't see the overall picture.

"I just try to free my mind completely of what is obvious. I try very hard to get away from the obvious and go to the abstract side and see what magic happens.

"I'm just as afraid [working] today as I was with the first picture I ever worked on. That gets the adrenalin going. The idea, 'If I can do this [sound effect], I can do anything,' is a line I've been saying to myself for years. You never stop [trying]."

Motion Picture Rater
Richard Heffner

Before a film is ready to be distributed and marketed, the producer will usually apply for a **rating** of the picture. The ratings system, as administered by the Motion Picture Association of America (MPAA), is a strictly voluntary procedure: no film screened in the United States is legally obligated to be classified. In fact, smaller distributors regularly decide to release films without any rating, preferring not to be subject to the opinions of the MPAA's Classification and Ratings Administration (CARA) as to what constitutes an acceptable film for different age groups.

But for all practical purposes, an MPAA rating has become a de facto requirement for any film intent on capturing a large audience and making a decent profit. While smaller, usually independent theaters in larger cities will play unrated movies, many large chains refuse to book any picture that does not come with an MPAA rating.

The Motion Picture Association of America introduced the now familiar ratings system in 1968. Several months after assuming the presidency of the MPAA in 1966, Jack Valenti, former press secretary to Lyndon Johnson, witnessed a sudden breakdown in the movie industry's decades-old system of self-censorship. Until then, all MPAA companies agreed not to release a film without its "Production Code" seal of approval. But now, by including provocative content, two films threatened to destroy the uneasy peace between artistic free expression and the demands of the marketplace.

Warner Bros. was ready to buck the system and release *Who's Afraid of Virginia Woolf,* a film that for the first time contained a forbidden word and phrase: *screw,* and "hump the hostess." After a three-hour meeting between Valenti and studio head Jack Warner, Warners agreed to remove *screw* but left the sexual phrase intact. Soon after, MGM (Metro-Goldwyn-Mayer) was set to release Antonioni's *Blow Up,* despite the fact that the Production Code seal had already been denied. This was the first studio film to contain explicit nudity. To release the picture without a seal could have dealt a fatal blow to the censorship system. To prevent that crisis, Valenti and others patched together a solution that allowed MGM to distribute the picture through a subsidiary, nonsignatory company.

Clearly, neither the rigid Production Code nor these ad hoc solutions were appropriate for an American society that, in the late 1960s, was experiencing a rapid change in its cultural mores. Rather, a systematized yet fluid response was needed—a ratings system, designed solely for parents, one that could inform them as to the nature of a film a child might wish to attend yet would not demand censorship of that film's content.

At the end of 1968, the MPAA, in conjunction with the National Association of Theater Owners and the International Film Importers and Distributors of America, introduced its first rating system. Films would be classified in one of four categories: G, a film acceptable to general audiences; M, all ages admitted, but the film is geared toward mature audiences and therefore parental guidance is advised; R, a restricted film, to which children under the age of sixteen would need to be accompanied by a parent; and X, no one under seventeen would be admitted.

Changes were made to the system soon after introduction. The age required to see an R film was raised from sixteen to seventeen. It was also quickly learned that parents actually misconstrued the meaning of the M designation, believing that it implied a film was intended for more mature audiences than one rated R. The designation was hence changed from M to GP (general audiences, parental guidance suggested.) The letters were later reversed: PG, or parental guidance.

In July, 1984, the PG rating was split into two: PG ("Parental guidance suggested; some material may not be suitable for children"); and PG-13 ("Parents strongly cautioned. Some material may be inappropriate for children under thirteen"). The latter implied that a film "had a higher level of intensity" than its lower-rated cousin but was still not so intense that children would be restricted from attending.

In September, 1990, the MPAA began to explain why a film received an R rating. The explanations, printed in reviews and distributed to theaters, used any words that the association's ratings board found appropriate to describe the rating; there was to be no prescribed list of explanatory phrases. (In 1992, films rated PG and PG-13 also began to include reasons for their classifications.) The X rating, which was intentionally never copyrighted and offered as a self-imposed category to any filmmaker, had long before become co-opted by the sex industry. In an attempt to reclaim a legitimate designation for films appropriate only for adults but not tinted by an implication of pornography, X was replaced by the copyrighted NC-17 designation, signifying a film to which "no children under 17 [are] admitted," due to "violence or sex or aberrational behavior or drug abuse or any other elements which, when present, most parents would consider too strong and therefore off limits for viewing by their children."

Many filmmakers and distributors decry the ratings board as a group of anonymous men and women who force companies to cut films if they want their pictures widely distributed. In fact, the current head of the ratings administration abhors the entire notion of censorship.

"De Tocqueville once said, 'If you fight the perceived will of the majority, that will of the majority would be transmuted into the tyranny of the majority,' " Richard Heffner, chairman of the Classification and Ratings Administration muses. "Thumb your noses enough at the people of this country and they will strike you down eventually."

That thought came to Heffner after he had been approached by Jack Valenti in 1974 to become the second head of the then nascent classification system. If Valenti expected the man who would ultimately be responsible for granting a film a G, R, or X rating to reflect the personality, temperament, and style widely found in the film business, then Heffner was the wrong choice. It would be hard to imagine a man more out of place in the Hollywood "community" of hyperbole, ostentatiousness, and deception than Richard Heffner. An academic and intellectual, Heffner was trained as an American historian, at Columbia University, and gained his teaching experience at the University of California at Berkeley, Rutgers, Columbia, and Sarah Lawrence College. As a public affairs director at New York's WRCA-TV in the 1950s, Heffner created *The Open Mind,* one of the nation's longest-running TV programs, still on the air (now on public television) after thirty-seven years.

Heffner's next stop was at CBS, where he helped develop the young television network's editorial structure. In 1961 he took a leave from that position to become the first general manager of WNET, New York's fledgling public television station. Heffner was soon back in academia, taking up a Rutgers University post as professor of communications and public policy. His duties took him to Salzburg, where, at the behest of the U.S. State Department, he traveled in the early 1970s to speak on Soviet attitudes toward the concept of transmitting, without interference, television programs from a satellite directly into citizens' homes.

To prepare his presentation, Heffner researched earlier United Nations debates on the efficacy of allowing broadcasts without prior state censorship. What he found saddened him. The Soviets demanded the right to censor any transmission beamed directly from a satellite. In the United Nations, ambassador after ambassador had agreed. "Walk down Forty-second Street," one said. "We don't want this garbage in *our* homes." In the UN, delegates approved the right to prior censorship by 101 to one, with only the United States voting against the resolution.

While in Salzburg, Heffner received a call from Valenti. Would Heffner consider joining the MPAA as its new ratings administration chairman? The idea, Heffner thought, was laughable.

"Frankly, Mr. Valenti, I'm not interested," Heffner said. "My mother did not raise me to count nipples."

"Mr. Heffner," Valenti countered, "since you produce a program called *The Open Mind,* I suggest you have one and discuss this further with me when you're in California."

Heffner wasn't interested, because he thought the CARA ratings system was another example of prior censorship. But once he met with the MPAA board, he began to change his mind.

"It became clear to me that the function of the ratings system was literally to keep the censor, to keep governmental interference, *away* from the door. So I began thinking the rating system was an ingenious creation. They weren't creating a system that would impose what it thought was good for children or the nation at large, but rather would try to perceive what most parents would consider appropriate for children, which had no force of law. If that succeeded, it would diminish the pressure for censorship. The motion picture industry would no longer be so susceptible to the Reverend Wildmons and others who say 'censor the bastards.' " And De Toqueville's warning about the "tyranny of the majority" would come to naught.

CARA attempts to reflect accurately the mores of society by picking board members (there are eleven, including Heffner) who are parents, have nothing to do with the film industry, are willing to set aside their full-time jobs and move to Los Angeles, and are representative of the society at large in terms of geographical location and profession. Board members are paid relocation expenses but are free to quit and return home at any time. Their salaries are not made public.

"We've got a concentration of people on the board originally from the Midwest, and I like that," Heffner says. "We've got a carpenter, a children's book writer, a couple of housewives, and a postal worker from Ohio. The age range is from the twenties up to two people who are grandparents. Many of the people in the film industry don't realize that there is something to this country besides Manhattan and Beverly Hills."

If the eleven board members decide that a film is appropriate for general audiences, it will receive the unrestricted G or PG label. If the members think a film should be seen by only certain age groups, then they will award it one of the restricted classifications: PG-13, R, or NC-17. The function of the ratings board, according to Heffner, is not to establish inflexible rules that will determine what rating a film will always receive, but rather to understand current American values, and, as best as possible, reflect those attitudes in its advisory ratings. The rules regarding what content demands a particular rating are fluid. "We change our standards, because our job is to reflect contemporary attitudes," Heffner says. "A film that was an X twenty years ago could be an R today [as is the case with the Dustin Hoffman–Jon Voight classic, *Midnight Cowboy*]. And a film that was an R twenty years ago could be an NC-17 today. Filmmakers tend to believe movement can take place only in the direction in which they want it to take place. Attitudes have hardened in the public's mind in some areas and softened in others. Twenty years ago, parents believed that lascivious sex and nudity constituted a threat to society. Now, they're much more concerned about violence."

Here's how the process works: Once a film is completed (a picture that is edited after it is rated must be rerated before it can be distributed with that particular classification), the distributor will call CARA's Los Angeles office to book a screening time.

CARA will send the distributor a form requesting technical information about the picture as well as a screening fee.

At least seven of the eleven CARA members must see a film; if fewer than five show up, the screening will be postponed. After the picture is viewed, each member is given a "green ballot" that states, "In my opinion most parents would think that this film, (a) need not be restricted, or (b) should be restricted." Once that is determined, the member decides on the appropriate rating within those two categories.

The ballots are filled out without any discussion. Years earlier, the board members would first discuss the film, but Heffner saw that the veteran members would often influence the neophytes, as they jumped up right after a film ended and announced, "Ah, that's an R." Now discussion takes place only after the first ballot. When discussion is completed, a final ballot is cast.

The rating is awarded based on a majority vote, with two exceptions. First, there's the "fucking rule." When Heffner first joined the board, if anybody in a film said *fuck*, even once, the picture automatically received an R.

"Time after time, this ruling would be appealed, and time after time, I'd get up and say, 'If I had my way, this film would be rated PG despite the word.' For this reason, our rating was overturned fifty-five times before we changed the rule."

Now, if a character in a film says "one of the harsher sexually derived words," it automatically rates a PG-13. Say the word more than once, and the picture gets an R. If one of the words is said only once, but in a sexual context, the picture still gets an R. "There's a difference between saying "fuck you" and "I want to fuck you," Heffner notes dryly. "If someone says 'you cocksucker,' or 'you motherfucker,' even once, we'll give it an R." Even so, all the language-related rules can be set aside by a two-thirds vote of the board.

The only other automatic rating was instituted during the Reagan administration, when Nancy Reagan's "Just Say No" antidrug campaign was popular. As a result, any drug use or content merits an automatic PG-13 rating, unless the board, by a three-fourths vote, decides to establish a less harsh classification.

As head of the board and a well-known figure, Heffner comes into regular contact with members of the film community. But he is adamant about protecting the privacy of his colleagues and the integrity of their work. Heffner does not want to diminish his board members' ability to give unbiased ratings of films by exposing them to the seductive charms of Hollywood.

Heffner has chosen to absorb that pressure. With most filmmakers contractually obligated to bring in a picture with no stronger than an R rating, no filmmaker wants to be forced to shred his or her vision just to make the grade. As a result, Heffner constantly receives telephone calls in the middle of the night, threats, and pressure to change the board's vote on a particular film.

But pressure doesn't stop with Heffner. Distributors and filmmakers constantly demand to know the names of the rating board's members, so that they can force them to vote in a particular way. Heffner refuses to make the names of the members known, but that doesn't stop the requests. "Those who use the word 'anonymous' to describe us, as if there's some kind of secretiveness about what we do, that's what I deplore. That's the kind of bullshit I don't like about Hollywood. Why do they want the names? Why do they want the phone numbers? When you want the names, you want to know them because you want to get to them.

"Never in my life have I experienced as much pressure as I do here. The way I respond to the pressure is basically, fuck you. When I'm gone, they can give out the names of the members, but not while I'm around. Because I know what it means to be called in the middle of the night and have a recording of a phone conversation played back to me and told 'we'll make mincemeat out of you.' "

Filmmakers don't have to accept the rating they receive.

First of all, they're given a detailed clinical list of changes that are necessary in order to get a less restrictive certificate. Distributors are regularly instructed to do such things as "cut out the scene where the woman is masturbating," or "remove the shot with the man wiping the blood off his penis after having sex," to change the rating.

If the filmmaker does not want to change the picture, he or she can appeal the rating before a larger, independent board, made up of members of the motion picture industry, representatives of member companies of the National Association of Theater Owners (NATO), and the MPAA. At the hearing, at which a quorem of at least eleven of the fourteen to eighteen members must be present, the film is shown, the picture's representative states why the desired rating is appropriate, and Heffner argues why the board's rating should be upheld.

The only supporting witnesses allowed are those who actually worked on the film. "In the past, the appellant would bring in three paid psychiatrists or film critics to bolster his case," Heffner notes. "Their presence was so irrelevant to the question 'What do most parents consider an appropriate rating?' that we eliminated that."

After a chance for rebuttal, both Heffner and the film's producer leave the room; a two-thirds vote of those present is necessary to overturn the original rating. There is no further appeal.

If a film is riddled with sex or violence, removing the offending portions to receive a less restrictive rating could leave a shell of a film, depleting its plot, nuances, character development, or simply making it too short. In that case, cutting makes no sense. When director Abel Ferrara received an NC-17 for his film *Bad Lieutenant*, a gritty tale of the life of a sordid policeman played by Harvey Keitel, Ferrara complained because he wasn't given specific information as to what sections of the film he should excise to receive an R. "I can't edit a mood," Ferrara told the press.

"That's more of the bullshit that the producers and directors will say and the press will print," says Heffner. "We never say that you have an NC-17 because of a mood. We say that you have such an accumulation of violence and sexuality that we couldn't begin to tell you what to cut. We'd have to tell you to burn the print—and that we won't say—or resubmit it in a less intense, less graphic, less sexual form. Or take the NC-17 rating. We'd love you to do that."

Despite the MPAA's attempt to neutralize the connotation of its most restrictive rating by ridding itself of the X designation, NC-17 has become equated with a film that is unplayable except in a small group of theaters. It's no wonder, then, that filmmakers are adamant about avoiding that most restrictive of ratings. And given the film industry's penchant for hyperbole, it's understandable that filmmakers, producers, and distributors are quick to see a conspiracy at hand when a rating does not go their way.

In an attempt to get the ratings board to reconsider its classification, Heffner and his colleagues are often barraged with excuses and explanations that don't ring true. "What I'm told so often is not real. Such things as, 'My violence is really anti-violence. I really put all this on the screen to show how awful violence is. Not to excite, not to exploit, but because I want to express my opposition to violence, so please don't give me an NC-17, give me an R.'

"Deny, deny, deny. You hear people deny reality so many times. So if I sound cynical, I am cynical, and I must say that seeing all the different forms and permutations that bullshit can take is something that keeps you going."

Heffner roils when he hears the criticism that the ratings board is soft on violence, giving violent films an R, but very tough on explicit sexuality, especially when males are shown naked on screen.

"One of the great canards of the rating system is that male frontal nudity automatically gets an NC-17 rating. You read that in every newspaper in the country, and it's totally untrue. The people in the film industry don't go to the movies. They don't see the penises hanging out that are not NC-17. Any filmmaker who doesn't get what he wants says, 'God damn it, they're so afraid of sex' or 'they're so afraid of violence.' It's absolutely fascinating, the power of the rumor that is transmitted in the film community.

"Have you not seen sexy movies [that are rated R]? Most of the tentative NC-17s we give have to do with violence. For god's sake, all you have to do is watch *Basic Instinct* to see the level of sexuality that we allow under an R."

As a broadcaster originally trained by Edward R. Murrow, Heffner is sickened by much of what he watches and hears on almost a daily basis. His comfort comes in knowing that he contributes to keeping the state from restricting free expression.

"By rating motion pictures, I'm doing something in the public interest. But there are times when I wish the earth would open up and swallow the people who make, distribute, and exhibit many of the films we see. I have never found the extent of lies, untruths, and exaggerations in other fields as in Hollywood. Because this is the world of fantasy. What you see on the screen is not real, and what I am told so often is not real."

Yet, Heffner still takes heart when he views a work that truly pushes the human mind and spirit. "When I see a film like *The Joy Luck Club*, I feel like I did when I was a kid on Riverside Drive looking at the George Washington Bridge. How, I wonder, did they manage to do that? These frequent enough acts of creativity and imagination are so wonderful, you marvel that human beings manage to do this. In the end, it makes up for all the bad you see."

Vice President of Publicity and Promotion, Independent Publicist, Unit Publicist, Unit Photographer

Cheryl Boone-Isaacs
Neil Koenigsberg

It's selling that matters in American filmmaking, sometimes more so than what you have *to* sell.

But the selling of a film can't wait until the picture is "in the can" and the actors and director have either gone on to other projects or the unemployment line. Unlike the promotion of most other products, be it a can of peas or a bottle of Perrier, a motion picture needs to be sold months before it's even ready to be bought.

The selling of a movie is an integral part of the filmmaking process, for without audiences future projects can be lost, and promising careers destroyed. The selling of a movie is the true business of show *business*. For that business to be profitable, the salespeople of films, those heads of studio publicity, advertising directors, and independent public relations agents, need to generate a groundswell of positive public opinion, a sense of anticipation among consumers and the press alike that, for whatever reason, a film must not be missed.

Salespeople need to convince consumers that their bigger-than-life movie project is even bigger than the next guy's bigger-than-life project; in essence, they must create a myth surrounding the mythical event of the film itself. The advertising and promotional processes—which together make up the **marketing** aspect of filmmaking—can't just begin shortly before the film hits the streets. If they did, some marketers might find their efforts lingering around longer than the film.

Rather, the job of selling a picture can begin years before, sometimes even before the script is written. In Los Angeles and New York, the two most important market cities for the film industry, promotion and advertising may start while an idea is still little more than a twinkle in some producer's wallet.

Extravagant billboards announcing a film's future appearance will pop up on Sunset Boulevard. Double-page glossy ads stating that a picture is about to begin production will be placed in *Variety* and *The Hollywood Reporter*, congratulating the filmmakers on their future bound-to-be-a-smash-hit film. Articles in trade publications will extoll the movie's star and production company, with the aim of giving the impression that all involved are on the cutting edge of the industry.

Nor are consumers spared the hype. One year before Dino De Laurentiis released his new improved version of *King Kong* in 1976, for example, Los Angeles newspapers were carrying ads for the blessed event, offering posters of the gorilla climbing atop that famous New York skyscraper.

But the fact remains that, despite all the carefully conceived advertising and promotional strategies, many films still turn out to be duds, financial and critical disasters; and some pictures, after receiving a lot of publicity, never even get made.

When everything goes well and the picture is a success, the studio deems the advertising and promotional campaigns to have been correct. But if a picture is a flop, for whatever artistic, commercial, or social reasons, the blame for that failure usually falls squarely on the shoulders of that same marketing and public-relations team.

Those are some of the frustrating aspects of being involved in the business of film promotion, according to Neil Koenigsberg, until early in 1987 the president of Pickwick, Maslansky, Koenigsberg (PMK), one of Hollywood's top public relations firms. Koenigsberg is now a talent manager and independent producer.

"Nobody knows what's important in the film promotion business to be successful, ever. Ever!" says Koenigsberg. "Ultimately, you don't know. Nobody knows anything. That's why everybody in this business is so crazy."

Koenigsberg seems to know what's important more often than not. After working as a public relations agent for ten years, Koenigsberg co-founded, along with Michael Maslansky, his own agency in 1974. They joined forces with New York's Pickwick agency in 1983, to form PMK Public Relations. The company today employs 125 public-relations specialists in Los Angeles and New York and manages to acquire many of the industry's top accounts.

PMK has represented and promoted some of this country's major films, including *Coming Home, Network, Dance with a Stranger, Modern Romance,* and *Hannah and Her Sisters.* Koenigsberg also counts among his more than one hundred clients some of the nation's top actors and directors, including John Schlesinger, Richard Chamberlain, William Hurt, Sally Field, Brian Kurland, and Christine Lahti.

Koenigsberg is a free-lance **public-relations executive** working outside of the actual studio system. He is called upon to represent both individual clients, such as actors and directors, as well as feature films for which a particular studio feels that it needs some additional help in generating publicity.

"Whether or not we bring in an outside public-relations agency to help us with publicity is so arbitrary," says Cheryl Boone-Isaacs, Paramount's **vice president of publicity and promotion.** "If an actor is represented by an outside agency, then we might think it's a good idea to bring the agency in on the film, to get a feel for the whole project and to keep everything in perspective."

Paramount's publicity department is headed by a senior vice president of publicity and promotion, operating out of the company's New York office. Boone-Isaacs heads the Los Angeles division, with ten people reporting to her. In addition to this formal structure, the company contracts with fifty-five independent public-relations offices in the top fifty-five markets around the country. These offices develop proposals and put into effect whatever publicity has been decided is necessary to increase interest in a film when it is released in that firm's local city.

Directing a staff of ten publicity people at Paramount prevents Boone-Isaacs from having the time she needs to keep an eye on every film that is being shot. Since Paramount is a corporation with a large bureaucracy, the organization can often get bogged down in procedural matters, in paperwork that must be filled out that can limit the effectiveness of the operation. A freelance agency such as PMK is not faced with those problems. With a large staff of its own, it can assign an individual to work on one particular motion picture, thereby devoting more undivided attention to a film.

When PMK picks up a new film as a client, the PR agent assigned to the picture, as well as one of the company principals, meet with the marketing executives at the studio producing the movie to map out promotional strategy. That meeting could involve anywhere from a few to a few score individuals. Every party to the production is equipped with his or her own personal PR agent, each fearing that without their own representative, their interests will not be adequately represented.

For the promotion of *Murphy's Romance*, a 1985 comedy starring James Garner and Sally Field, Neil Koenigsberg regularly met not only with the in-house public relations staff at Columbia pictures, but also with Field's and Garner's own press people. All in all, five separate public-relations firms worked to promote the film.

A studio's approach to maximizing publicity around a new project follows a standard formula, with only a few variations based on the special needs of an extraordinary picture. As head of the West Coast office, it is Boone-Isaacs's responsibility to keep abreast of all new feature films, to prepare to issue publicity on them as soon as their production is deemed to be public knowledge.

In weekly meetings attended by advertising, publicity, and promotion executives, a joint decision is taken on the best way to "position" a movie before the public. As soon as a deal is struck to produce a film, the publicity department gears up to issue the first of what will be a multitude of press releases. Working in conjunction with the studio **production executive** developing the project, as well as with the director himself, Boone-Isaacs will position this first release to reflect the tone of the entire publicity campaign. In addition, this first piece of material will describe the facts of the film: the producer, director, and stars, its release date, shooting location, and the essence of the story.

When Paramount announced the start of production of John Hughes's film, *Pretty in Pink*, Boone-Isaacs and her team decided to emphasize the facts that this was the first film that Hughes was doing under his new production deal with Paramount; that it was his first film after his very successful pictures, *Breakfast Club* and *Sixteen Candles*; and that it starred Molly Ringwald. "We wanted to let everyone know by way of the press that John Hughes was making another movie with Molly Ringwald. The audience was going to have another good time. Great music. Fun. A fun movie, but in the vein of seriousness of John Hughes."

The press release announcing these facts was written, as is always the case, by one of Boone-Isaacs's **senior** or **junior publicists**. It was sent to over two thousand outlets across the country, to journalists attached to newspapers, magazines, and television and radio stations, as well as to wire services. A release was also sent to the industry trade papers, *Variety* and *The Hollywood Reporter*, to ensure that the film was added to their weekly lists of movies in production.

Various periodicals that cater to the age group most likely to see the film, such as *Seventeen, Glamour, Teen* magazine, and *Teen Beat* were contacted and offered the opportunity to interview the stars and director of the project. Those interviews were coordinated by a free-lance **unit publicist**. The publicist acts as point person, setting up star interviews or accompanying a reporter if he or she just wants to watch the filming. The publicist also works with the studio PR team in deciding which elements of the film to publicize.

In addition to the unit publicist, the set had its own **unit photographer,** an individual in charge of shooting color and black-and-white stills of all the scenes of the film. The photographer was chosen based on his ability to recreate the mood of the film in still photographs. For instance, if a director likes to shoot scenes that look dark and ominous, then it is important that the unit photographer knows how to obtain that look in his photographs.

Those unit photographers' seventy rolls of stills were then made available to the marketing people for possible use in their advertisements, and were sent nationwide to reporters for periodicals that might want to run them in conjunction with an article about the film.

Paramount also uses the photographs in a booklet it issues twice a year to journalists, just prior to the summer and Christmas holiday seasons, featuring all of its upcoming motion picture projects.

The press is continually wooed for one simple reason: well-known actors have little trouble getting publicity; but new films and young actors just starting out do. To ensure that people start taking notice of an up-and-coming actor, to ensure that word-of-mouth begins to build, that a film gets attention, public-relations people first have to reach the nation's press, for it is the press that is the essential intermediary in the marketing process. Nobody in the film business ever forgets that. The press is wooed, wined, and dined by press agents and public-relations people, all eager to gain the extra edge over every other new film in town.

That edge pays off every time a client's film or cast are mentioned on *Entertainment Tonight*, with every celebrity cover story successfully placed in *Playboy* or *Rolling Stone*, or every guest appearance on *The Tonight Show*.

Editors and talent coordinators of magazines and television shows play ball with the public-relations agents because publicity benefits them as well. They know that their readers or viewers like to see certain stars and clips from new films. And the more readers or viewers a publication or show has, the more money they can charge for advertising or commercial time.

Public relations was not Neil Koenigsberg's first career goal, although for as long as he can recall he has held a love for Hollywood. Growing up on New York's Long Island, he remembers always holding a fascination for things theatrical, so much so that, as an adolescent, he used to get his father to drive him miles away to Hempstead or Forest Hills every week so that he could buy the latest copy of *Variety*.

"On Saturdays, when other kids were playing football, I went to movies by myself, especially foreign films. I'd go to a double feature and have lunch alone. To this day, the joy for me of being in a big city like London or Boston or New York is a day alone, going to movies—sometimes two—and reading a book."

Koenigsberg became interested in the theater while a student at Boston University. Reading the programs for plays, he noticed there were always listings for "press agents" and "public relations agents." In his senior year at school he decided, as so many college students have done, to apprentice at a summer-stock theater. But Koenigsberg did not go after one of the myriad numbers of technical positions advertised in the weekly theater publication, *Backstage*. Instead, he went looking for a public-relations job. After answering a slew of ads and "walking down a lot of dark corridors in upper Manhattan," Koenigsberg landed a fifty-dollar-per-week apprenticeship position at an Equity summer theater in Michigan.

Returning to New York, Koenigsberg picked up a seventy-five-dollar-per-week job as a junior PR man. "I worked out of an office above Sardi's. After ten days, I quit."

Next came a stint at the prestigious New York–based Lee Solters Agency, and then a move to Cinema Center Films and its successor, National General. Two years after starting in the business, Koenigsberg moved to Hollywood, hired by the head of publicity at Paramount to act as in-house PR staff.

Tired of the day-to-day routine, Koenigsberg left Paramount, but continued working for the studio as a unit publicity director for a number of its motion pictures. An executive at MGM called to say that the studio was producing a picture called *The Passenger*, starring Jack Nicholson and Maria Schneider. They needed someone to handle publicity but wanted someone familiar with the Italian director, who was a man by the name of Antonioni. Had he ever heard of him?

"Had I ever heard of him?" Koenigsberg laughed. "I'd seen every film he ever made!" Hired for a three-month stint to direct the campaign from the West Coast, Koenigsberg became involved in planning a major tribute to Antonioni. To generate publicity about the release of the film, the director would be brought over from Italy for a reception sponsored by the American Film Institute at its glorious Greystoke Mansion in Beverly Hills. All of the top press people would be invited. It was expected that the event would attract a lot of attention because Jack Nicholson had agreed to serve as host.

At the same time, Koenigsberg ran into his old friend, Michael Maslansky, who had just returned from living in London and was acting as publicity agent for the film *Embryo*, the adaptation of the Robin Cook thriller. Realizing that he could use all the help he could get, Koenigsberg took a page out of his own promotional book and devised a scheme whereby he and Maslansky would form their own company, and claim to the world of

Hollywood that *The Passenger* and *Embryo* were in actuality their firm's first two accounts. The strategy worked. With their new "name" clients, other business began to trickle in.

Working out of the back room of Maslansky's apartment, the new team of Maslansky and Koenigsberg slowly began to build a reputation, never sure of what their success would be. "Everyone was telling us that we wouldn't make it," Koenigsberg recalls. "I can't tell you how thrilling it is to pick out letterhead stationery, not knowing if you'll ever need more than ten sheets."

But Koenigsberg wound up needing a lot more than ten sheets. He and his partner were successful at devising special strategies that went beyond the expected studio approach and ensured that their movies would receive the attention they needed.

With so much competition from other pictures, the successful independent press agent must add to the studio's foundation of press releases and star interviews with innovative programs of his own.

While James Garner was filming *Murphy's Romance*, he was also actively involved in preventing the Occidental Petroleum Corporation from gaining drilling rights along the California coastline adjoining the Los Angeles suburb of Pacific Palisades. The pipeline to pump the oil from the drilling site to the refinery would have gone through some of the most affluent neighborhoods in the city, including the Palisades, Bel-Air, and Brentwood.

Koenigsberg used *Murphy's Romance* as a fundraiser for No Oil, the lobbying group in which Garner and his wife Lois were active. Contributors paid to come to a special screening, with most of the proceeds going to the group. An *Entertainment Tonight* crew filmed the entire event, and gave it and the film prominent mention in one of that week's episodes.

During a marathon four-hour strategy meeting ("The longest I've ever been in," said Koenigsberg), for *The Chipmunk Adventure*, the first feature film based on the successful 1950s *Chipmunks* record albums, Koenigsberg proposed to the assembled throngs of marketing people, salespeople, advertising staffs, and production executives from the Samuel Goldwyn Company, that they try to ensure that a large helium float of the Alvin character join the annual Macy's Thanksgiving parade, which would be taking place just one month prior to the film's then-expected Christmas, 1986 release (the film's release was later postponed to the spring of 1987). He also suggested that an Alvin-suited character be booked as a guest on *The Tonight Show*, and that an effort be made to have Alvin light the Christmas tree at the White House, or at least host a charity affair for government workers' children in Washington. If they were really lucky, they could score a coup by convincing Nancy Reagan to attend. Due to the film's postponed release, these suggestions were not carried through.

Prior to the film's production, a press kit, complete with a specially designed cover and containing various releases on the stars, director, producer, and animators would be sent to all the relevant press workers. Tours of the animation factory in Culver City, California, would be set up in the hope that a writer would break a story about the husband-and-wife animation team at the time of the picture's release.

PMK's plan for a big Alvin event, one that would get a "fabulous" amount of attention, involved the staging of a celebrity screening for the members of the Motion Picture Academy, including famous producers, directors, actors, and all their children. "We'll have Alvin giving out balloons," Koenigsberg said. "We'll have all the reporters from the television shows, from the newspapers, from the wire services. We'll have [someone like] Richard Dreyfuss holding his daughter while she shakes hands with Alvin [and the cameras capture the scene]."

The studios as well are always looking for innovative promotional devices. One of the strong selling points of *Pretty in Pink* was its music. To exploit this, Paramount set up a promotional tie-in with MTV, whereby the music video network was given the exclusive rights to film a special *Pretty in Pink* party, to be hosted by an MTV veejay. The party took place after a pre-

miere screening of the film for stars and studio executives at
Mann's Chinese Theater in Hollywood. MTV then edited the
footage and aired the show after the film opened, reinforcing the
notion amongst viewers that this film had great music and a fun
story.

Paramount and MTV split the costs of the production—a
good way for MTV to get an exclusive program for a small
amount of money. And Paramount picked up an hour's worth of
free advertising, a promotion of one of their films by an enthusiastic MTV veejay, an individual that the MTV viewing audience
identifies with and trusts.

Prior to *Pretty in Pink*'s opening in nine hundred theaters
across the United States, Paramount's fifty-five free-lance agencies set up screenings for its local journalists and encouraged
radio stations to promote the film by giving away tickets to it.
While the studio may have lost money in the short term by letting people in for free, it hoped that those individuals who saw
the film early on would like it and generate "positive word of
mouth," that is, they would tell their friends to go and see it.

While the assembled guests at the then-proposed *The Chipmunk Adventure* Christmas screening and the *Pretty in Pink*
party would surely have an enjoyable time, their presence at
those events was of only secondary importance to the promotional goals of PMK and Paramount. They were invited because if
they didn't come, neither would the press; no press, then no
publicity. "We're out there projecting images," Koenigsberg says.
"That's what our work is all about."

But what works for one film may not work at all for another.
Do the stars of a particular picture have drawing power? If so,
then get them on the cover of a glossy magazine when the picture first opens. Are the actors involved in any activities that will
draw media attention? Then use the film as a promotional tie-in
to increase awareness and draw attention to the picture.

PMK convinced *Playboy* to alter its policy for the first time
and run a cover picture of Sally Field, even though she wouldn't
appear nude within the magazine. Instead, *Playboy* agreed to

make her the focus of one of the magazine's celebrity interviews in an issue coinciding with the opening of *Murphy's Romance*.

During the promotion of the feature film *Network*, a scathing attack on network television news, Koenigsberg held a special advance screening of the movie for former CBS correspondent Daniel Schorr, who then wrote a piece about the film for *Rolling Stone*. And when *Coming Home*, the Jane Fonda–Jon Voight antiwar film set in the Vietnam era, was released, Koenigsberg arranged to have the film used as a fundraiser for groups of Vietnam veterans. The showings not only raised money, but also raised awareness of the existence of the picture among the general population.

Paramount faced a particularly challenging problem with its release of *Crocodile Dundee*, an Australian comedy starring Paul Hogan. The picture had several things fighting its success. For starters, it was an Australian film and, with a few big-city exceptions, foreign films in general do not do well across the broad spectrum of the American population. In addition, its star, Paul Hogan, was an unknown personality in the United States. The picture was opening in September, and it was now already June–not a long time to plan and launch a promotional campaign.

Paramount's Boone-Isaacs had a meeting with the Australian Tourist Commission, which had been using Hogan in American TV commercials to promote their country. She discovered that, while his face had became familiar to people in ten different markets through his commercials, those ads had run the longest in Los Angeles. And even people who knew who he was and what he was representing didn't know his name.

But Boone-Isaacs also learned that those spots were very successful. "Qantas [the Australian airline] was having full planes every day. People liked Hogan, which I assumed they would. He's a very pleasing person."

The studio's entire marketing staff met to decide how best to use Hogan in promoting the picture. They decided that the best thing they could do was to emphasize Hogan himself as the biggest reason to see the film. Newspaper ads were designed that featured a giant smiling countenance of Hogan towering over and peering out from behind the skyscrapers of New York, pulling them apart like Samson in the temple. His head topped with an archetypal Australian bush hat, Hogan immediately gave the impression of a friendly, charming, somewhat naïve visitor, someone making his impression on one of the most challenging of cities.

The promotional people decided to ask Hogan to travel around the United States for them, extolling the film. Over the course of six weeks, he hit twelve cities, booked by Paramount on local television and radio talk shows, and interviewed by the press.

The media in smaller cities and towns are usually happy for the opportunity to interview celebrities. Unlike the handful of major American communities that are inundated with movie and television stars, the presence of a well-known personality in a town the size of Baton Rouge genuinely creates a stir among the media, who will often welcome the change of pace that this person will provide to their local news and talk shows.

Before his itinerary was locked in, each of the fifty-five independent public-relations agencies around the country submitted proposals to Paramount, spelling out how they would get publicity for the film, which local talk shows he would be booked onto, which newspapers he would appear in. From that group of proposals, Hogan's travel plans were formulated; his stops included such cities as New York, San Francisco, Chicago, Washington, Montreal, Boston, and Minneapolis.

Paramount also formulated a tie-in radio advertising campaign with Qantas, whereby the airline agreed to give away a number of free trips to Australia in exchange for a mention of their company by Hogan. Qantas was interested in the arrangement because, as a carrier operating out of only a few American gateway cities, they remained a relatively unknown entity to many citizens. Hogan sat down one day in a recording studio and taped a personal, customized spot for each market in which the ad ran, including in each version the words "Hi, I'm Paul Hogan, star of *Crocodile Dundee*. Win a free trip to Australia on Qantas."

After the film opened, Boone-Isaacs began working with *Newsweek* editors, hoping to persuade them to put together a cover story of Hogan and the Australian phenomenon. Thanks to the efforts of Paramount's publicity people, Hogan had already been seen on the *Today* show, *Good Morning America*, *The Tonight Show*, *The David Letterman Show*, CNN, and *Entertainment Tonight*. "He was everywhere," boasts Boone-Isaacs.

But one place he wouldn't be was on the cover of *Newsweek*. The staff had agreed to prepare a cover article but, at the last minute, it was replaced by extensive coverage of the then-exploding story about the illegal arms shipments to Iran and the diversion of funds to the Nicaraguan counterrevolutionaries. The Hogan story ran, but as an inside article.

All of these appearances are of immeasurable importance to a studio. They constitute nothing less than nationwide free advertising, but without the hard sell seen in actual commercials or print advertisements.

A good film or one that has certain strong "elements," such as a well-known cast, is already one step ahead of the game. While publicity can help generate initial interest, enthusiasm among filmgoers will take over, providing the word of mouth that a film needs for survival. A "bad" film, on the other hand, a low-budget picture, or one without any known actors, is a different story. If, after reading the script, all of the PR people agree that the film is "small" or a stinker, then the firm has to try and salvage its integrity, to try to head off the expected bad or nonexistent reviews at the pass.

Sometimes that strategy takes the form of an attempt to redirect the media perception of a film, to make something "hot" out of something that might have been little more than a minor picture of passing interest. With *Dawn of the Dead*, a small horror film was turned into a cult classic thanks to a carefully thought-out promotional campaign. Koenigsberg and his colleagues "came from cold status and we got people like Roger Ebert and Rona Barrett raving about the director, George Romero. We said that this is an important film, this isn't just a low-budget horror movie. This is a satire, it's socially significant, George Romero is an important filmmaker. We screened the hell out of it, we gave it attention in the way that you would give a major studio's film.

"We did the same thing with John Carpenter's *Halloween*. All of his press was to build up something big out of something small. And that's exciting because that's something that's not being treated by the studios in that way. They're not thinking that way; it's the independent press agent who's thinking that way."

Yet, according to Koenigsberg, there is no formula to ensure that any picture—be it good or bad—will succeed, regardless of the publicity it receives. "Too many people get involved in the big-star syndrome," he says. "I've got a client who's the star of a top television show, he's recently been on the cover of a major national magazine, but because he doesn't have a feature film role he thinks he's done something wrong. I've had clients end our contract because we only helped them get their film nominated for an Academy Award, not win one."

While PMK has become one of the most successful public-relations firms in the motion pictures business, it still doesn't expect to receive a carte blanche entrée into the nation's media. "You've got to create a reason for a client to come with you. Every time I shake hands with a new client and tell them 'I'm going to help make your film successful,' I'm always terrified that I'm not going to get the [press] outlets I need," Koenigsberg says. "There's just so much space for films in *Vogue* and other magazines each month; in fact, I'm always amazed that there's enough to deliver to keep the clients happy.

"You've got to get a client to understand that it's not just one magazine cover that's important. It's the process that's important."

Film Trailer Producer and Graphic Designer

Chris Arnold
Jeff Bacon

While film promotion is an essential part of marketing, every producer, director, and distributor hopes to create a motion picture so compelling that moviegoers tell their friends to see it. This "positive word-of-mouth" is a filmmaker's dream; it's glowing, unsolicited, and ultimately *believable* advertising that money can't buy. For the fact is, people tend to trust their friends' opinions much more than the exhortations of an anonymous advertising agency.

It's rewarding to create a film that everyone eventually loves; the challenge, however, is to get early audiences to see a movie before there's any word of it on the street. That's where the producers of **motion picture trailers** and **advertising**, in addition to the publicists and public relations heads discussed in the previous chapter, are essential. A film distributor must create a campaign that encourages the first moviegoers to show up. The campaign must tease, excite, hype, inform, and motivate without ever disappointing the customer. Just as positive word-of-mouth can help raise a film above the pack, an advertising campaign that promises more than the film ultimately delivers can quickly destroy it.

When audiences saw the British film, *The Crying Game*, many were shocked to learn that the main female lead was really a male. Yet they kept that fact secret from their friends; most people were more than happy to be drawn into a conspiracy of silence actively encouraged by the producers and Miramax, the film's American distributor, in their ad campaign. The word-of-mouth effort was a smashing success; it worked because the film actually delivered what it promised: a compelling story with excellent acting, as well as a surprising twist.

It's no coincidence that the creators of the best movie advertising campaigns remain independent of Madison Avenue, nor that Madison Avenue agencies have never succeeded in breaking into Hollywood. Advertising a new film, creating interest in and anticipation of its arrival, requires skills different from those required to promote a new bar of soap.

Most makers of motion picture trailers and advertisements come out of the film industry, not the advertising business. They understand the power of the medium, and how to script, structure, and edit the hundreds of hours of footage into a distilled, thirty-second message that conveys the essence of the film.

"Advertising movies is unlike advertising any other product," says Christopher Arnold, a partner in Cimarron/Bacon/O'Brien (CBO), one of Hollywood's most successful film marketing firms. Arnold, along with business partner Bob Farina and creative partner Jeff Bacon, are in charge of an operation that employs more than seventy people and creates trailers, TV commercials, newspaper and magazine ads, stationery, typefaces, logos, hats, T-shirts, and arcade games for some of America's biggest movies. Its films have included *Terminator 2*, *True Lies*, *Mrs. Doubtfire*, and *Legends of the Fall*.

"In film advertising, you're really giving away free samples of your product. You can't do that if you're advertising chewing gum or a car. For us, the movie *is* the product. In the trailer you create, you can give someone a scare or make them laugh or excite the hell out of them. The people who are good at advertising movies didn't start out doing that work, they started as filmmakers, they had a hands-on role in the medium."

CBO employees, unlike other advertising agency workers, are mad about the products they promote. They don't need to be told to watch a film on which they're about to start an assignment; most probably already know the director's work. They're avid fans of the medium, spending much of their time reviewing cassettes and laser disks of their favorite pictures.

Arnold studied at the now defunct London Film School, which during the 1960s was a popular way station for a large number of Americans looking for a place to learn the art of filmmaking in an unstructured atmosphere. Arnold produced several documentaries in the U.K. before returning to the U.S. to work as a film editor. Bacon, on the other hand, has spent his entire life in California. Terrible at standard academic subjects, he excelled in music and the creative arts. An independent study course at Cal State Fullerton gave him the chance to experiment on design ideas. Soon Bacon was creating theater brochures and college catalogues. Once out of school, Bacon got his first break, when everyone at the design shop where he was employed got the flu. Suddenly he was creating a brochure for the Jane Fonda–Dolly Parton film, *Nine to Five*.

Neither Arnold nor Bacon was interested in devoting years to a single project. Instead, they longed for the ability to delve into a job with great intensity for a short period of time, to juggle several projects simultaneously.

"What's nice about what we do is we do it, experience it, and then move on," Arnold says. "Filmmakers live and breathe a picture for two years. It's hard to believe they do it. That's why directors are the last people on earth who, at the end of the process, should tell you what their films are about. They just can't do that. I can name directors who have the most exciting thriller you've ever seen, and they think it's a love story."

If the creators of a film's trailer and its subsequent ad campaign are to steer the right kind of audience to the picture, it's essential that they correctly determine the nature of a film. Trailer makers are in the business of compression: they take a ninety-minute film and reduce its elements to a thirty-second segment. In that process, they have two jobs: they must make the audience aware of an upcoming film, and they must get them to want to see it.

The film world is filled with trailers that do neither, that bore or anger an audience, that show so much of the film that the customer sees no reason to pay anything to see the rest, that look interesting the first time they're seen but by the fifth viewing begin to look silly and the movie not worth the ticket price. A good trailer campaign creates initial awareness, leaves the audience wanting more, and, as the film gets closer to release, elevates "want-to-see" to a fever pitch.

If the trailer for *Thelma and Louise* had concentrated only on the violence in the film, it would have given audiences a false and negative impression of the picture. Such a trailer would be exciting to watch but would imply that the film was about two crazy women who loved to shoot men. In truth, their violence stemmed from the fact that a man had raped one of them. To leave that out of the trailer would distort the film; yet including it could give away too much of the story. The film is about the relationship of the two women, not about their violent acts, and that's what a successful trailer would have to convey. "The information that we give in a trailer," says CBO partner Jeff Bacon, "includes a list of ingredients of the picture, without being so narrow in focus that it limits which audience would be interested in seeing it."

A great deal of information must be conveyed in a thirty-second commercial, and it's essential that the trailer producers get it right. They have to set the tone for the film, and they must present it in such a way that it will appeal to audiences conditioned by a decade of the quick cuts and fast action of MTV music videos.

That's why computer effects have become the norm for CBO, which has outfitted its shop with top-of-the-line Macintoshes to create the necessary high-tech look, to produce and evaluate various graphic and video options, and to edit the final version of everything from film trailers to their one-sheet advertising posters (so named because they're printed on one sheet of paper) hung outside of theaters. "MTV has changed the palette of communications," Jeff Bacon points out. "Even in TV commercials there's exciting typography, music, and design that's part of the minimum requirements of trailer productions."

To convey ever-increasing amounts of information to an audience possessing a brief attention span, trailer producers have started to include splashy graphics in their visuals, with multiple layers of information displayed simultaneously. Rather than just show one scene or one title, Bacon will often incorporate the visual *within* the title. "We can animate any combination of typography, film footage, and graphic pieces of art," he said. "We can take a title and spin it, make it three-dimensional, reverse it, modify its colors, and morph it [visually dissolve one object into another, a technique pioneered in Michael Jackson's *Black and White* music video]; everything that used to cost an arm and a leg can be done cheaply with our computers. In fact, morphing has become so passé and simple that anyone can do it."

Arnold and Bacon are capable of supervising all aspects of a film's marketing campaign. When a producer requires only a new name for a picture, CBO will generate a list of a few hundred possible titles. Or the company may be called upon to hype a project before it's ever sold. When a producer needed a package that would help his new script to stand out visually from the scores that weekly pass a studio executive's eyes, CBO encased the script in thick paper with its own typeface and logo. "When Jeffrey Katzenberg [the former head of production at Walt Disney

studios] received it, we wanted him to say, 'This I've got to read,' "
says Arnold.

When a distributor commissions CBO to create a campaign,
the three principals quickly read the film's script; if they don't
know the director's earlier work, they'll watch other films to get
a sense of his or her style. Positioning is everything, so the distributor will tell CBO what they believe the film is about, what they
want the advertising campaign to emphasize, and what subjects
the campaign can not broach.

"Every producer presents us with his wish list and his list
of no-nos," says Arnold. "They'll tell us they're really worried that
their picture will be made to look like it's X-rated, that it will be
seen as too violent when they're trying to get a younger audience
to attend. They all are horrified to think that instead of having
the next Arnold Schwarzenegger film, they really have the next
Heaven's Gate [a major financial disaster].

"Then, we fill our minds with all that information and figure out how to combine all those wishes and eliminate the nega-
tives. With some research that tells us the likely audience, we
choose how to pitch the ball. Will we make the advertising campaign young and zany, or will we try to make it more intelligent?"

The final campaign for a high-budget "A" film will often
consist of a package of trailers and advertisements. The first
"teaser" trailer will attack the issue of awareness: initially shown
six months before the film is in theaters, it will introduce the
picture's title, its director and stars, and the date of release. It
may not include any footage from the film.

Three months before the film is due, the first of the "real"
trailers will appear. Its purpose is to create a high want-to-see
quotient. It will be the first trailer to incorporate footage, special
effects, and enough aspects of the picture to raise expectations
and excitement. (A film may have more than one version of a
trailer, depending on the picture's budget and the needs of the
advertising campaign. However, they will never run simultaneously; the first will always be pulled before the second is shown.)

A few weeks before the film is released, print ads will appear. The print campaign will play an even more important role: to develop one single still image that will draw customers to the theater.

The higher a film's budget, the more energy and resources will be spent on advertising. With so much money at stake, it's essential that the distributors increase the odds that enough people will see the film, tell their friends, and even come back to see it a second time.

When director James Cameron was shooting the Arnold Schwarzenegger film *Terminator 2*, he knew that advertising was going to be key to generating interest. Cameron needed a company that would be capable of understanding and packaging a story that contained a large amount of complex scientific material. While he hadn't used CBO for a full campaign, the company had been hired to recreate trailers for an earlier film, *Total Recall*, after Tri-Star had decided that the original trailers weren't working.

"Tri-Star came to us with a lot of frustrations, because they hadn't been able to get a trailer that told the story of *Total Recall* in a simple way that everyone could understand," Jeff Bacon says. "The public's perception was that this story was a crazy, mixed-up thing that was incomprehensible. Yet it wasn't a very complicated story. We put it in simple and dramatic terms, and suddenly everything took off."

After that successful experience, Cameron, along with executive producer Mario Kassar and *Terminator 2*'s distributor, Tri-Star, decided to give CBO a shot. The picture had a number of important and also potentially treacherous elements: the public already knew that some sort of *Terminator* sequel was in the works; they knew the director, the star, but not the story line. Rumors circulated that the film had cost an enormous amount of money to create. If this high-budget picture didn't look as good as expected, moviegoers would feel cheated.

Cameron was determined that the marketing campaign

would reveal just enough of the film without exposing any essential elements. While it happens regularly, Arnold and Bacon rail against those film trailers that show too much, that practically give away the entire story. They understand why those trailers continue to be made but are convinced that they discourage viewers from going to see the film.

"The problem is, research has come into our lives in a big way, and marketing executives know that a trailer that tells the whole story will test better. That goes back to awareness and want-to-see. If I showed a viewer three minutes that teased and frustrated but made him or her want more, or if we showed that person three minutes that told what was going on and delivered all the great jokes, the viewer would give the one that told everything a ten and the one that teased a five. We've gone to the wall many times to defend the trailer that tells less, and we're told to tell more. It takes the courage of someone like James Cameron or Steven Spielberg to say 'I know people will like the trailer if it tells the story, but there has to be magic when you walk into a movie theater.' "

Fortunately, with *Terminator 2*, that problem would not arise. After lengthy discussions, it was decided that the campaign would be kicked off with a teaser announcing that there was a new *Terminator* film. A second would reveal that there were not one but two Terminators. A third would state that one of the Terminators was good and one bad but not reveal who was who. A fourth and final trailer would clear the mystery. Schwarzenegger was the hero.

"This was a clever approach," says Bacon. "It was one of the most unique marketing situations. We were taking the ultimate bad guy from *Terminator* and making him the ultimate good guy in *Terminator 2*. We had to do it in a stepped way so the audience wasn't deluged with information."

The first trailer had already been created by Cameron solely to take to the Cannes Film Festival as an advertising adjunct to help raise money for the film from foreign sales. Its for-

mat was simple: The ninety-second scene portrayed Schwarzenegger, as the Terminator, rising up out of the mold that created
him. "He's back," stated the narrator. The two words said it all.

Bacon and Arnold read the script several weeks after shooting began and then discussed it with Cameron, as well as Tri-Star
executives Buffy Shutt and Cathy Jones. Like the initial trailer, the
first print ad was created solely for film executives; it was a simple announcement appearing in *Variety* and *The Hollywood Reporter*, the industry trade papers, stating that filming had begun.
The ad was a shot of Schwarzenegger combined with the abbre-
viation *T2*.

T2 ultimately became the shorthand name for the film, one
that eventually replaced the complete "Terminator" moniker.
The filmmakers were lauded for their brilliance in creating this
concise, easy-to-remember title; in actuality, the name was an
accident. Director Cameron, having failed to secure permission
to use the Terminator name to raise money during the Cannes
Film Festival, decided to use the shortened version until the reg-
istration was complete. The name stuck.

While the film was shot, the CBO staff was simultaneously
creating written copy for the trailer. The group came up with
close to one hundred variations, sent them to Tri-Star, and received approval to develop ten.

The studio and the creative advertising people were working so closely that it became impossible to determine which
camp had generated an idea. "Often everyone comes up with the
same things at the same time," says Bacon. "You start seeing that
our second idea—revealing the fact that there were two Terminators—and the studio's fifth idea were identical.

"We also decided not to stress the science fiction aspects
of the film," said Chris Arnold. "The first Terminator movie was
a big hit mainly because the sci-fi crowd loved it. But Jim had a
human story as much as a sci-fi story. By the time *T2* came along,
the only science fiction movie making money was *Star Trek*.

"We wanted to make a real human story, we wanted to

bring the Linda Hamilton character out to center stage. And we wanted to play down the horrendous violence that people were expecting from *T2*. Even though every second Schwarzenegger film was a comedy, people felt that Arnold's movies were getting more and more violent; he was becoming known as someone who went out and killed hundreds with automatic weapons. So bringing the character of the mother out onto center stage was a way to solve that problem. We were constantly trying to put heart and soul into the trailers. We created TV spots that were almost entirely emotional and nonviolent."

Chris Arnold began his work by screening 165 hours of dailies in six days. He devoted all his time to watching numerous takes of several scenes, while noting which shots he'd like to include in his trailers. "More than an entire day was spent watching the boy chased by a truck and Arnold pulling him off. My word, they shot that forever. Watching the dailies was exhausting and frustrating," Arnold says, "because you may love something that eventually will be cut out of the movie."

Eventually, Arnold completed his first trailer, using one of the film's famous action sequences. First, the building in which the Terminator is in is attacked; Schwarzenegger comes to the window and fires. Then, the "bad" Terminator motorcycles out of the building toward a waiting helicopter. He grabs on to the ship's runner, enters it by "morphing" himself into and out of a molten blob, removes the pilot, and sets off after a truck. At Tri-Star, all loved the trailer and approved its use. But when Arnold showed it to Cameron, the director absolutely refused to let him use the sequence.

"I don't want you to reveal what happens in the film," Cameron told Arnold. "You can take a piece of the action, but you must cut it against something else that's out of context. I want people excited, but I don't want people to see what happens in the film. If I let you do that, why would anyone come?"

Cameron agreed that the T1000, the "bad" Terminator, could be shown driving but that he could not be seen entering the helicopter, nor could the audience know that that was the same helicopter he then used to chase the truck. "The way the trailer is currently cut, as soon as someone sees that bike come out of the window, the viewer will know the next ten minutes of the film," Cameron complained.

Ultimately, Arnold used most of the shots, but he made sure not to show the Terminator's face once inside the helicopter. In addition, all of the shots were purposely cut together out of context. "You got a flavor of what the movie was, you got a flavor of the characters and the conflicts, but you didn't know who would be the final victor." CBO's goal was to work against what the audience assumed they knew about the Terminator character, to increase the film's potential viewership. "We'd say, 'You think this is violent? Well, look at this. You think Arnold's a machine? Well, he's not.' If all we came out with were trailers that showed Arnold with a gun, that might be great for eighteen-year-old males, but what about thirty-two-year-old women?"

While Chris Arnold was cutting trailers, his partner Jeff Bacon had hired a number of **sketch artists** to draw rough black-and-white one-sheets of virtually every possible permutation of the three main characters in the film: the Terminator, the mother, and the child, played by Schwarzenegger, Linda Hamilton, and Edward Furlong.

"Paper's cheap. We brought in clips from the movie and told the artists to draw whatever they wanted. We had Arnold on the bike, Arnold in the building, Arnold protecting the kid, Eddie; or Arnold and Linda and Eddie. We had Arnold with the gun; Arnold with the gun and Eddie; Arnold with the gun, Linda, and Eddie; Arnold without Linda, without Eddie, gun only; Arnold with glasses; Arnold without glasses. We did hundreds and hundreds of drawings."

Meanwhile, another group of artists was at work creating the logo and metallic-looking typeface that would be used in the ads. With the Macintoshes, the team could quickly explore variations on the font's color, its striations, size, and texture. "Before computers, we had to get actual pieces of metal, cut the material, and then shoot it. With the computer, if we wanted the metal to be 200 lines per square inch, we'd just punch it in. If we wanted, we could quickly change the type's striations, add more shadow, make the highlights come from behind or from any other direction."

To succeed, a still graphic has to impart one single, quickly grasped message. Unlike the trailer campaign, the print campaign would have one simple theme: the Terminator's back. "If we said, 'the Terminator's back, there are two of them, one is good and one is bad and the good one protects the kid,' we would have lost the ability for a one-second read," says Bacon. "In print, you can't explore all the options. I think of the one-sheet as the invitation, the teaser trailer as the extension of that, and the actual trailers are like the ingredients on a cereal box that you'd read before you opened it."

After a meeting between CBO and the Tri-Star executives, the print campaign options were narrowed to seven: Arnold on the motorbike alone; Arnold protecting Linda as he led the way and Linda looked back; Arnold leading a retreat with Linda and Eddie; Arnold armed with a machine gun using his strength to protect Eddie, who stood behind; a tight head shot of Arnold, with the city reflected in his sunglasses; as well as several long-angled shots of him.

Not everyone agreed on the efficacy of each treatment. "The movie's about Arnold, why would you show anyone but him?" some people from Tri-Star and CBO asked. Others argued against showing Arnold protecting a child. "You must have Linda in the shot, she adds so much to the film," said one camp. "No, the movie is about Arnold, it's not about Arnold and his date," several countered.

Ultimately it was agreed that all seven possibilities would be shot and meticulously blown up into a final form, as if they were all destined to become one-sheets. That way, when it came to finally picking the shot, none would be discarded because of inferior technical quality.

Bacon wanted to shoot Schwarzenegger while he was still in costume and mentally in the Terminator role. Once he finished shooting, Schwarzenegger would be involved with other projects; he'd then be impossible to pin down.

Finding time to get Schwarzenegger to the photo shoot during filming was difficult. Film production often involves very long days, along with six- or seven-day work weeks, and *Terminator 2* was no exception. The only time that the actor could squeeze the shoot in was just two hours on a Friday evening when he wouldn't be needed on the set.

Rather than make Schwarzenegger wait while they set up each successive shot, the pair decided to have the seven sets pre-assembled and ready. Two days before the shoot, Bacon and Chris Arnold set up the necessary props in their warehouse. As seven different poses would be taken, the two brought in seven Hasselblad cameras, seven tripods, seven backgrounds, and seven lighting setups. Test shots were taken with Polaroid cameras using doubles for the actors, so they knew that every set would be properly positioned.

Unfortunately, Linda Hamilton was working on a different schedule and couldn't be at the warehouse with Schwarzenegger and Eddie, so Bacon decided to shoot the adults separately and then make a composite photo of them. As they were never supposed to touch each other in the shot, this would be easy to accomplish.

The CBO people had perfected this assembly-line strategy on an earlier shoot, when time was also at a premium. Commissioned to create the poster for *Look Who's Talking*, the company had decided to create an image of an infant champing down on the film's logo. Knowing that babies were notorious for having attention spans measurable in milliseconds, the company decided to bring in twenty-two babies for the session, hoping that at least one would produce a usable image.

"We had twenty-two babies here, with twenty-two mothers and, as the law requires, twenty-two social workers. We divided the whole place up: babies ready to go were in one area; babies that needed changing were in another area; babies crying were in a third. After four minutes of flashbulbs popping the kids were freaking out and their eyes were dilating." It took twenty crying and uncooperative babies before baby number twenty-one, placidly decked out in a pair of oversize sunglasses, faced the camera, bit down hard on the sweetened piece of foam, and looked straight into the lens.

Schwarzenegger's automobile arrived on cue, at six on a rainy Friday evening. He entered the studio and stepped to his marks on the floor. Within minutes, all seven setups were taken. A few days later, the finished posters were brought to a meeting among Tri-Star executives, Schwarzenegger, James Cameron, and Jeff Bacon. The shots were discussed for twenty minutes; it quickly became clear that all were gravitating toward the same scene: the motorcycle. "It had that calm-before-the-storm, cool, hip quality," Bacon says. "It was unique in that we had bleached out all the warm tones. The one-sheet only had blue, cool colors. You got a sense that he's this icy cold machine who's arrived on his motorcycle to take care of the situation."

While planning was underway for the one-sheet, writers were devising numerous lines to use with the ad. They agreed on "This time, it's nothing personal." In newspaper ads, the photograph showed a tight shot of Schwarzenegger's face, with copy stating "This time, the fireworks start July 3," the date of the film's release.

After months of work, many hundred-hour work weeks, and many missed birthdays, holidays, and trips, Cimarron/Bacon/O'Brien created three film trailers, twenty television spots, one-sheets, video box art, video game art, a new typeface, and I'LL BE BACK T-shirts. The film became one of the box office hits for 1991, and "T2" and "I'll be back" became part of the vernacular.

"We start at a pretty dangerous time in the filmmaking

process," Bacon says. "A filmmaker is in the middle of his passion. When we're making trailers, we're playing with his unborn child. Sometimes it's pretty nerve-wracking for them."

Bacon and Arnold play an integral role in the process of educating the public about a new motion picture. "Our job is to go back to that person's experience and figure out what was their idea at the beginning that made this director say, 'I'll give up three years of my life for this.' If there was an idea back there, we ought to, through our own creative work, be able to figure out how to get somebody else to pay seven fifty to see it. After all, these are dreams—and they're for sale."

Motion Picture Sales Executive

Sigrid Davison
Eric Taub

The motion picture has been conceived, written, produced, and edited. The music has been composed, the sound track mixed, the trailers, publicity, and advertising campaigns created. Now, the final job begins: the unglamorous, tedious but essential task of selling the film throughout the world.

No matter how good the movie, the work that went into creating it is useless if the picture isn't seen. Pictures made by the major Hollywood studios have little trouble getting booked into American theaters, duplicated on video, and sold to pay and free television at home. But abroad, not even major motion pictures are guaranteed a wide audience in every country. Local customs, laws, tastes, and morals may create widely differing commercial outcomes for a picture that might be a smash hit in the U.S.

These big-budget "A" pictures still have an inherent advantage over smaller, independently made titles. At home and abroad, they're usually distributed by major corporations, either a Hollywood studio or its well-bankrolled overseas subsidiary. With their extensive staffed sales operations and subsidiary offices around the world, these companies have the clout to place a film where others can't.

As an independent film distributor, I learned years ago that the makers of lower-budget titles produced without the financial backing of Hollywood face an even greater uphill battle to earn back investors' money. These smaller concerns may hire a sales team, attempt to sell their films on their own, or if they become discouraged about their prospects, sell off the rights to their pictures to another, established distributor, seduced by the great fortunes that their newfound business partner promises will soon come but all too often don't.

No matter who ultimately does the selling, both major and minor filmmakers and distributors will, for several years after a film is finished, find themselves in a world of late-night international phone calls, blizzards of paperwork topped by scores of faxes, and exhausting amounts of overseas travel, as they attempt to negotiate and close deals in many countries. And then, once the sale is made, the real work begins. Long-form contracts must still be negotiated, prints and materials must be shipped, plans for each country's advertising and marketing must be discussed and supervised.

Today, the overseas market often accounts for as much and sometimes more revenue than that obtained in the United States, so foreign sales is given top priority. Before a film is produced, its creators will attempt to estimate how much revenue is likely to be available from theatrical, video, and television licensing in all the major countries. It's an estimate that often must be taken with several ounces of salt. There is no way to ensure that, once a film is finished one or two years hence, the movie's genre or stars will continue to be popular, the video market won't have collapsed due to rampant piracy, or laws restricting the number of American films that can be shown on television won't have been enacted, as has already happened in France.

As film budgets continue to rise faster than the rate of inflation, big and small producers look to cover their costs by sharing their investment with a number of companies in different countries, divvying up the distribution rights in exchange for a guarantee to contribute part of the budget.

In many instances, the sale of those rights may not even be made directly to the end user, be it a theater owner, video distributor, or television station. Before the picture hits the screen, another middleman may have entered the scene, a locally-based company that will in turn sell off the rights piece-meal to various cinemas and local TV outlets in that country. By the time a film actually is available to consumers up to three intermediaries—an agent in both the selling and the buying countries, plus an advisor to the buying agent—may have taken their own bit of profit out of the film.

The actual techniques used to sell a film depend as much on the type of picture being offered as on the personality of the salesperson doing the work. Big-budget movies with a well-known cast and director will be carefully introduced at the world's major film-selling markets, such as springtime's Cannes Film Festival. Large ads in the trade newspapers, T-shirts, base-ball caps emblazoned with the film's name, and other promo-tional merchandise may all be used to drum up enthusiasm and sear the name of the film into a buyer's head.

For every $30-million A title that the worldwide film indus-try produces and promotes each year, scores of other pictures with much lower budgets will be on the auction block. Thanks to the legalization of private television stations in many countries that have previously forbidden them, as well as the growth in home video, the market for cheap American-made action-adventure films remains strong. Most of these films will never be seen in the United States, yet they often star well-known Ameri-cans who need the work. With a tiny enough budget, the distrib-utors can make a profit on foreign sales alone.

These smaller pictures do not receive the A films' lavish promotional and advertising campaigns. Rather, they're sold strictly as commodities, in bulk, and snapped up by a local distributor who will make his or her buying decision on as little information as can be gleaned from the illustration on a video box, the film's printed brochure, or a ninety-second trailer carefully edited to show only the best shots. More often than not, the only person who will ever fully watch a minor motion picture is the film's maker. Once a small picture is completed, neither its seller, its buyer, nor the oft distracted television viewer may ever give it much of a second's thought. Clearly, it's no accident that film salespeople always refer to motion pictures and television programs as "product."

It's a concept that distresses many film enthusiasts, but it is a sad fact of show *business*. What interests and excites filmmakers may be unsalable. To make matters worse, even when a marketable film is created, the piece of work that its creator has labored over for as much as a decade often becomes used as little more than a tool to sell other films, thrown in with ten more to close the deal, its story and theme often irrelevant to a sales staff whose main goal is to make the numbers and earn the commission.

Sigrid Davison has seen both sides of the film sales business. As a former **senior vice president of international sales** for Skouras Pictures, she often dealt with small movies costing as little as $250,000 to produce. Davison now holds the same position at Cinevox, a German-based production and distribution company in Los Angeles, but her job responsibilities are dramatically different. Instead of packaging minor titles, she has crafted an international sales strategy for a $25-million feature film that will be released in the United States by Warner Bros.

"Selling those low-budget exploitation films was like selling soap," Davison said. "Buyers from around the world would purchase anything based on the promotional film and the artwork. I would go to a film market and hear the same thing from 200 people: 'No action, I don't want. No star, I don't want.' If there was a car crash, a pretty blond babe, special effects or horror, that's all they needed."

Motion picture sales was not an occupation that either Davison or I had ever sought. Davison had hoped to become a film producer and attended the University of Southern California's Peter Stark producer's program for that purpose. After graduating, she landed an interview with the president of Universal Pictures. "He told me that if I wanted a job in production, to forget it, there were so many others who wanted the same thing. But if I wanted a job in distribution or sales, they'd hire me. It was purely a fluke," she says.

In 1986, I was hired as the vice president of programming for WesternWorld Television, a small production-distribution company boasting key relationships with major foreign television broadcasters, such as ABC Australia and the British Broadcasting Corporation. (The company's most memorable work was a BBC coproduction called *Threads*, the story of life after a nuclear attack.) During a cost-cutting campaign, partially brought about by heavy borrowing from Credit Lyonnais bank, WesternWorld began firing key personnel and doubling up on responsibilities. Overnight I went from vice president of programming to vice president of programming and sales. While the change was unwelcome, I learned that I had a skill for negotiating. Clients trusted me; they knew that no matter what I was asking them to buy, I would honestly assess the programming and not deceive them.

For the past two years, Davison has spent all her time at the up-market end of the business preselling *Never Ending Story, Part III*, a sequel to the original film produced by Cinevox's owner, Dieter Geisler. Released in late 1994, this $25-million children's fantasy film, complete with creatures created by Jim Henson's company, is one part of a planned programming and merchandising package that includes an animated television series, interactive games, toys, clothing, and one more movie sequel.

With a children's fantasy film, Davison knew that she was on safe ground; buyers couldn't reject the film due to its content, as had often happened to her in her previous positions. Children's and family films are popular in all countries, but that's not necessarily true for other genres. Extremely violent films sell well in Asian countries, but they're strongly frowned upon in Scandinavia, where film buyers actually show undisguised disgust when they look at them. When I offered a low-budget comedy with some sexual scenes to a buyer in Saudi Arabia, he pointed out that all the nudity would have to be excised before it could be shown on television. Yet that same film was considered as perfect primetime programming for free TV in Scandinavia, nudity and all. "This will be very popular with children," the Scandinavian buyer assured me.

While the programming standards for certain countries are discernible, they are not always immutable. While at Skouras Pictures, Davison had great success selling a low-budget ($250,000) "shlock movie" to Japan. But the success turned into a short-lived opportunity. "The Japanese wanted horror films. But suddenly there was a case of a man who was murdering children, who blamed his predilection on the viewing of violent films. Overnight, Japan's distributors did not want to buy any more violent films."

Children's films such as *Never Ending Story* would not be subject to these marketplace twists. Yet it was essential for Davison to nail down distribution deals before the picture was completed. With such a high-budget film, her company needed to know that sufficient worldwide sales would exist to cover its costs. To protect its financial integrity, Cinevox had to have much of its financing in place before the cameras rolled.

Preselling refers to the act of selling distribution rights to a film before it is shot. It's done as a way to raise money to make the picture, but there are inherent dangers to the strategy. If the film isn't as good as the buyer hoped or doesn't have the promised cast, he can demand money back and may refuse to enter into the same kind of relationship again.

Davison knew the dangers of preselling but felt confident because of the talent already committed to the project. She was also buoyed by the fact that Dieter Geisler had a strong track record: he had already delivered parts one and two of *The Never Ending Story*, which were very successful films in a number of countries, and hence was perceived as a producer who lived up to his promises.

Before Davison set out on her quest, she already had the ammunition to convince buyers her film would be a money-maker: the picture would be directed by Peter MacDonald, director of *MoMoney* and *Rambo III*, and the second unit director of *Batman*. It would star Jason James Richter, fresh from the film *Free Willy*. And the first two pictures had grossed $150 million, the original grossing $40 million in Japan alone, one of Davison's key territories for this new sequel.

Several of the original distributors quickly signed up, including companies in Italy, Spain, Korea, and Japan. Each deal called for that company to agree to pay a **minimum guarantee** "against" a percentage of future royalties. That is, once the company recouped from ticket sales the money they were paying Cinevox for distribution rights, they would then split any additional earnings according to a formula negotiated by the two parties.

Davison felt confident in her ability to presell the film, both because of the picture's promise and because of her own skills as a saleswoman. "To be a good salesperson, you need to do a lot of hard work, and then a lot of follow-up," she said. "You need an outgoing personality, but you also need to maintain your contacts and make them satisfied with your product. You have to be straight and honest, or else it will eventually come back to haunt you."

Selling films also requires a knowledge of and sensitivity to other cultures, traits xenophobic Americans often lack when compared to their foreign counterparts. While American businesspeople may like to slap each other on the back and speak loudly, it's a practice that doesn't always go over well with people from more inhibited cultures. Americans doing business overseas are fortunate that English has become the language of commerce and the U.S. dollar its unofficial currency, but even the simple words *yes* and *no* may mean different things in different cultures.

"In Japan, it's very impolite to say no," Davison points out. "So when they say maybe they're really saying no, but you think they're saying yes. Then an American will mistakenly say to himself, 'Well, he's not saying no, so I'll keep trying to close the deal.' In India, it's the opposite. When you say no to them, they think you mean maybe."

With several of her key agreements in hand, Davison made plans to attend the Marché International du Film, the International Film Market, held in conjunction with the better-known Cannes Film Festival each spring. The market is just one way station for film buyers and sellers. Reminiscent of itinerant peddlers traveling to small villages in the last century, filmmakers and distributors will make regular visits to a clutch of film, video, and television sales markets held throughout the world.

In addition to Cannes, the year begins with NATPE, the National Association of Television Program Executives market held in various U.S. cities. The Monte Carlo film market begins a few weeks later. In February, the American Film Market holds its annual meet in Santa Monica. April sees MIP-TV *(Marché International des Programmes de Télévision)* in Cannes, then, two weeks after that, the Cannes Film Festival and market. After a summer hiatus comes MIPCOM, MIP's sister market, and then one week later, the year ends with Milan's MIFED gathering in late October.

Markets are five to ten days of nonstop meetings, business lunches, cocktail parties, and late dinners, all coupled with endless handshaking, superficial smiles that often disappear as soon as the recipient departs, and never ending cigarette smoke. After dinner you often meet with your company colleagues to discuss the day's events and plan the next day's strategy. Then the cycle starts over again. For a distributor, the entire ordeal can cost between $20,000 and 150,000 per market, depending on the size of your stand, the number of support staff you bring, and the amount of money as needed to bribe recalcitrant hotel managers unable to secure you a room without receiving something under the table.

If the distribution company hosts a party or brings a famous movie star to impress the international buyers, then costs mount even higher. An actor requires his or her own entourage, first-class plane ticket and hotels, bodyguards, and a public relations campaign to alert the local media to his or her presence.

Some film salespeople attend every market, leaving little time at home for the follow-up work necessary to fulfill a distribution deal. Yet all the traveling is a necessary evil; the markets provide a centralized meeting place for program buyers and sellers, a setting where you can track down someone who's been avoiding your telephone calls and faxes for weeks, where the fine points of a contract can be ironed out, where films can be easily screened in their entirety, often to the chagrin of a seller who hoped that a deal could be made based on the trailer alone. Film markets are the place where some deals come together and others fall apart. As Irmgard Strehle, a well-known saleswoman for Cine International, director Werner Herzog's Munich-based distributor, cynically points out, "You make a deal at Cannes, you renegotiate it at MIFED, and then you cancel it at AFM."

Before going to Cannes, Davison made a list of expected prices for every territory that she needed to sell. The cost to license a picture in a particular country depends on a number of factors: its size, the wealth of its population, the current currency exchange rate, the film's cast and their popularity in that country. A motion picture that would have been worth a several-hundred-thousand-dollar license fee in the United States was worth just $20,000 to me four years ago in the countries of the former Soviet Union. While populations are similar, the Russians and their neighbors earn about $80 per month, and a cinema ticket there costs twenty cents. Two years later, the value of the ruble fell from 460 to 1600 per dollar; prices dropped to the $15,000 range, a fall that would have been greater if so many Russians didn't keep vast sums of money in overseas dollar bank accounts.

If sellers aren't sure how much a territory is worth, they'll often demand a much higher price than they expect as a way to gauge the buyer's reaction. And for those who haven't a clue as to how much to ask (and that's often true, especially when dealing with smaller countries) price charts published by the trade magazines give them a starting point.

While most countries' prices are fairly stable, each market usually produces one new wild card, a country where the home video or cable television business is beginning to take off, and everyone is making a grab to buy as much programming as possible for the cheapest prices. Rights owners with a large library of older, unsellable films will gladly dump them on often naive buyers for a low per-film price, but one that adds up when a lot of films are involved. Other sellers, aware that panic buying is at hand, may decide to hold off, letting competitors bid up the prices before they agree to sell and make a killing on material that otherwise would have been useless.

At the beginning of the 1990s, Korea was the new hot territory. Hundred of Korean buyers, some of whom had been clothing manufacturers and fire extinguisher salespeople a few months earlier, were suddenly film distributors, paying exorbitant prices for junk. We film sellers welcomed them with open arms, knowing that we could unload everything in our inventories to them. What we didn't make on each film we'd make up for in bulk. Most of these Korean entertainment industry entrepreneurs are now out of business and prices have fallen to more earthly levels. Now it's Taiwan's turn, as the government has recently announced its intention of permitting private cable television channels on an experimental basis. Two years ago, I was offered $1,000 per film for a package of five-year-old B horror films. Today, the price has risen to $4,000 as the channels come on-air, and their owners become more desperate to find programming to fill the broadcasting day. Once again, we're more than happy to do business with them.

No matter what the scale of the film—a high-budget epic, or low-budget exploitation—the actual negotiating process is the same. Americans and West Europeans may eschew haggling in most business dealings, but they become enthusiastic practitioners when selling movies. Hoping to get more than they expect, sellers begin negotiations by asking for a license fee that only the most naive buyer would agree to pay. Wanting to pay less than a film is worth, buyers go through all sorts of machinations, contortions, and emotional appeals in an attempt to convince the seller that the asking price is absurd and impossible. "You get people falling on the floor, flailing their arms in shock" over the asking price, says Davison. "That's part of the game."

Buyers have told me that I would bankrupt their families, that my asking prices were higher for low-budget films than they had paid for *E.T.*, that the prices I wanted were fine for five years ago, but absurd today. The fact is, both buyer and seller know they ultimately will agree on a price fairly close to the midpoint between their first offers.

"A Middle Eastern distributor offered me $500 for *Blood Simple* [one of the first films by Ethan and Joel Coen, producer and director of *Miller's Crossing* and *Barton Fink*]," Davison says. "I said $7,000, knowing it was worth $5,000. He said no and left. The next day, he came back and offered $600. I said no. Over the next five days, we finally settled on $5,000, the price I always wanted. But you had to go through the process. For him, it was like buying a rug."

Some local companies have no intention of actually buying the film rights but negotiate anyway, hoping to strike a deal in principal. Then once they do, they "shop" the film to an end-user in their own country: a theater owner, video distributor, or television station. Only when they know they have a deal will they actually make the required down payment and sign the contract.

With video piracy rampant in many countries, buyers often negotiate contracts for films that they have already released illegally, and then they fail to pay the license fee. Until they're caught and the contract is canceled, they will use the paperwork as "proof" to the local government agencies that they do indeed hold a film's rights. They can then continue to sell the picture without fear of reprisals.

Speaking no English, a well-known European distributor negotiated a deal with me by writing his buying price on a piece of paper. We went back and forth, each of us erasing and rewriting figures, until we agreed on a price. He signed my deal memo (a short form detailing the basic terms of the contract), never made the down payment, and never returned my phone calls. When I saw him at a television market a year later and asked why he broke the contract, he shrugged, smiled, and walked on.

Presales for *Never Ending Story, Part III* went quickly. With its desirable director and cast and the success of its predecessors, Davison managed to sell seventy percent of the world's territories within six months of introducing the film. Little more than one year later, every territory but two, Scandinavia and Benelux (the Dutch-speaking areas of Belgium and Luxembourg, plus the Netherlands) had been sold. "I'm asking a lot of money in those two territories," Davison said. "I've got all the money I need to finance the film, so I'm not in any hurry to close deals there, until I get the price I want."

Once a deal is signed, the difficult work begins. In addition to working out fine points in a more formal, "long-form" agreement that often runs to thirty pages, the distributor must be paid a negotiated down payment. The sum, usually around twenty percent of the total license fee, secures the right to the contract, and gives an early indication of how likely it is that the buyer will actually honor the deal.

The motion picture sales business often seems to be about one thing only: money. "How much money will you pay me for this license? How much money will I accept? How much money will I receive for a deposit? When do I need the money?" And all too often, a deal deteriorates into, "Where's my money? When are you sending it? You promised it last week."

Film buyers use every modern variation of "the check's in the mail" to explain why they have not paid their bills. After selling a package of twenty films to a large private company in Eastern Europe, I quickly received payment in full for half of them. After waiting weeks for the rest, which was promised to me on a daily basis, I was told that the money had indeed been sent. Then I was told that it hadn't actually been sent but would be soon, as there was a delay at the bank. Then, the bank wasn't wiring any funds abroad, as there had been a run on dollars. Then the bank was closed for a holiday. I couldn't reach the president of the company to whom I had sold the films, for he was out of the country launching his country's first private airline. Then he was out of the country meeting with President Reagan. Then, the company went bankrupt, leaving scores of people like myself holding worthless contracts. Several months later, the president of the company was jailed for illegal business activities. (A year later, he wrote to me asking for a recommendation vouching for his character and professional business activities.)

Another overseas distributor took a twenty-second look at ten film brochures and immediately signed a contract with me to buy them all for video release. Six months later, he still had not paid. Each fax to him resulted in a promise to pay the following week. When I confronted him at the MIFED trade show in Milan, he told me it was actually the responsibility of his partner to pay, but he hadn't been able to reach him for weeks. Faxes to his partner resulted in letters telling me it was the first partner's responsibility to pay. The distributor was eventually placed on the American Film Marketing Association's list of unethical buyers.

Another distributor who owed Cinevox's Davison a royalty report and possibly additional commissions told her that lightning had struck his computer, jumbling all the information. He sent her a page of gibberish and said it was the best data he could give her. One Pacific-based buyer told Davison he couldn't pay the money owed because his son had been kidnapped and he needed the funds for ransom. "I laughed," Davison says. "You have to have a sense of humor about this. You also have to yell and scream, rant and rave, beg, and sometimes be sweet to get your money," Davison says. "You have to be pushy, even though it's not my way. She who bugs most, gets paid. But I still never got paid by that particular buyer."

Assuming all goes well and the client turns out to be reliable and trustworthy, the sales executive (the U.S. distributor) will work with the local buyer to ensure that the picture will be released in such a way as to maximize sales. Regardless of his own personal feelings, the buyer must order a sufficient number of prints to make sure that enough theaters will screen it. The distributor also approves the local company's advertising campaign, to guarantee that the picture is being properly promoted, and to prevent so much money from being spent that the distributor will never see any additional profits.

The distributor also approves all artwork. The buyer must adhere to the distributor's requirements regarding the look of the artwork used on a video box, and the size and placement of the names of all the film's key personnel in any advertising. It is the sales executive's job to act as a representative of the actor, who often has "face approval," the right to reject any photo or drawing of him or herself used to promote the film.

The actual work of shipping prints and advertising material falls to the distributor's **traffic manager.** This person invoices customers for all materials, orders the prints to be struck from the film's **internegative** (a second negative, made to be used in place of the original), and then boxes and ships everything in time for release in the local country. Each step requires purchase orders, payment transfers, and quality-control checks. If several buyers require materials simultaneously, the task becomes monumental. When Davison worked as sales head for Odyssey Pictures, she was in charge of selling *1492*, the story of Christopher Columbus, to worldwide markets. The picture was timed to be available in October, 1992, to coincide with the anniversary of Columbus's landing in the Americas. Every countrywanted to release the film on the same date. "We had eight internegatives simultaneously circulating throughout the world," Davison says. "And the director demanded that he have approval of all the voices used to dub the film in different languages. Our traffic manager had to be extremely well organized and conscientious."

Davison met with her foreign clients at Cannes, the AFM, and MIFED to discuss the support needed from her to help make *Never Ending Story, Part III* a children's marketing phenomenon on a par with the Muppets. Plans called for a large merchandising line, consisting of plush toys, pajamas, and interactive games, to be in place by the time the film was ready for delivery. That meant that Davison and her colleagues had to pick manufacturing sites and negotiate licenses, interview game creators and supervise their development, and find the right group to record the film's theme. Full-size Henson-created characters would be constructed and sent on worldwide promotional trips prior to the film's opening. Careful coordination of the creatures' trips was necessary because only a few models would be created, due to the high cost of production.

Cinevox's plan was to take advantage of every conceivable revenue-generating and marketing opportunity. Tens of millions of dollars and thousands of hours had been spent on the film's development, writing, production, and promotion. It was Cinevox's assignment to generate the profits—from all sources, worldwide—that would turn this huge expenditure of time and money into a worthwhile investment.

No matter what a film costs—no matter what its genre, social value, or quality—in countries where filmmakers live by their salaries and not by state subsidies, it all comes down to a single bottom line: will enough people see the film for it to make money? If you sell films, you have only one job. And part of that

job is to check your feelings, your personal judgments, your scruples, and your power at the door.

"I've sold wonderful and not so wonderful films," Davison
says. "Maybe I won't like a film—I don't like films that are too
violent. But it still will make money. I haven't liked everything I've
sold. How do you do that? You just do it. You go with the flow.
We all have to eat."

Glossary

Above the Line. That part of the budget that includes expenditures for so-called talent-related costs, i.e., producer; director, writer, and actors.

Agent. An individual who acts as an intermediary in the motion picture process. Some agents typically negotiate their client's employment contracts; others try to sell their client's scripts to feature film production companies, help find financing for a film, or act as an intermediary for two or more companies that need to work together to get a project off the ground.

Ambiance. The collection of sounds that normally remain unnoticed but actually contribute to the mood of a scene through its very presence.

Apprentice Editor. A new entrant into the profession, the apprentice editor is charged with the more mundane tasks of the editing process, such as synchronizing the visuals of the dailies with their respective sound tracks, and coding each soundtrack and picture.

Art Director. The individual who supervises the construction of the film set; it is his job to ensure that the actual location looks the way that the production designer has envisaged it.

Aspect ratio. The ratio of the height of a motion picture screen to its width.

Assistant Editor. Working alongside the film editor, it is the assistant's job to take care of the physical tasks of editing: inspecting the footage for scratches; transporting the film to the processing laboratory; categorizing and separating the unedited scenes.

Assistant Production Manager. The individual in charge of arranging and scheduling a postproduction facility's resources.

Associate Producer. See **Production Manager.**

Barn Doors. Metal flaps surrounding a stage fixture that restrict the amount and spread of light onto a scene.

Below the Line. Those budget expenses assigned to production and crew costs, as opposed to "above-the-line" items, i.e., costs associated with "creative" elements: producers; writers; directors; and actors.

Best Boy. The assistant to the gaffer. It is the best boy's job to oversee the lighting crews, to order all necessary lighting equipment, to keep track of employee time cards and other paperwork. The term "best boy" probably originally referred to the fact that the person in that position was the "best" boy capable of keeping everyone else in line.

Boom. The pole that holds the microphone above a scene and out of the shot.

Boom Operator. The individual who manipulates the boom—raising, lowering, and turning it to ensure it is in the best position to record sound.

Budgeter. The person who prepares the film's budget prior to start of production, determining how all monies need to be spent.

Business Affairs Dept. Those people in a studio or production company who negotiate and prepare contracts.

Cable Person. The crew member who handles all sound-related cables; also called the "third man."

Camera Operator. That person who actually operates the motion picture camera, on the instructions of the director of photography.

Carbon Arcs. Large, very intense lamps utilizing two pieces of carbon across which a spark is created. They are used to light exterior night scenes.

Carpenter. The person in charge of actually constructing the set. The carpenter reports to the construction coordinator.

Carpenter's Assistant. This person reports to the carpenter in the building of a set.

Casting Director. Working in conjunction with the producer or director, the casting director ferrets out appropriate talent for a film, set ups meetings with the actor and the producer/director, and suggests and evaluates potential actors.

Changed-Elements Clause. A contractual clause that allows studios or other production entities to reconsider a project that they may have previously rejected, e.g., if a new star suddenly becomes involved with it.

Coding. The imprinting of tiny sequential numbers alongside the visual images and sound tracks to allow sound and picture to be easily synchronized.

Compositor. The individual in charge of adding various layers of computer-generated background and action scenes to create an ultimate sense of reality.

(Computer) Animation Supervisor. The individual who ensures that the computer animators are creating objects that mimic those found in reality.

Computer Animator. The craftsperson responsible for using a computer to draw objects that can mimic, in look and movement, those objects in real life.

Computer Graphics ("CG"). Objects, backgrounds and scenes that are created digitally, using a computer and appropriate software.

Construction Coordinator. The individual who oversees the construction of a film's set. The construction coordinator reports to the art director.

Continuity. The act of keeping the dialogue and physical movement of an actor identical from angle to angle, from long shot to closeup, to allow for smooth editing between shots.

Coverage. Recording a scene from a number of different angles, to ensure that the scene will edit well.

Credits. The formal acknowledgment of an individual's contribution to the film production. The size as well as the placement of a screen credit within a movie often becomes a major bone of contention between the executive and the creative person.

Dailies (rushes). Unedited motion picture film developed overnight and delivered to the film production company the next morning for both physical and artistic inspection.

Deal Memo. A short written contract that sets down the basic terms agreed to between two parties for the licensing of a film's distribution rights. The Deal Memo is eventually superseded by the Long-Form Agreement.

Digital Rotoscoper. The individual responsible for removing from the final screen image various masks and extraneous marks used to create and position a computer-generated object.

Director of Photography. An individual charged with the job of interpreting the director's point of view into a visual form. The DP designs lighting, frames shots, and oversees the actions of the subordinate lighting and electrical staffs of the film.

Dolly. A piece of equipment that allows a motion picture camera to be pushed smoothly around the set to avoid any jarring bumps while shooting.

Dolly Grip. This is the individual charged with operating the dolly.

Dollying. The act of pushing the dolly to its appointed physical space.

Electrical Best Boy. The assistant, right-hand man to the gaffer; as such, he is responsible for supervising the lighting crews and for ordering all necessary lighting equipment.

Electrician. Working on a film's lighting crew, these people find the source of electricity, tap into it, or set up independent electrical generators.

Elements. Those factors, such as the inclusion of a well-known director or actor in a project, that increase a project's interest in the eyes of decision makers.

Entertainment Attorney. A lawyer who specializes in matters relating to the entertainment industry, such as negotiating agreements for actors and directors, and resolving disputes between his or her clients and the contracting production company.

Equalization. Equalization involves the adjustment of various frequency levels in the audio tracks to increase or decrease the perception of a voice or a sound effect.

Executive Producer. A fluid job title, one often granted to an individual who secures the funding necessary to get a film into production. The executive producer is usually not involved in a film's day-to-day decision making.

Face Approval. The right of an actor to approve any likeness of himself or herself that will be used in advertising and marketing the film in which they appeared. Face approval is usually only granted to well-known stars who have earned producers large profits at the box office.

Film Editor. See **Apprentice Editor** and **Supervising Editor**.

Final Cut. The last edited version of a film before its release. It is rare for a director, working within a motion picture studio, to receive the right to a final cut.

Foley Stage. Situated within a sound studio, this stage consists of several large trays filled with various materials that allow technicians to simulate the sounds of various walking surfaces.

G. The Motion Picture Association of America's rating that advises parents that a film is acceptable to audiences of all ages. It, along with PG, is one of three unrestricted ratings granted by the MPAA.

Gaffer. This is the individual charged with the shaping of a location to fit the director's and the director of photography's needs. A gaffer typically scouts locations, determines lighting requirements, and helps all technical aspects of a production to run smoothly. The term probably originates from European carnivals, when people were in charge of "gaffing," or herding, customers inside the tent.

Go-Motion Photography. A variant of stop-motion photography, in which the camera shutter remains open in between each frame, resulting in a slight blur to the photographed image. This removes the stilted look prevalent in stop-motion animation.

Grip. A grip is a technician who supervises all work except for electrical tasks. It is the grip who manipulates various equipment stands and who sets up light-diffusing material in front of lamps. The term originates from the necessity of "gripping" various pieces of equipment, "putting a grip on a wall" as it's moved backstage.

Grip Best Boy. The grip best boy is assistant to the key grip.

High-Concept Films. An idea for a motion picture that can be told in just a few simple sentences and, due to its emphasis on action and melodrama, is thought likely to be a commercial success.

Hot Seat. This refers to the operating seat of a camera crane.

Independent Production Cos. These are production companies outside of the major film studios, the latter of which are represented by Columbia, Disney, Twentieth Century-Fox, Warner Bros., Paramount, and Universal.

Interiors. These are scenes filmed inside a sound stage or building.

Internegative. A second negative struck from the original. The internegative is then used to create a film's release prints, thereby reducing wear on the negative.

Junior and Senior Publicist. Working for a public relations executive, these lower-level employees write press releases, organize press conferences, and arrange interviews with the stars of a soon-to-be-released motion picture.

KEM. A KEM is a type of film editing machine.

Key Grip. This is another name for the head grip.

Lamp Operator. The individual responsible for maintaining, adjusting, and operating a film lamp.

Lead Man. This individual—also known as the assistant set director—takes the lead in tracking down various artifacts with which to decorate the set.

Line Producer. Often called the production manager, this individual is charged with overseeing the day-to-day functioning of the production.

Literary Property. A book or screenplay that may be made into a film.

Location Manager. The individual charged with scouting out shooting locations.

Long Form Agreement. The formal multi-page contract signed by a film distributor and licensor, that sets forth all the points involved in the licensing of distribution rights to a motion picture.

Long shot. The name for a scene photographed from a long distance.

Main Title Credits. The film credits that appear prior to the start of the picture.

Match Mover. The individual responsible for ensuring that the perspective at which computer-generated objects are drawn is the same as that used by the director of photography to shoot the background. If the angles do not match, the foreground objects will not appear to fit in the scene.

MIFED. An Italian acronym which originally meant "International Market for Films and Documentaries." Held each Fall in Milan, this sales market is attended by buyers from around the world searching for theatrical and home video distribution rights.

Minimum Guarantee (MG). A sum initially paid by the licensee of distribution rights. Any future royalties which might be due the rights licensor will be offset by this MG.

MIP-TV. A French acronym for Marché Internationale du Film (International Film Market). An international television and video rights market held each April in Cannes.

MIPCOM. MIP-TV's sister market, held each October in Cannes.

Mix; mixer. The process during which a film's various audio elements, including live sound, effects, and music are combined and adjusted; the individual carrying out this process.

Modeler. That individual responsible for creating computer-generated three-dimensional objects.

Montage. A rapid succession of related or disparate filmed images
that, when cut together, illustrate a
particular mood or idea.

Motion picture trailer. A short montage of film clips and narration, used
in theaters and on television to advertise a film about to be released.

Movieola. This is a type of film editing machine.

MPAA. The Motion Picture Association
of America, an industry trade group.

Nagra. The name for a highly sensitive
tape recorder used for recording
live, location sound, as well as
sound effects.

NATO. National Association of Theater
Owners. In association with the
MPAA and the International Film
Importers and Distributors of
America (IFIDA), NATO is responsi-
ble for the administration of the
MPAA's film rating system.

NATPE. An acronym for "National Association of Television Program Executives." An annual market, held in
various cities throughout the United
States, at which local American television stations and some foreign
broadcasters purchase transmission
rights to U.S.-produced TV programs
and feature films.

NC-17. "No children under 17 admitted." A Rating Board designation
stating that a motion picture's content is such that no children under
the age of 17 will be permitted entry
to a theater to view it.

Negative Sound. Negative sound is
the absence of sound, the purpose
of which is to enhance future effects.

Noise abatement. Noise abatement is
the removal or lessening of unwanted sounds during shooting.

Nursery Man. This is the individual
who provides plants to the set.

One-liner. This is a script breakdown,
used by the gaffer, that tells him
which scenes will be shot each day,
their scene numbers, and what kind
of action occurs in each shot.

Optical House. This is a technical facility capable of manipulating motion picture film to provide special
effects, such as slow motion, the su-
perimposition of titles on top of action, and the recropping of a
scene's image.

Option. An option is the temporary
purchase of rights to a literary property. An option lasts for a set period
of time, and is less expensive than
an actual outright purchase.

Over-the-Shoulder Shot. This is a
camera angle that typically includes
the shoulder and the back of the
head of one individual, as well as the
full face of another who is facing
the camera.

PG. "Parental guidance suggested;
some material may not be suitable
for children." A Rating Board designation implying that parental guidance should be exercised before
allowing a child to see the particular film.

PG-13. "Parents strongly cautioned.
Some material may be inappropriate
for children under 13." Along with R
and NC-17, one of the three restricted MPAA ratings. PG-13 implies
that a motion picture's content is
such that parents are advised to
consider if the film is appropriate for
their children 12 and under.

Pitch Meeting. This is a meeting between a producer and a studio executive in which the producer attempts to convince the executive to
get involved in a particular film
project.

Planted microphones. A "planted
microphone" is hidden in an object
to conceal it during shooting.

Positive word-of-mouth. When a
high proportion of moviegoers speak
positively about a film to their friends,
the movie is said to have generated
"positive word-of-mouth."

Preproduction. This describes the period before a film begins shooting, during which casting, hiring, script rewriting, set construction, and location scouting are all accomplished.

Preselling. The selling of distribution rights to a film before it is actually made. Pre-selling is one way of raising money to start and/or complete production.

Producer. The individual responsible for bringing a film project to fruition. The producer often is the person who options the literary property, finds a director and/or star, and convinces a studio to fund the film.

Product. The term by which motion picture sales executives refer to movies and television programs.

Production Designer. This is the individual charged with creating an integrated visual "look" to a film, one that interprets the needs of the script and of the director.

Production Executive (Vice President of Production). This is the person who, representing the production company, oversees a film project, working with writers, directors, and producers in shaping it to fit the company's needs.

Production Manager. Often also called the Associate Producer, this individual runs a film project's day-to-day operations.

Public Relations Executive. An individual working either as a freelancer or an employee of a motion picture studio who is responsible for promoting a film and/or its stars to the print and electronic media.

R. "Restricted, under 17 requires accompanying parent or adult guardian." One of the three restricted MPAA ratings. An R rating is given to a film that contains various types of adult behavior, including nudity within sensual scenes, excessive violence, drug use, or hard language.

Rating. A letter code assigned to a film by the MPAA's Rating Board, as an attempt to offer parents advance information about movies that they may or may not want their children to see.

Reader. See **Story Analyst.**

Release Print. A color-corrected copy of the completed film, used for projection in movie theaters.

Rendered. The computerized combination of digital elements, such as movement, light, shadow, and texturing, that will make a digitally created object look as if it exists in real time and space.

Screen test. A screen test is sample footage shot of an actor or actress to see how they look on film.

Scrim. Scrim is the name for the material, used to diffuse light, placed in front of lamps to give the illumination a softer, often more pleasing effect.

Script Supervisor. This is the individual who follows the script during shooting, to ensure that the actors say the same lines and make the same physical movements, each time the camera rolls. See **continuity.**

Second Unit Director. This individual is charged with overseeing the shooting of scenes ancillary to the main action. A second unit may be photographing additional shots, buildings, or action scenes, at the same time that the director is shooting the scenes involving the actors.

Senior Vice President of International Sales. An individual responsible for the sale of motion picture distribution rights throughout the world.

Set Decorator. This is a person experienced in interior design who actually finds appropriate objects to place within a set to give it that "lived in" look. He/she carries out the tasks based on the needs of the set, as decided by the production designer.

Set Dresser. This individual physically places objects within a set.

Sound Blanket. This is the name for a blanket placed on walls to reduce unwanted reverberations as sounds are recorded.

Sound Designer. This person oversees all of the audio elements of a film, similar to the work a production designer carries out for the visual portion of a motion picture.

Sound Effects Editor. This person is charged with reshaping sound to conform to the emotional needs of each scene.

Sound Mixer. The sound mixer is the head of the on-location sound recording team, which also includes the boom operator and third man.

Spotting Run. This is the name for a viewing of the nearly completed film by the sound effects editor, in order to determine the type of sound effects that must be added.

Stand-in. This individual substitutes for the actor while the director of photography is composing the shot and lighting is being tested.

Stand-By Painter. This individual ensures that various physical objects within a scene are touched up to prevent any extraneous reflections or unwanted colors during shooting.

Sticks. This is the name for the wooden legs upon which the camera is place during shooting.

Stop-motion photography. A special effects technique in which an object, such as a model of a dinosaur, is photographed one frame at a time. After each shot, the object is moved slightly and then reshot. The resulting sequence simulates movement.

Story Analyst. Also known as a reader, this person reads and evaluates all literary material submitted to a production company or literary agency for consideration.

Storyboard. This is a sketched depiction of each important scene in a film.

Stuntperson. A gender-neutral variant of "stuntman," the stuntperson substitutes for an actor and performs physical activities that would be too difficult or dangerous for an untrained individual to attempt.

Stunt Coordinator. The stunt coordinator maps out all the places in a film where stunts will need to be performed.

Supervising Editor. This is the person charged with the actual editing of the film, in consultations with the director and producer.

Swing Gang. This group of people, dispatched by the lead man, acquires the various necessary objects for set decoration.

Take. This is the name for one of the number of particular recordings of a scene.

Talent. A term that, in the vernacular, refers to those individuals appearing in front of the camera (i.e., actors and actresses).

Traffic Manager. The individual responsible for coordinating the shipment of feature film prints, video masters, slides, dialogue lists, posters, and any other material necessary for a licensee to properly market and release a feature film in a particular territory.

Third Man. See **Cable Person.**

Tripod. This object holds the camera during shooting.

Turnaround. Turnaround describes the point at which the rights to a script revert back to the producer from the studio, because the studio has not been able to put the project in production.

2-D Painter. The individual who creates a computer-generated object's surface textures and colors.

Unit Photographer. This is the name for the still photographer assigned to take publicity photos of a particular film.

Unit Publicist. This is the public relations person assigned to write press and publicity releases for a particular film.

Utility Stuntperson. An individual who performs physical feats, not as a substitute for an actor, but as part of the scene's activity. It is the utility stuntperson who will drive a car that crashes into the star's, for example.

Visual Effects Producer. The individual responsible for overseeing the budgeting and progress of special effects on a particular film or group of films.

Visual Effects Supervisor. The individual responsible for overseeing the creation of visual effects on one particular film. The visual effects supervisor reports to the visual effects producer.

Wild lines. Dialogue recorded on the set immediately after a scene has been shot, used as substitutes for words or phrases that were poorly registered during filming.

Wire and Rig Remover. The individual responsible for removing from the final computer image wires and other extraneous marks created by apparatus used to position an object while photographed.

Wireless Microphones. A microphone that uses radio waves, rather than a direct, "hard"connection, to transmit sound to a tape recorder. Wireless microphones enable actors to be filmed from great distances, but with the sound quality one would otherwise expect only from a closeup shot.

Work print. A positive copy of the dailies, made from the negative, solely for editing purposes. The work print will be cut and reassembled many times until the picture is deemed complete.

X. A rating formerly given to films that were not suitable for children under 17. As the only rating purposely never copyrighted by the MPAA, the X rating eventually was co-opted by pornographers as a positive indication of a film's strong sexual content.

Index